Houghton
Mifflin
Harcourt

SCIENCE FUSiON

fusion [FYOO • zhuhn] a combination of two or more things that releases energy

This **Interactive Student Edition** belongs to

_____

Teacher/Room

_____

Consulting Authors

Michael A. DiSpezio

Global Educator
North Falmouth, Massachusetts

Michael DiSpezio is a renaissance educator who moved from the research laboratory of a Nobel Prize winner to the K–12 science classroom. He has authored or co-authored numerous textbooks and written more than 25 trade books. For nearly a decade he worked with the JASON Project, under the auspices of the National Geographic Society, where he designed curriculum, wrote lessons, and hosted dozens of studio and location broadcasts. Over the past two decades, he has developed supplementary material for organizations and shows that include PBS *Scientific American Frontiers, Discover* magazine, and the Discovery Channel. He has extended his reach outside the United States and into topics of crucial importance today. To all his projects, he brings his extensive background in science and his expertise in classroom teaching at the elementary, middle, and high school levels.

Marjorie Frank

Science Writer and Content-Area Reading Specialist
Brooklyn, New York

An educator and linguist by training, a writer and poet by nature, Marjorie Frank has authored and designed a generation of instructional materials in all subject areas, including past HMH Science programs. Her other credits include authoring science issues of an award-winning children's magazine; writing game-based digital assessments in math, reading, and language arts; and serving as instructional designer and co-author of pioneering school-to-work software for Classroom Inc., a nonprofit organization dedicated to improving reading and math skills for middle and high school learners. She wrote lyrics and music for *SCIENCE SONGS,* which was an American Library Association nominee for notable recording. In addition, she has served on the adjunct faculty of Hunter, Manhattan, and Brooklyn Colleges, teaching courses in science methods, literacy, and writing.

Acknowledgments for Covers

Front cover: *Iceberg* (bg) ©Hans Reinhard/Corbis

ISBN 978-0-544-77847-4

7 8 9 10 0928 24 23 22 21 20 19

4500785594   B C D E F G

Michael R. Heithaus

Dean, College of Arts, Sciences & Education
Florida International University
North Miami, Florida

Mike Heithaus joined the Florida International University Biology Department in 2003. He is a professor in the Department of Biological Sciences and has served as Director of the Marine Sciences Program and Executive Director of the School of Environment and Society. His research focuses on predator-prey interactions and the ecological roles of large marine species including sharks, sea turtles, and marine mammals. His long-term studies include the Shark Bay Ecosystem Project in Western Australia. He also served as a Research Fellow with National Geographic, using remote imaging in his research and hosting a *Crittercam* television series on the National Geographic Channel.

Donna M. Ogle

Professor of Reading and Language
National-Louis University
Chicago, Illinois

Creator of the well-known KWL strategy, Donna Ogle has directed many staff development projects translating theory and research into school practice in middle and secondary schools throughout the United States. She is a past president of the International Reading Association and has served as a consultant on literacy projects worldwide. Her extensive international experience includes coordinating the Reading and Writing for Critical Thinking Project in Eastern Europe, developing an integrated curriculum for a USAID Afghan Education Project, and speaking and consulting on projects in several Latin American countries and in Asia. Her books include *Coming Together as Readers; Reading Comprehension: Strategies for Independent Learners; All Children Read;* and *Literacy for a Democratic Society.*

Program Reviewers

Content Reviewers

Paul D. Asimow, PhD
Professor of Geology and Geochemistry
Division of Geological and Planetary Sciences
California Institute of Technology
Pasadena, CA

Laura K. Baumgartner, PhD
Postdoctoral Researcher
Molecular, Cellular, and Developmental Biology
University of Colorado
Boulder, CO

Eileen Cashman, PhD
Professor
Department of Environmental Resources Engineering
Humboldt State University
Arcata, CA

Hilary Clement Olson, PhD
Research Scientist Associate V
Institute for Geophysics, Jackson School of Geosciences
The University of Texas at Austin
Austin, TX

Joe W. Crim, PhD
Professor Emeritus
Department of Cellular Biology
The University of Georgia
Athens, GA

Elizabeth A. De Stasio, PhD
Raymond H. Herzog Professor of Science
Professor of Biology
Department of Biology
Lawrence University
Appleton, WI

Dan Franck, PhD
Botany Education Consultant
Chatham, NY

Julia R. Greer, PhD
Assistant Professor of Materials Science and Mechanics
Division of Engineering and Applied Science
California Institute of Technology
Pasadena, CA

John E. Hoover, PhD
Professor
Department of Biology
Millersville University
Millersville, PA

William H. Ingham, PhD
Professor (Emeritus)
Department of Physics and Astronomy
James Madison University
Harrisonburg, VA

Charles W. Johnson, PhD
Chairman, Division of Natural Sciences, Mathematics, and Physical Education
Associate Professor of Physics
South Georgia College
Douglas, GA

Program Reviewers *(continued)*

Tatiana A. Krivosheev, PhD
Associate Professor of Physics
Department of Natural Sciences
Clayton State University
Morrow, GA

Joseph A. McClure, PhD
Associate Professor Emeritus
Department of Physics
Georgetown University
Washington, DC

Mark Moldwin, PhD
Professor of Space Sciences
Atmospheric, Oceanic, and
Space Sciences
University of Michigan
Ann Arbor, MI

Russell Patrick, PhD
Professor of Physics
Department of Biology,
Chemistry, and Physics
Southern Polytechnic State
University
Marietta, GA

Patricia M. Pauley, PhD
*Meteorologist, Data Assimilation
Group*
Naval Research Laboratory
Monterey, CA

Stephen F. Pavkovic, PhD
Professor Emeritus
Department of Chemistry
Loyola University of Chicago
Chicago, IL

L. Jeanne Perry, PhD
Director (Retired)
Protein Expression Technology
Center
Institute for Genomics and
Proteomics
University of California, Los
Angeles
Los Angeles, CA

Kenneth H. Rubin, PhD
Professor
Department of Geology and
Geophysics
University of Hawaii
Honolulu, HI

Brandon E. Schwab, PhD
Associate Professor
Department of Geology
Humboldt State University
Arcata, CA

Marllin L. Simon, Ph.D.
Associate Professor
Department of Physics
Auburn University
Auburn, AL

Larry Stookey, PE
Upper Iowa University
Wausau, WI

Kim Withers, PhD
Associate Research Scientist
Center for Coastal Studies
Texas A&M University-Corpus
Christi
Corpus Christi, TX

Matthew A. Wood, PhD
Professor
Department of Physics & Space
Sciences
Florida Institute of Technology
Melbourne, FL

Adam D. Woods, PhD
Associate Professor
Department of Geological
Sciences
California State University,
Fullerton
Fullerton, CA

Natalie Zayas, MS, EdD
Lecturer
Division of Science and
Environmental Policy
California State University,
Monterey Bay
Seaside, CA

Teacher Reviewers

Ann Barrette, MST
Whitman Middle School
Wauwatosa, WI

Barbara Brege
Crestwood Middle School
Kentwood, MI

**Katherine Eaton Campbell,
M Ed**
Chicago Public Schools-Area 2
Office
Chicago, IL

**Karen Cavalluzzi, M Ed,
NBCT**
Sunny Vale Middle School
Blue Springs, MO

Katie Demorest, MA Ed Tech
Marshall Middle School
Marshall, MI

Jennifer Eddy, M Ed
Lindale Middle School
Linthicum, MD

Tully Fenner
George Fox Middle School
Pasadena, MD

Dave Grabski, MS Ed
PJ Jacobs Junior High School
Stevens Point, WI

Amelia C. Holm, M Ed
McKinley Middle School
Kenosha, WI

Ben Hondorp
Creekside Middle School
Zeeland, MI

George E. Hunkele, M Ed
Harborside Middle School
Milford, CT

Jude Kesl
Science Teaching Specialist 6–8
Milwaukee Public Schools
Milwaukee, WI

Joe Kubasta, M Ed
Rockwood Valley Middle School
St. Louis, MO

Mary Larsen
Science Instructional Coach
Helena Public Schools
Helena, MT

Angie Larson
Bernard Campbell Middle School
Lee's Summit, MO

Christy Leier
Horizon Middle School
Moorhead, MN

Helen Mihm, NBCT
Crofton Middle School
Crofton, MD

Jeff Moravec, Sr., MS Ed
Teaching Specialist
Milwaukee Public Schools
Milwaukee, WI

**Nancy Kawecki Nega, MST,
NBCT, PAESMT**
Churchville Middle School
Elmhurst, IL

Mark E. Poggensee, MS Ed
Elkhorn Middle School
Elkhorn, WI

Sherry Rich
Bernard Campbell Middle School
Lee's Summit, MO

Mike Szydlowski, M Ed
Science Coordinator
Columbia Public Schools
Columbia, MO

Nichole Trzasko, M Ed
Clarkston Junior High School
Clarkston, MI

Heather Wares, M Ed
Traverse City West Middle School
Traverse City, MI

© Houghton Mifflin Harcourt Publishing Company

Contents
in Brief

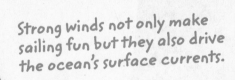

Strong winds not only make sailing fun but they also drive the ocean's surface currents.

Contents

These rafters are on a wild ride downriver! They are using the river currents that form as water flows from higher elevations to lower elevations.

Assignments:

_____
_____
_____
_____
_____
_____
_____
_____

Some green sea turtles migrate over 2,000 km on ocean currents in the Atlantic Ocean.

Surfers love riding ocean waves before they break near shore. The taller the wave, the faster a surfer can travel.

Contents (continued)

What happens when solar wind particles reach the upper atmosphere over the Arctic? The aurora borealis!

Assignments:

_____

_____

_____

_____

_____

_____

Although humans don't have thick fur or the ability to survive without drinking water for months, we have found other ways to live in extreme climates.

© Houghton Mifflin Harcourt Publishing Company • Image Credits: (tr) ©Mitchell Kanashkevich/The Image Bank/Getty Images; (c) ©Wayne R Bilenduke/Photographer's Choice/Getty Images

Power up with Science Fusion!

Your program fuses...

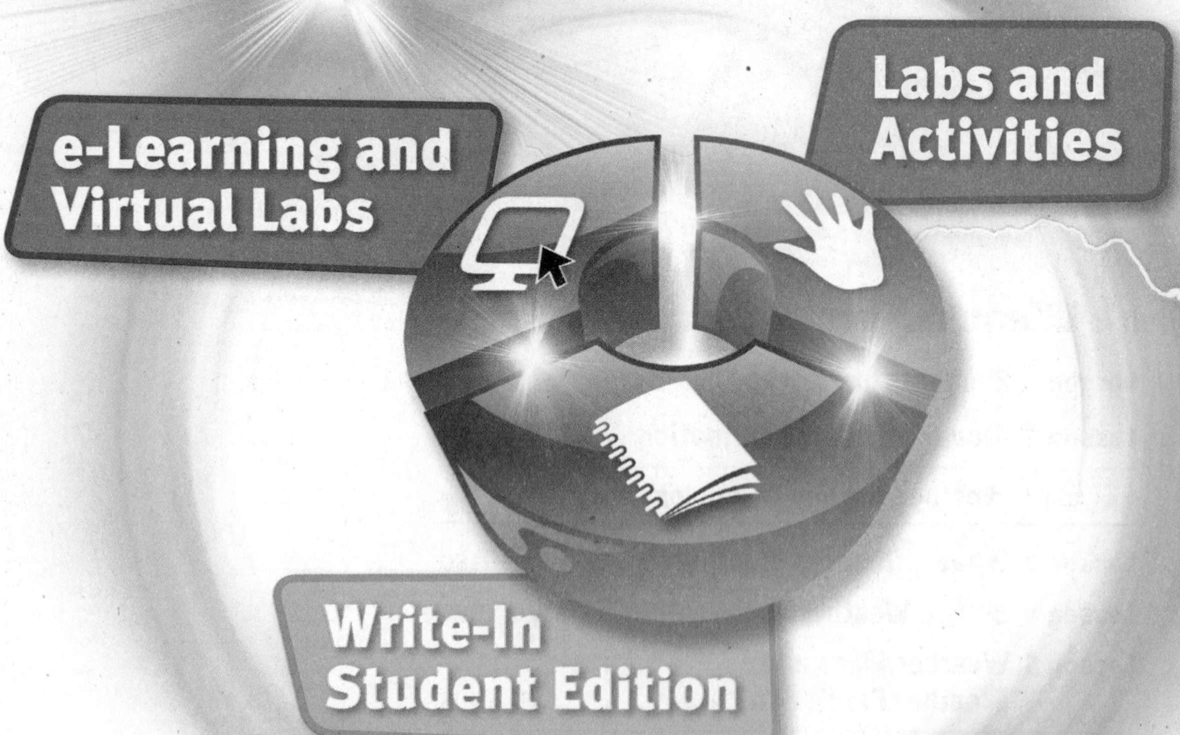

e-Learning and Virtual Labs

Labs and Activities

Write-In Student Edition

...to generate energy for today's science learner — *you*.

S.T.E.M. activities throughout the program!

Write-In Student Edition

Be an active reader and make this book your own!

You can answer questions, ask questions, create graphs, make notes, write your own ideas, and highlight information right in your book.

Learn science concepts and skills by interacting with every page.

Labs and Activities

ScienceFusion includes lots of exciting hands-on inquiry labs and activities, each one designed to bring science skills and concepts to life and get you involved.

By asking questions, testing your ideas, organizing and analyzing data, drawing conclusions, and sharing what you learn...

You are the scientist!

e-Learning and Virtual Labs

Digital lessons and virtual labs provide e-learning options for every lesson of Science Fusion.

On your own or with a group, explore science concepts in a digital world.

360° of Inquiry

Earth's Water

Big Idea

Water moves through Earth's atmosphere, oceans, and land in a cycle and is essential for life on Earth.

Waterfalls show the important role gravity plays in moving Earth's water.

What do you think?

Fresh water is found in ponds, lakes, streams, rivers, and underground in aquifers. Where does the water in your school come from?

Humans rely on water to stay healthy.

Unit 1
Earth's Water

Conserving Water

Fresh water evaporates into the air and then condenses to form clouds. It falls from the sky as precipitation and then flows over Earth's surface in streams and rivers. It seeps underground through soil and rocks. Fresh water makes up only a small fraction of Earth's water and is not evenly distributed.

Some watering methods lose a great deal of water to evaporation.

1 Think About It

A Take a quick survey of your classmates. Ask them where the fresh water they use every day at home and at school comes from.

_____

_____

_____

B Ask your classmates to identify different uses of water at your school.

_____

_____

_____

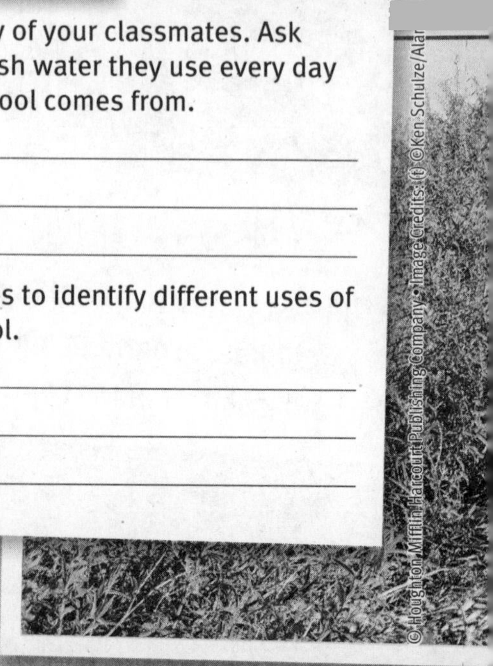

How do you conserve water?

Water is an essential resource for everyone, but it is a limited resource. What are some ways that your school may be wasting water?

_____
_____
_____
_____
_____
_____
_____
_____
_____

Xeriscaping is a method of landscaping by using plants that require less water.

A Make a list of five ways in which the school can conserve water.

_____
_____
_____
_____
_____

B In the space below, sketch out a design for a pamphlet or a poster that you can place in the hallways to promote water conservation at your school.

Take It Home

Take a pamphlet or a poster home. With an adult, talk about ways in which water can be conserved in and around your home. See *ScienceSaurus®* for more information about conservation.

Water and Its Properties

ESSENTIAL QUESTION

What makes water so important?

By the end of this lesson, you should be able to describe water's structure, its properties, and its importance to Earth's systems.

Not all liquids form round droplets, but water does. Water's unique properties have to do with the way water molecules interact.

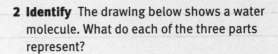
Engage Your Brain

1 Predict Check T or F to show whether you think each statement is true or false.

T	F	
☐	☐	Most of the water on Earth is fresh water.
☐	☐	Water exists in three different states on Earth.
☐	☐	Water can dissolve many different substances, such as salt.
☐	☐	Flowing water can be used to generate electricity.

2 Identify The drawing below shows a water molecule. What do each of the three parts represent?

_____

_____

_____

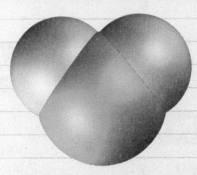

Active Reading

3 Synthesize You can often define an unknown word if you know the meaning of its word parts. Use the word parts and sentence below to make an educated guess about the meaning of the word *cohesion*.

Word part	Meaning
co-	with, together
-hesion	sticking, joined

Example sentence
When water forms droplets, it is displaying the property of <u>cohesion</u>.

Cohesion:

_____

_____

_____

_____

Vocabulary Terms
- polarity
- cohesion
- adhesion
- specific heat
- solvent

4 Apply As you learn the definition of each vocabulary term in this lesson, create your own definition or sketch to help you remember the meaning of the term.

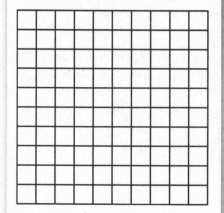

Watered Down

What are some of water's roles on Earth?

Water shapes Earth's surface and influences Earth's weather. Water is also vital for life. Without water, your body could not regulate its temperature or convert food into a usable form of energy. Only about 3% of water on Earth is fresh water. Of this 3% of water that is drinkable, about 69% is frozen in glaciers and icecaps and is not readily available for our use. Therefore, it is important that we protect our water resources.

Influencing Weather

 **Active Reading** 6 **Identify** As you read, underline four different forms of water that fall on Earth's surface.

Weather is related to water. Water constantly moves from Earth's surface to the atmosphere, where it may form clouds. Water falls back to Earth's surface again as rain, snow, hail, or sleet. Weather also depends on the amount of moisture in the air.

Shaping Earth's Surface

Over time, water can completely reshape a landscape. Water slowly wears away rock and carries away sediment and soil. Flowing rivers and pounding ocean waves are also examples of water shaping Earth's surface. Frozen water shapes Earth's surface, too. Glaciers, for example, scrape away rock and soil, depositing these materials elsewhere when the glacier melts.

Do the Math

You Try It

5 **Graph** About 3% of water on Earth is fresh water. The rest is salt water. Fill out the percentage grid to show the percentage of fresh water on Earth.

© Houghton Mifflin Harcourt Publishing Company • Image Credits: ©Scott Barrow/Corbis

Supporting Life

Every living thing is largely made up of water, and nearly all biological processes use water. All of an organism's cellular chemistry depends on water. Water regulates temperature and helps transport substances. Without water, animals and plants would dry up and die.

For humans, clean water is vital for good health. People must have clean water to drink in order to survive. Contaminated water sources are a major public health problem in many countries. Contaminated water is also harmful to plants, animals, and can affect crops that provide food for humans.

Supporting Human Activities

Clean drinking water is necessary for all humans. Many humans use water at home for bathing, cleaning, and watering lawns and gardens.

More fresh water is used in industry than is used in homes. Over 20% of the fresh water used by humans is used for industrial purposes—to manufacture goods, cool power stations, clean industrial products, extract minerals, and generate energy by using hydroelectric dams.

More water is used for agriculture than industry. Most water used for agriculture is used to irrigate crops. It is also used to care for farm animals.

Visualize It!

7 List List at least four roles of water in this scene.

_____

_____

_____

_____

_____

Molecular Attraction

What is the structure of a water molecule?

Matter is made up of tiny particles called *atoms*. Atoms can join with other atoms to make molecules. A water molecule is made up of two hydrogen atoms and one oxygen atom—in other words, H_2O. Each hydrogen atom is linked to the oxygen atom, forming a shape like a cartoon mouse's ears sticking out from its head.

What makes water a polar molecule?

In a water molecule, the hydrogen atoms have a small positive charge. The oxygen atom has a small negative charge. So the water molecule has a partial positive charge at one end (mouse ears) and a partial negative charge at the other (mouse chin). Anything that has a positive charge at one end and negative charge at the other end is said to have **polarity**. A water molecule is therefore a polar molecule. In liquid water, the negative end of one water molecule is attracted to the positive end of another water molecule. Each water molecule interacts with the surrounding water molecules.

👁 Visualize It!

8 Label Indicate the polarity of water by writing a + or − next to each atom that makes up the water molecule.

Because of polarity, the positive end of one water molecule interacts with the negative end of another molecule.

Water molecules have a positive end and a negative end.

What states of water occur on Earth?

Active Reading **9 Identify** As you read, underline the three states of water that occur on Earth.

Most of Earth's water is in liquid form. Earth is the only planet in our solar system with abundant liquid water. Gravity causes liquid water to flow downhill and to rest in low-lying areas. As a result, Earth has rivers, lakes, and oceans. Like other liquids, liquid water takes the shape of whatever contains it.

Liquid water can change into an invisible gas called water vapor, or it can freeze into solid ice or snow. Like liquid water, water vapor and ice also have the chemical formula H_2O. So liquid water, water vapor, and ice are simply varieties, or states, of water. Conditions on Earth allow water to exist in these three different states. The three states of water can change into one another. When water changes state, it either takes up or releases energy.

Water vapor is a gas, so most water vapor is found in Earth's atmosphere. Water vapor cannot be seen. Clouds form when water vapor in the atmosphere condenses into liquid water droplets. Like all gases, water vapor expands or contracts to fill available space.

Unlike other liquids, water expands when it freezes. Molecules in liquid water, therefore, are closer together than are the molecules of solid water. In other words, there is more open space between the water molecules in ice. Due to this fact, solid water, or ice, is less dense than liquid water. So ice floats on liquid water.

Visualize It!

10 Describe Using your own words in the spaces provided, identify the state of water, and describe the properties of each state of water.

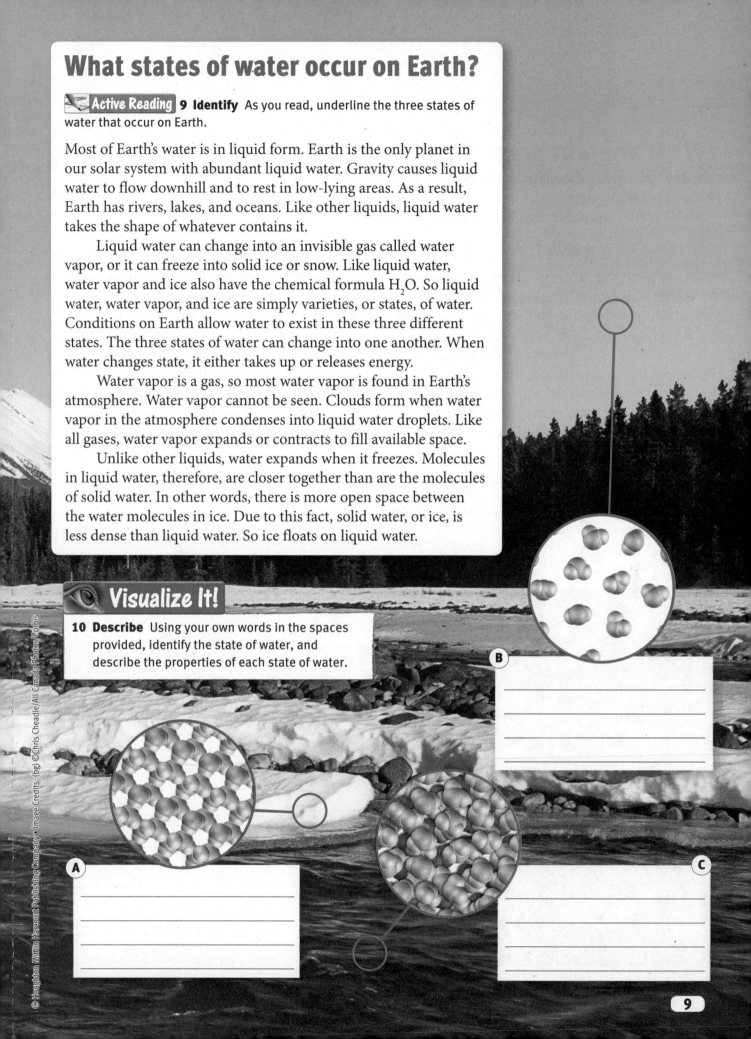

A

B

C

The Universal Solvent

What are four properties of water?

The polarity of water molecules affects the properties of water. This is because water's polarity affects how water molecules interact with one another and with other types of molecules.

It Sticks to Itself

The property that holds molecules of a substance together is **cohesion**. Water molecules stick together tightly because of their polarity, so water has high cohesion. Because of cohesion, water forms droplets. And water poured gently into a glass can fill it above the rim because cohesion holds the water molecules together. Some insects can walk on still water because their weight does not break the cohesion of the water molecules.

It Sticks to Other Substances

The property that holds molecules of different substances together is **adhesion**. Polar substances other than water can attract water molecules more strongly than water molecules attract each other. These substances are called "wettable" because water adheres, or sticks, to them so tightly. Paper towels, for example, are wettable. Water drops roll off unwettable, or "waterproof," surfaces, which are made of non-polar molecules.

Visualize It!

11 Label Identify each photo as representing either adhesion or cohesion. Then write captions explaining the properties of water shown by each photo.

A

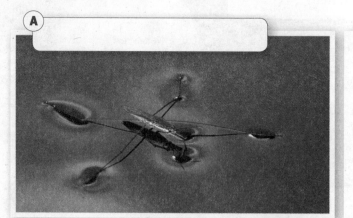

_____

_____

_____

_____

_____

_____

B

_____

_____

_____

_____

_____

_____

These stalactites formed as water dripped down and left dissolved minerals behind.

It Can Absorb Large Amounts of Energy

The energy needed to heat a substance by a particular amount is called its **specific heat**. As water is warmed, its molecules are separated a little as the water expands. The attraction between polar water molecules means that separating them takes a great deal of energy, so the specific heat of water is very high. Because of its high specific heat, water can absorb more energy than many other substances can.

Warm water stores more energy than cold water does. And water vapor stores much more energy than liquid water does. The stored energy is released when warm water cools and when water vapor cools to form liquid. This ability of water to store and release heat is very important in weather and climate.

It Dissolves Many Things

A liquid that dissolves substances is called a **solvent**. Because of its polarity, water dissolves many substances. Therefore, water is often called the universal solvent. Salt, or NaCl, is a familiar substance that water dissolves.

Water as a solvent is very important to living things. Water transports vital dissolved substances through organisms. And most of the chemical reactions that take place inside organisms involve substances dissolved in water.

Only this one doesn't dissolve quickly in water.

12 Summarize What characteristic of water accounts for its properties of adhesion, cohesion, high specific heat, and nature as a solvent?

_____

_____

Think Outside the Book Inquiry

13 Apply Water dissolves a substance until the water becomes saturated and can dissolve no more of the substance. Starting with 100 ml water, determine how much salt or sugar can be dissolved before the solution is saturated.

© Houghton Mifflin Harcourt Publishing Company • Image Credits: (bg) ©Alrendo Travel/Getty Images; (r) ©HMH

Visual Summary

To complete this summary, fill in the blanks. Then use the key below to check your answers. You can use this page to review the main concepts of the lesson.

Water and Its Properties

Water plays many roles in Earth's systems.

14 Water has the following four major roles on Earth:

_____

_____

_____

_____

Water has high cohesion, high adhesion to polar substances, high specific heat, and is a good solvent.

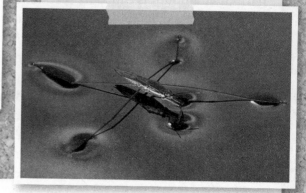

17 Water gets soaked up by a paper towel because of the property of

_____

18 Water is a commonly used _____ because it dissolves most substances.

Water is a polar molecule. On Earth, water may be found as a liquid, a solid, and a gas.

15 Water is made up of two _____ atoms and one _____ atom.

16 Because water molecules have a negative end and a positive end, they have

_____

19 Synthesize Which properties of water make it useful for washing and cleaning? Explain your answer.

_____

Lesson Review

Vocabulary

Fill in the blanks with the terms that best complete the following sentences.

1 Because a water molecule has a negative end and a positive end, it displays _____

2 Water's high _____ means that a large amount of energy is required to change the water's temperature.

3 When water molecules stick to the molecules of other substances, the molecules are displaying _____

Key Concepts

4 Summarize Why is water important to living things?

_____
_____
_____
_____
_____

5 Describe Draw a water molecule in the space below. Label the atoms that make up the molecule, as well as their partial charges.

6 Explain Why does water have high cohesion?

_____
_____
_____
_____

Critical Thinking

Use the graph to answer the following questions.

Household Water Use in the United States

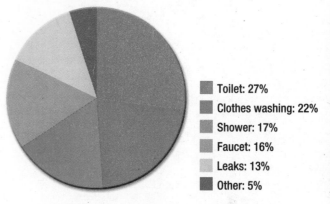

- Toilet: 27%
- Clothes washing: 22%
- Shower: 17%
- Faucet: 16%
- Leaks: 13%
- Other: 5%

Source: American Water Works Association Research Foundation, 1999

7 Identify In an average household, what is most water used for?

_____

8 Infer What do you think are the three biggest changes a household could make to reduce its use of water?

_____
_____
_____
_____

9 Explain Why do you think conserving fresh water might be important?

_____
_____
_____

10 Evaluate Which states of water can you find in your home? Explain.

_____
_____
_____
_____
_____
_____

My Notes

The Water Cycle

ESSENTIAL QUESTION

How does water change state and move around on Earth?

By the end of this lesson, you should be able to describe the water cycle and the different processes that are part of the water cycle on Earth.

Water from the ocean evaporates, forms clouds, then falls back into the ocean when it rains. Can you think of other ways water travels between Earth and Earth's atmosphere?

 **Lesson Labs**

Quick Labs
• Modeling the Water Cycle
• Can You Make It Rain in a Jar?

Exploration Lab
• Changes in Water

Engage Your Brain

1 Predict Circle the word or phrase that best completes the following sentences.

The air inside a glass of ice would feel *warm/cold/room temperature*.

Ice would *melt/evaporate/remain frozen* if it were left outside on a hot day.

Water vapor will *condense on/evaporate from/ melt into* the glass of ice from the air.

The ice *absorbs energy from/maintains its energy/releases energy into* the surroundings when it melts.

2 Analyze Using the photo above, solve the word scramble to answer the question: What happens to ice as it warms up?

TI GACNSEH EASTT

_____

Active Reading

3 Synthesize You can often define an unknown word if you know the meaning of the word's origin. Use the meaning of the words' origins and the sentence below to make an educated guess about the meaning of *precipitation* and *evaporation*.

Latin word	Meaning
praecipitare	fall
evaporare	spread out in vapor or steam

Example sentence
Precipitation, in the form of rain, helps replace the water lost by evaporation from the lake.

precipitation:

_____

evaporation:

_____

Vocabulary Terms

- water cycle
- evaporation
- transpiration
- sublimation
- condensation
- precipitation

4 Apply As you learn the definition of each vocabulary term in this lesson, write out a sentence using that term to help you remember the meaning of the term.

What goes up...

What is the water cycle?

Movement of water between the atmosphere, land, oceans, and even living things makes up the **water cycle**. Rain, snow, and hail fall on the oceans and land because of gravity. On land, ice and water flow downhill. Water flows in streams, rivers, and waterfalls such as the one in the photo, because of gravity. If the land is flat, water will collect in certain areas forming ponds, lakes, and marshland. Some water will soak through the ground and collect underground as groundwater. Even groundwater flows downhill.

Water and snow can move upward if they turn into water vapor and rise into the air. Plants and animals also release water vapor into the air. In the air, water vapor can travel great distances with the wind. Winds can also move the water in the surface layer of the ocean by creating ocean currents. When ocean currents reach the shore or colder climates, the water will sink if it is cold enough or salty enough. The sinking water creates currents at different depths in the ocean. These are some of the ways in which water travels all over Earth.

Visualize It!

5 Analyze What is the relationship between gravity and water in this image?

_____

_____

_____

_____

How does water change state?

Water is found in three states on Earth: as liquid water, as solid water ice, and as gaseous water vapor. Water is visible as a liquid or a solid, but it is invisible as a gas in the air. Water can change from one state to another as energy is absorbed or released.

Water absorbs energy from its surroundings as it *melts* from solid to liquid. Water also absorbs energy when it *evaporates* from liquid to gas, or when it *sublimates* from solid to gas. Water releases energy into its surroundings when it *condenses* from gas to liquid. Water also releases energy when it *freezes* from liquid to solid, or *deposits* from gas to solid. No water is lost during these changes.

Active Reading

6 Identify As you read, underline each process in which energy is absorbed or released.

Visualize It!

7 Analyze Under each photo, write an example of where you might find water in that state of matter.

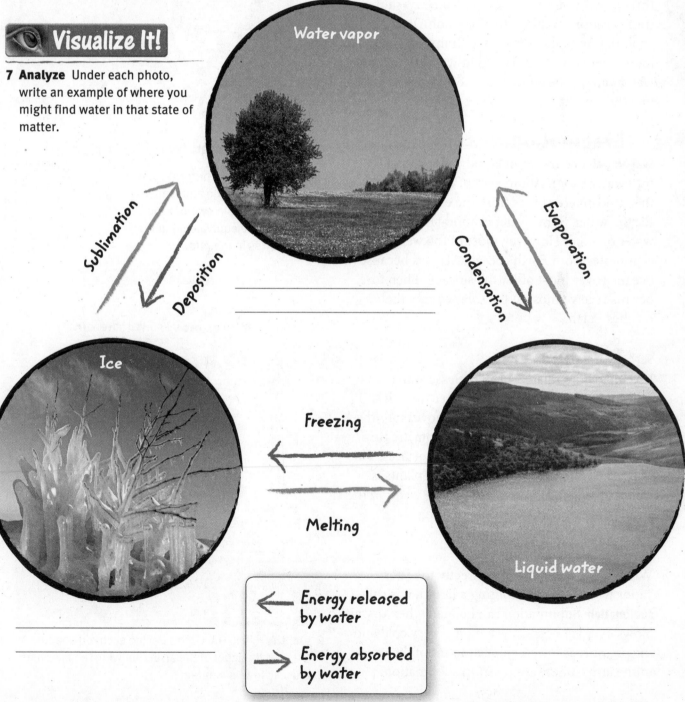

Water vapor

Sublimation

Deposition

Condensation

Evaporation

Ice

Freezing

Melting

Liquid water

← Energy released by water

→ Energy absorbed by water

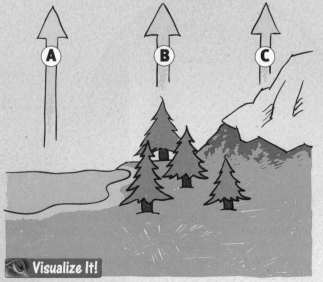

The evaporating water leaves behind a dry, cracked lake bed.

How does water reach the atmosphere?

Water reaches the atmosphere as water vapor in three ways: evaporation (i•VAP•uh•ray•shuhn), transpiration (tran•spuh•RAY•shuhn), and sublimation (suhb•luh•MAY•shuhn). It takes a lot of energy for liquid or solid water to turn into water vapor. The energy for these changes comes mostly from the sun, as solar energy.

◯ Evaporation

Evaporation occurs when liquid water changes into water vapor. About 90% of the water in the atmosphere comes from the evaporation of Earth's water. Some water evaporates from the water on land. However, most of the water vapor evaporates from Earth's oceans. This is because oceans cover most of Earth's surface. Therefore, oceans receive most of the solar energy that reaches Earth.

◯ Transpiration

Like many organisms, plants release water into the environment. Liquid water turns into water vapor inside the plant and moves into the atmosphere through stomata. Stomata are tiny holes that are found on some plant surfaces. This release of water vapor into the air by plants is called **transpiration**. About 10% of the water in the atmosphere comes from transpiration.

◯ Sublimation

When solid water changes directly to water vapor without first becoming a liquid, it is called **sublimation**. Sublimation can happen when dry air blows over ice or snow, where it is very cold and the pressure is low. A small amount of the water in the atmosphere comes from sublimation.

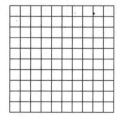

Do the Math **You Try It**

8 Graph Show the percentage of water vapor in the atmosphere that comes from evaporation by coloring the equivalent number of squares in the grid.

Water moves into the air.

A   B   C

Visualize It!

9 Identify Fill in the circles beside each red heading at left with the label of the arrow showing the matching process in this diagram.

What happens to water in the atmosphere?

Water reaches the atmosphere as water vapor. In the atmosphere, water vapor mixes with other gases. To leave the atmosphere, water vapor must change into liquid or solid water. Then the liquid or solid water can fall to Earth's surface.

◯ Condensation

Remember, **condensation** (kahn•den•SAY•shuhn) is the change of state from a gas to a liquid. If air that contains water vapor is cooled enough, condensation occurs. Some of the water vapor condenses on small particles, such as dust, forming little balls or tiny droplets of water. These water droplets float in the air as clouds, fog, or mist. At the ground level, water vapor may condense on cool surfaces as dew.

◯ Precipitation

In clouds, water droplets may collide and "stick" together to become larger. If a droplet becomes large enough, it falls to Earth's surface as precipitation (pri•sip•i•TAY•shuhn). **Precipitation** is any form of water that falls to Earth from clouds. Three common kinds of precipitation shown in the photos are rain, snow, and hail. Snow and hail form if the water droplets freeze. Most rain falls into the oceans because most water evaporates from ocean surfaces and oceans cover most of Earth's surface. But winds carry clouds from the ocean over land, increasing the amount of precipitation that falls on land.

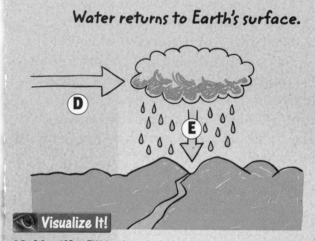

Water returns to Earth's surface.

Visualize It!

10 Identify Fill in the circle beside each red heading at left with the label of the arrow showing the matching process in this diagram.

Hail

Snow

Rain

11 Summarize Fill in the boxes to describe how precipitation forms.

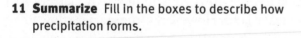

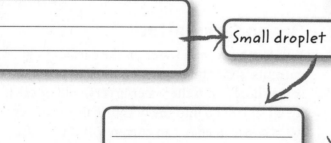

Small droplet

Large droplet falls to Earth.

How does water move on land and in the oceans?

After water falls to Earth, it flows and circulates all over Earth. On land, water flows downhill, both on the surface and underground. However, most of Earth's precipitation falls into the oceans. Ocean currents move water around the oceans.

Runoff and Infiltration

All of the water on land flows downhill because of gravity. Streams, rivers, and the water that flows over land are types of *runoff*. Runoff flows downhill toward oceans, lakes, and marshlands.

Some of the water on land seeps into the ground. This process is called *infiltration* (in•fil•TRAY•shuhn). Once undergound, the water is called *groundwater*. Groundwater also flows downhill through soil and rock.

 **Active Reading**

12 Compare How do runoff and groundwater differ?

_____

_____

_____

Visualize It!

13 Summarize Write a caption describing how water is moving in the diagram above.

_____

_____

Ice Flow

Much of Earth's ice is stored in large ice caps in Antarctica and Greenland. Some ice is stored in glaciers at high altitudes all over Earth. Glaciers cover about 10% of Earth's surface. Glaciers can be called "rivers of ice" because gravity also causes glaciers to flow slowly downhill. Many glaciers never leave land. However, some glaciers flow to the ocean, where pieces may break off, as seen in the photo, and float far out to sea as icebergs.

Ocean Circulation

Winds move ocean water on the surface in great currents, sometimes for thousands of miles. At some shores, or if the water is very cold or salty, it will sink deep into the ocean. This movement helps create deep ocean currents. Both surface currents and deep ocean currents transport large amounts of water from ocean to ocean.

Icebergs can be carried over long distances by ocean currents.

Water Works

What does the water cycle transport?

In the water cycle, each state of water has some energy in it. This energy is released into or absorbed from its surroundings as water changes state. The energy in each state of water is then transported as the water moves from place to place. Matter is also transported as water and the materials in the water move all over Earth. Therefore, the water cycle moves energy and matter through Earth's atmosphere, land, oceans, and living things.

Think Outside the Book

14 Apply With a classmate, discuss how the water cycle transfers energy.

Energy

Energy is transported in the water cycle through changes of state and by the movement of water from place to place. For example, water that evaporates from the ocean carries energy into the atmosphere. This movement of energy can generate hurricanes. Also, cold ocean currents can cool the air along a coastline by absorbing the energy from the air and leaving the air cooler. This energy is carried away quickly as the current continues on its path. Such processes affect the weather and climate of an area.

Matter

Earth's ocean currents move vast amounts of water all over the world. These currents also transport the solids in the water and the dissolved salts and gases. Rivers transfer water from land into the ocean. Rivers also carry large amounts of sand, mud, and gravel as shown below. Rivers form deltas and floodplains, where some of the materials from upstream collect in areas downstream. Rivers also carve valleys and canyons, and carry the excess materials downstream. Glaciers also grind away rock and carry the ground rock with them as they flow.

Visualize It!

15 Identify What do rivers, such as the ones in the photo, transport?

_____

_____

© Houghton Mifflin Harcourt Publishing Company • Image Credits: ©Yann Arthus-Bertrand/Corbis

Water is continuously changing state and moving from place to place in the water cycle. This diagram shows these processes and movements.

16 Identify Label each arrow to show which process the arrow represents.

17 Identify Shade in the arrows that indicate where water is changing state.

Condensation

Evaporation

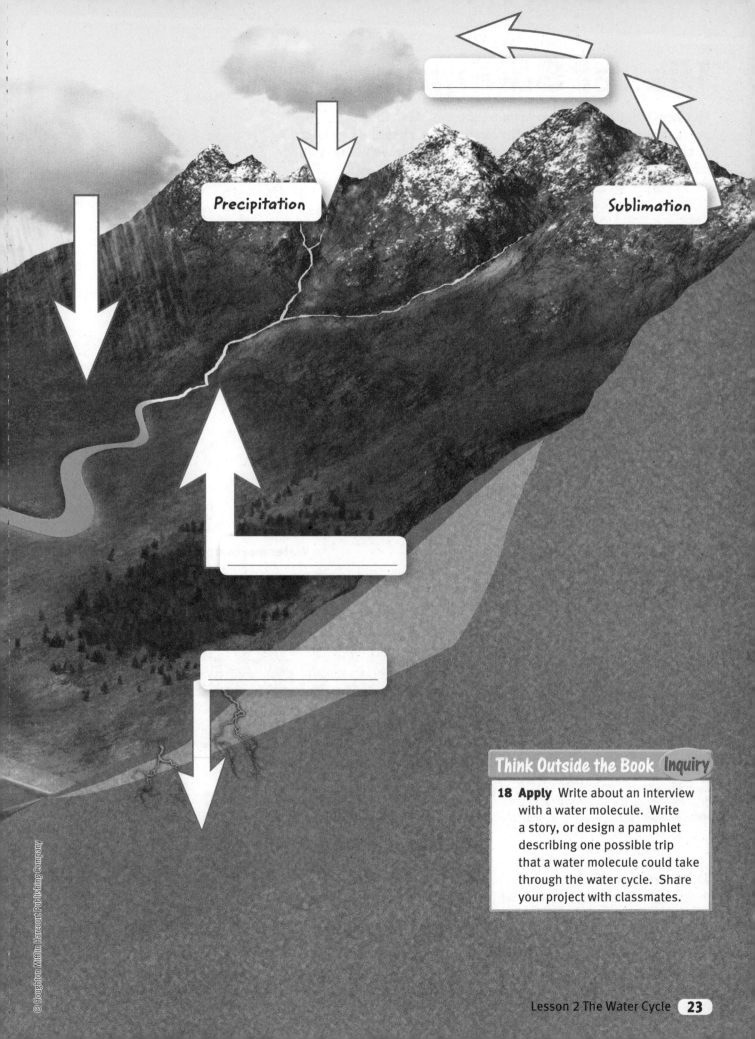

Precipitation

Sublimation

Think Outside the Book Inquiry

18 Apply Write about an interview with a water molecule. Write a story, or design a pamphlet describing one possible trip that a water molecule could take through the water cycle. Share your project with classmates.

Visual Summary

To complete this summary, write a term that describes the process happening in each of the images. Then use the key below to check your answers. You can use this page to review the main concepts of the lesson.

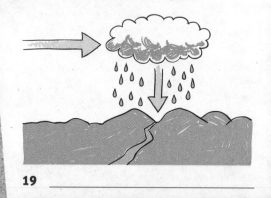

Water moves in the atmosphere.

19 _____

The Water Cycle

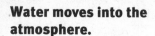

Water moves into the atmosphere.

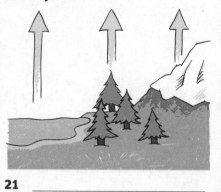

21 _____

Water moves on land and in oceans.

20 _____

Answers: 19 condensation or precipitation; 20 iceflow, runoff, infiltration, or ocean current; 21 evaporation, transpiration, or sublimation

22 **Predict** Describe what might happen to the water cycle if less solar energy reached Earth and how Earth's climate would be affected.

Lesson Review

Vocabulary

Write the correct label A, B, C, or D under each term to indicate the definition of that term.

1 water cycle

_____

2 evaporation

_____

3 precipitation

_____

4 condensation

_____

A The change of state from a liquid to a gas

B The change of state from a gas to a liquid

C The movement of water between the atmosphere, land, oceans, and living things

D Any form of water that falls to Earth's surface from the clouds

Key Concepts

5 Identify List the three ways in which water reaches the atmosphere and tell which way accounts for most of the water in the atmosphere.

_____

_____

_____

6 Classify Which of the processes of the water cycle occur by releasing energy?

_____

_____

7 Identify What happens to water once it reaches Earth's surface?

_____

_____

_____

8 Summarize Describe how three common types of precipitation form.

_____

_____

_____

_____

_____

Critical Thinking

Use the image below to answer the following question.

9 Apply Describe the energy changes occurring in the process shown above.

_____

_____

10 Infer Why does the amount of water that flows in a river change during the year?

_____

_____

11 Predict During a storm, a tree fell over into a river. What might happen to this tree?

_____

_____

_____

12 Evaluate Warm ocean currents cool as they flow along a coastline, away from the equator. Explain what is transported and how.

_____

_____

_____

_____

My Notes

Evaluating Technological Systems

Skills
✓ Identify inputs
✓ Identify outputs
Identify system processes
✓ Evaluate system feedback
✓ Apply system controls
✓ Communicate results

Objectives

- Analyze a hydroelectric power plant as a system.
- Identify the inputs and outputs of a system.
- Identify and evaluate feedback in a system.
- Examine how controls are used to regulate a system.

Analyzing Water Power

A system is a group of interacting parts that work together to do a job. Technological systems process inputs and generate outputs. An input is any matter, energy, or information that goes into a system. Outputs are matter, energy, or information that come out of the system. Most systems also generate some waste as an output.

Inputs and Outputs

Energy from moving water is the most common renewable source of electrical energy in the United States. A hydroelectric dam is a system that changes the mechanical energy in moving water into electrical energy. Water is the input to a hydroelectric dam. Huge tunnels, called *penstocks*, carry water into the dam to fan-like turbines. Water flowing past the blades of the turbines causes the turbines to spin. This causes wire coils in the generator to spin. Spinning coiled wire in a magnetic field produces an electric current. Electric current is one output of the hydroelectric dam system. Water flowing out of the dam is another output. In a hydroelectric dam, some of the energy from the flowing water is wasted in the form of heat from the friction of the spinning turbines and coils.

1 Identify What are the inputs and outputs of a hydroelectric dam?

_____

_____

"Workers use bicycles or tricycles to travel from one turbine to the next over the length of the dam because the turbines are so large."

Feedback and Control

Feedback is information from one step in a process that affects a previous step in the process. Feedback can be used to regulate a system by applying controls. In a hydroelectric dam system, information about how much electricity is produced is sent back into the system. This information is used to regulate the amount of electricity that is produced. When more electricity is needed, giant gates, called *sluice gates,* are opened to allow water to flow. When less electricity is required, some gates are closed. The sluice gates act as the control in this system.

2 Analyze In the image below, place the terms *input*, *output*, and *control* in the boxes that correspond to the correct part of the hydroelectric dam system.

Reservoir

Sluice gates

Dam

Generator

Power plant

Transformer

A

Penstock

Turbine

Power transmission cables

B

Downstream outlet

C

Water flowing through a dam spins a turbine. This spins a generator, which produces electric current. Transformers convert the current so that it can be used in homes, businesses, and factories.

 You Try It!

Now it's your turn to identify inputs, outputs, feedback, and controls.

 You Try It!

Now it's your turn to identify inputs, outputs, feedback and controls in a system that uses water power. Working with a partner, think of another way that you could use moving water to do a job. For example, flowing water in water mills has been used to spin large cutting blades in saw mills or to grind grain in flour mills. You can use one of these systems or use your imagination to create your own system that uses moving water to do a job.

(1) Identify Inputs

In the oval below, enter a name for your system. Recall that inputs can be matter, energy, or information. List the inputs into your system on the lines above the arrows. If there are more than three inputs, you can add more arrows.

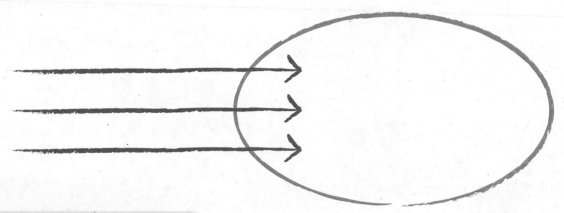

(2) Identify Outputs

As with the inputs, the outputs of a system can be matter, energy, or information. Keep in mind that most systems also generate some waste as an output. In the oval, write the name of your system. Use the arrows below to list the outputs of your system. If there are more than three outputs, you can add more arrows.

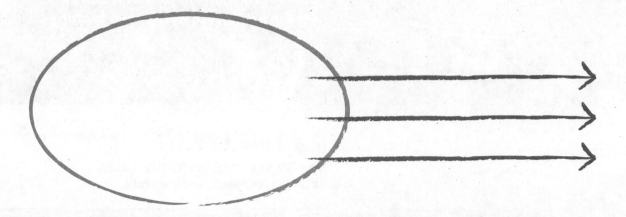

③ Evaluate System Feedback

Now, consider which steps in your system could be used as feedback to regulate the system. Which outputs need to be monitored and why?

_____

_____

_____

_____

④ Apply System Controls

Using the feedback you identified in the last step, propose one or more controls for your system that will keep the system working properly.

_____

_____

_____

_____

⑤ Communicate Results

In the space below, draw a sketch of the system you developed. Label the inputs, outputs, feedback and controls.

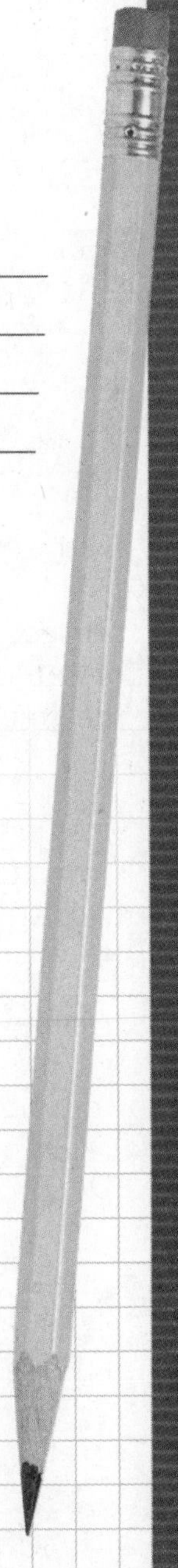

Surface Water and Groundwater

ESSENTIAL QUESTION

How does fresh water flow on Earth?

By the end of this lesson, you should be able to explain the processes involved in the flow of water, both above and below the ground.

Fresh water flows on Earth's surface, sometimes tumbling over waterfalls like these.

Lesson Labs

Quick Labs
• Modeling Groundwater
• Model a Stream

Exploration Lab
• Aquifers and Development

Engage Your Brain

1 Identify Read over the following vocabulary terms. In the spaces provided, place a + if you know the term well, a ~ if you have heard of the term but are not sure what it means, and a ? if you are unfamiliar with the term. Then write a sentence that includes one of the words you are most familiar with.

_____ tributary
_____ surface water
_____ aquifer

Sentence using known word:
_____
_____
_____

2 Describe Write your own caption for this photo.

_____
_____
_____
_____

Active Reading

3 Apply Many scientific words, such as *channel*, also have everyday meanings. Use context clues to write your own definition for each meaning of the word *channel*.

Example sentence:
She didn't like the TV show, so she changed the <u>channel</u>.

channel:
_____
_____

Example sentence:
The <u>channel</u> of the river was broad and deep.

channel:
_____
_____

Vocabulary Terms

• surface water • tributary
• groundwater • watershed
• water table • divide
• channel • aquifer

4 Identify As you read, create a reference card for each vocabulary term. On one side of the card, write the term and its meaning. On the other side, draw an image that illustrates or makes a connection to the term. These cards can be used as bookmarks in the text so that you can refer to them while studying.

Where on Earth is fresh water found?

About 97% of Earth's water is salty, which leaves only 3% as fresh water. Most of that small amount of fresh water is frozen as ice and snow, so only about 1% of Earth's water is fresh liquid water. This fresh liquid water is found both on and below Earth's surface.

This tiny percentage of Earth's water must meet the large demand that all living things have for fresh, clean water. In addition to providing drinking water, fresh water is used for agriculture, industry, transportation, and recreation. It also provides a place to live for many plants and animals.

On Earth's Surface

Active Reading **5 Identify** As you read, underline three examples of surface water.

Water above Earth's surface is called **surface water**. Surface water is found in streams, rivers, and lakes. It either comes from precipitation, such as rain, or from water that comes up from the ground to Earth's surface. Springs are an example of underground water coming up to the surface. Surface water flows from higher ground to lower ground. Water that flows across Earth's surface is called *runoff*. Eventually, runoff can enter bodies of water.

Beneath Earth's Surface

Active Reading **6 Identify** As you read, underline how surface water becomes groundwater.

Not all runoff becomes surface water. Some runoff and surface water seep down into the ground. Water drains through the soil and filters down into underground rock, collecting in spaces between rock particles. The water found in the spaces between rock particles below Earth's surface is called **groundwater**.

Most drinking water in the United States comes from groundwater supplies. To use these supplies, people drill down to the water table to reach reservoirs of groundwater. The **water table** is the upper boundary, or surface, of groundwater.

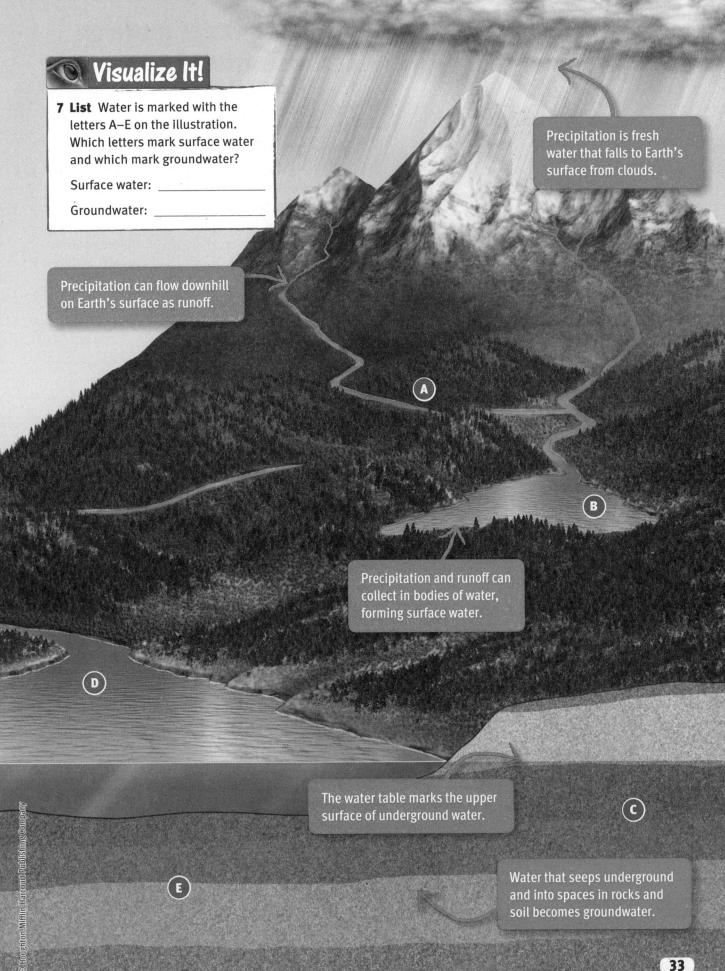

Visualize It!

7 List Water is marked with the letters A–E on the illustration. Which letters mark surface water and which mark groundwater?

Surface water: _____

Groundwater: _____

Precipitation is fresh water that falls to Earth's surface from clouds.

Precipitation can flow downhill on Earth's surface as runoff.

Precipitation and runoff can collect in bodies of water, forming surface water.

The water table marks the upper surface of underground water.

Water that seeps underground and into spaces in rocks and soil becomes groundwater.

Cry Me a River

How does water move on Earth's surface?

As precipitation falls on Earth's surface, it flows from higher to lower areas. The water that does not seep below the surface flows together and forms streams. The water erodes rocks and soil, eventually forming channels. A **channel** is the path that a stream follows. Over time, a channel gets wider and deeper, as the stream continues to erode rock and soil.

A **tributary** is a smaller stream that feeds into a river and eventually into a river system. A river system is a network of streams and rivers that drains an area of its runoff.

B

A

👁 Visualize It!

8 Identify Label *tributary*, *river*, *divide*, and *stream load* in the spaces provided on the illustration.

C

Within Watersheds

A **watershed** is the area of land that is drained by a river system. Streams, rivers, flood plains, lakes, ponds, wetlands, and groundwater all contribute water to a watershed. Watersheds are separated from one other by a ridge or an area of higher ground called a **divide**. Precipitation that falls on one side of a divide enters one watershed while the precipitation that falls on the other side of a divide enters another watershed.

The largest watershed in the United States is the Mississippi River watershed. It has hundreds of tributaries. It extends from the Rocky Mountains, in the west, to the Appalachian Mountains, in the east, and down the length of the United States, from north to south.

Many factors affect the flow of water in a watershed. For example, plants slow runoff and reduce erosion. The porosity and permeability of rocks and sediment determine how much water can seep down into the ground. The steepness of land affects how fast water flows over a watershed.

Active Reading **9 State** Which land feature separates watersheds?

_____

In Rivers and Streams

Gradient is a measure of the change in elevation over a certain distance. In other words, gradient describes the steepness, or slope, of the land. The higher the gradient of a river or stream, the faster the water moves. The faster the water moves, the more energy it has to erode rock and soil.

A river's *flow* is the amount of water that moves through the river channel in a given amount of time. Flow increases during a major storm or when warm weather rapidly melts snow. An increase in flow causes an increase in a river's speed.

Materials carried by a stream are called *stream load*. Streams with a high flow carry a larger stream load. The size of the particles depends on water speed. Faster streams can carry larger particles. Streams eventually deposit their stream loads where the speed of the water decreases. This commonly happens as streams enter lakes and oceans.

Active Reading **10 Summarize** How would an increase in gradient affect the speed of water?

_____

D

How does groundwater flow?

Although you can see some of Earth's fresh water in streams and lakes, you cannot see the large amount of water that flows underground as groundwater. Earth has much more fresh groundwater than fresh surface water.

It Trickles Down from Earth's Surface

Water from precipitation or streams may seep below the surface and become groundwater. Groundwater is either stored or it flows underground. It can enter back into streams and lakes, becoming surface water again. An **aquifer** is a body of rock or sediment that stores groundwater and allows it to flow.

Recall that the water table is the upper surface of underground water. The water table can rise or fall depending on the amount of water in the aquifer. In wet regions, the water table can be at or just beneath the soil's surface. In wetland areas, the water table is above the soil's surface.

It Fills Tiny Spaces Underground

An aquifer stores water in open spaces, or *pores,* between particles of rock or sediment. The storage space in an aquifer is measured by *porosity,* the percentage of the rock that is composed of pore space. The greater the pore space is, the higher the porosity is. A cup of gravel, for example, has higher porosity than a cup of sand does.

Permeability is a measure of how easily water can flow through an aquifer. High permeability means that many pores in the aquifer are connected, so water can flow easily. Aquifers with both high porosity and high permeability are useful as a water resource.

👁 Visualize It!

11 Label Draw an arrow, ↑ (high) or ↓ (low), to indicate the porosity and permeability of each rock sample. One is already completed as an example.

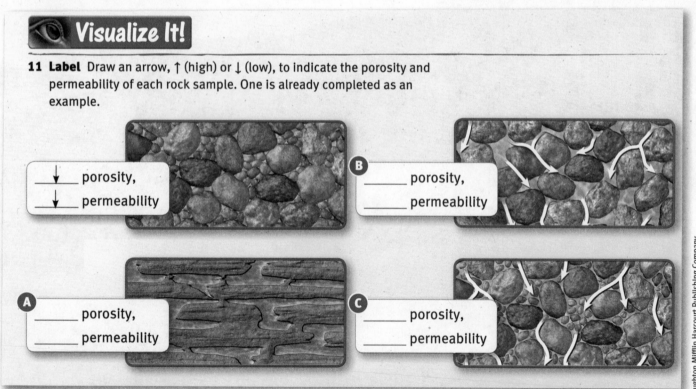

____↓____ porosity,
____↓____ permeability

B _____ porosity,
_____ permeability

A _____ porosity,
_____ permeability

C _____ porosity,
_____ permeability

It Is Recharged and Discharged

Surface water that trickles down into the ground can reach the water table and enter an aquifer. This process is called *recharge,* and occurs in an area called the *recharge zone.*

Where the water table meets the surface, water may pool to form a wetland or may flow out as a spring. The process by which groundwater becomes surface water is called *discharge* and happens in *discharge zones.* Discharge can feed rivers, streams, and lakes. Groundwater is also discharged where water is extracted from wells that are drilled down into the water table. Through discharge and recharge, the same water circulates between surface water and groundwater.

Think Outside the Book (Inquiry)

13 Debate During times of little or no rainfall, many communities have regulations limiting water use. Imagine that you live in a community with a depleted aquifer. As a class, develop a set of regulations that you think residents should follow. Start by brainstorming as many uses of water as you can. Then decide which uses should be regulated and to what extent.

 **Visualize It!**

12 Label On the illustration below, write a caption for *discharge zone* and for *aquifer.*

Water enters an aquifer in recharge zones.

Making a Splash

Active Reading

14 Identify As you read this page, underline how water is used in a typical home.

These rafters enjoy the exhilaration of river rapids.

How do people use surface water and groundwater?

About 75% of all the fresh water used in the United States comes from surface water. The other 25% comes from groundwater. But surface water and groundwater are connected. In human terms, they are one resource. People use this freshwater resource in many different ways.

For Drinking and Use at Home

Groundwater is an important source of drinking water. Surface water is used for drinking, too. Fresh water is also used in many other ways in homes. In a typical home, about 50% of all water used is for washing clothes, bathing, washing dishes, and flushing toilets. About 33% is used to water lawns and gardens. The rest is used for drinking, cooking, and washing hands.

For Agriculture

Activities like growing crops and raising livestock use about 40% of fresh water used in the United States. These activities account for about 70% of all groundwater use. A little over half the water used in agriculture comes from surface water. A little less than half comes from groundwater.

For Industry

Almost half of the fresh water used in the United States is used for industry. Only about 20% of this water comes from groundwater. The rest is surface water. About 40% of water used in industry helps cool elements in power plants.

For Transportation and Recreation

Surface water is also used to transport products and people from place to place. In addition, people use rivers, streams, and lakes for swimming, sailing, kayaking, water skiing, and other types of recreation.

Troubled Waters

Each hour, about 15,114 babies are born around the world. The human population has skyrocketed over the last few hundred years. But the amount of fresh water on Earth has remained roughly the same. The limited supply of fresh water is an important resource that must be managed so that it can meet the demands of a growing population.

Scientists are developing technologies for obtaining clean, fresh water to meet global needs. Here, a boy uses a water purifier straw that filters disease-causing microbes and certain other contaminants from surface water. The straw is inexpensive and can filter 700 L of water before it needs to be replaced—that's about how much water the average person drinks in one year.

Like many places on Earth, Zimbabwe is experiencing severe water shortages. The country has been plagued by droughts since the 1980s. Scientists estimate that about 1 billion people around the world do not have an adequate supply of clean, fresh water.

Extend

Inquiry

15 Infer Most of Earth is covered by water. How can we be experiencing shortages of drinking water?

16 Research Find out which diseases are caused by microbes found in untreated surface water. How might the water purifier straw reduce the number of people getting these diseases?

17 Recommend Conserving water is one way to ensure adequate supplies of drinking water. Work with a group to develop a plan to reduce water use at school. Present your plan to the class. As a class, select the best aspects of each group's plan. Combine the best suggestions into a document to present to the school administration.

Visual Summary

To complete this summary, fill in the blank with the correct word or phrase. Then, use the key below to check your answers. You can use this page to review the main concepts of the lesson.

Surface Water and Groundwater

Fresh surface water is found in streams, rivers, and lakes.

18 Smaller streams, or _____, flow into the main river channel.

Groundwater is found in pore spaces in rocks and sediment below Earth's surface.

19 The surface area where water enters an aquifer is called the _____ zone.

People use fresh water in homes, agriculture, and industry, for transportation, and for recreation.

20 Most industrial fresh water comes from rivers and other sources of _____

21 Relate Describe how a raindrop could become surface water, then groundwater, and then end up back on Earth's surface again.

Lesson Review

Vocabulary

In your own words, define the following terms.

1 surface water

_____

_____

2 watershed

_____

_____

3 groundwater

_____

_____

4 water table

_____

_____

5 aquifer

_____

_____

Key Concepts

6 Identify What three factors describe the movement of surface water in streams and rivers?

_____

_____

_____

7 Explain How does the gradient of a river affect its flow?

_____

_____

_____

8 Describe How quickly would groundwater flow through rock with high porosity and high permeability? Explain your answer.

_____

_____

_____

_____

Critical Thinking

9 Conclude An area's rate of groundwater recharge exceeds its rate of groundwater discharge. What can you conclude about the area's groundwater supply?

_____

_____

_____

_____

Use this graph to answer the following questions.

Average Water-Level Changes in the High Plains Aquifer by State (1980–2013)

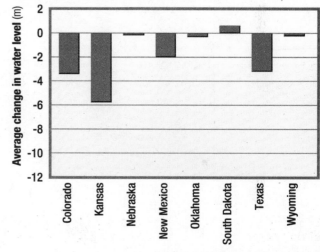

State *Source:* USGS, 2013

10 Analyze What has happened to the amount of water in the High Plains Aquifer over time?

_____

_____

11 Infer What might account for the changes described in question 10?

_____

_____

_____

_____

_____

My Notes

Unit 1 Big Idea ◀ Water moves through Earth's atmosphere, oceans, and land in a cycle and is essential for life on Earth.

Lesson 1

ESSENTIAL QUESTION
What makes water so important?

Describe water's structure, its properties, and its importance to Earth's system.

Lesson 2

ESSENTIAL QUESTION
How does water change state and move around on Earth?

Describe the water cycle and the different processes that are part of the water cycle on Earth.

Lesson 3

ESSENTIAL QUESTION
How does fresh water flow on Earth?

Explain the processes involved in the flow of water, both above and below the ground.

Connect ESSENTIAL QUESTIONS
Lessons 2 and 3

1 Synthesize Explain why precipitation on Earth's surface is less common on land than it is over the oceans. Base your answer on the water cycle.

_____

_____

_____

_____

Think Outside the Book

2 Synthesize Choose one of these activities to help synthesize what you have learned in this unit.

☐ Using what you learned in lessons 1 and 2, make a poster to show how the stored energy in water is released to the environment during certain changes in state.

☐ Using what you learned in lessons 1, 2, and 3, make a flipbook to show how gravity affects the movement and flow of water.

Unit 1 Review

Name _____

Vocabulary

Fill in each blank with the term that best completes the following sentences.

1 Water is a _____ molecule because its hydrogen atoms have a small positive charge and its oxygen atom has a small negative charge.

2 Water is called the universal _____ because it dissolves a large number of substances.

3 The continuous movement of water between the atmosphere, the land, the oceans, and living things is called the _____.

4 Any form of water that falls to Earth's surface from the clouds is called _____.

5 A _____ is the area of land that is drained by a river system.

Key Concepts

Read each question below, and circle the best answer.

6 A glass of ice water is shown below before and after it reaches room temperature.

Which of the following correctly explains something that occurred in the time between these two images?

A The ice cubes expanded in volume as they melted into liquid water.

B As water vapor condensed on the glass, it absorbed energy.

C The water droplets outside the glass absorbed energy as they evaporated.

D Some liquid water inside the glass sublimated into water vapor in the air.

7 Which of these circle graphs most correctly shows the approximate proportions of fresh water and salt water on the surface of the earth?

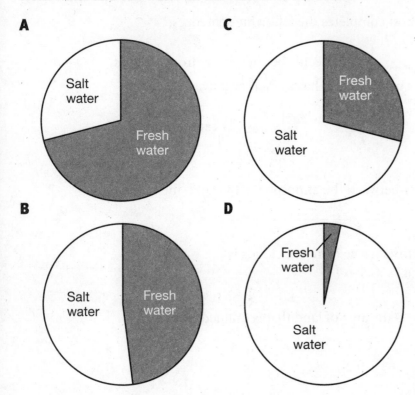

A

C

B

D

8 Which of the following is not a way that water reaches Earth's atmosphere?

A condensation

C sublimation

B evaporation

D transpiration

9 Which of the following correctly explains why icebergs float in the ocean?

A Ice is less dense than liquid water because water contracts when it freezes, filling in open space between molecules.

B Ice is less dense than liquid water because there is more open space between molecules in ice than in liquid water.

C Ice is more dense than liquid water because there is less open space between molecules in ice than in water.

D Water is a polar molecule, so the net positive electrical charges in the water repel the net positive electrical charges inside the iceberg.

10 A certain percentage of water that falls to Earth's surface as precipitation does not become surface water or groundwater and does not evaporate back into the atmosphere. Which of the following most likely explains what happens to this water?

A The water falls into the ocean, where it evaporates back into the atmosphere.

B The water is stored as snow and ice on Earth's surface.

C The water molecules are broken down into hydrogen and oxygen atoms.

D The water is absorbed and used by plants.

11 Which of the following is an incorrect statement about the flow of water through watersheds?

A A watershed can be fed by groundwater.

B The boundary separating two watersheds is called a divide.

C Plant life often alters the flow of water in a watershed by causing erosion.

D The gradient of the land can affect the flow of water through a watershed.

12 Which of the following is the name for all the materials carried by a stream other than the water itself?

A discharge   **C** gradient

B flow   **D** stream load

Critical Thinking

Answer the following questions in the space provided.

13 Give two examples of the importance of water to human activities, explaining how the water is used.

_____

_____

_____

_____

_____

_____

14 The diagram below shows the changes among the three states of water.

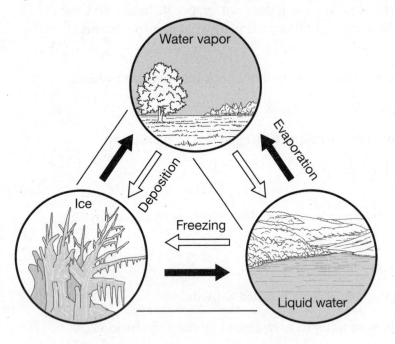

$\Longleftarrow$ Energy absorbed / released by water

$\longrightarrow$ Energy absorbed / released by water

Fill in each of the three blank lines with the correct term for the change of state shown by the arrows. In the key, circle the correct word to show whether water absorbs or releases energy in the changes of state shown by that type of arrow.

Connect ESSENTIAL QUESTIONS
Lessons 1, 2, and 3

Answer the following question in the space provided.

15 Describe what happens to a molecule of water as it moves through the water cycle along any path you choose. Be sure to mention the movement of the water molecule, any changes of state, and the absorption or release of energy.

_____

_____

_____

_____

_____

_____

_____

_____

_____

Oceanography

© Houghton Mifflin Harcourt Publishing Company • Image Credits: (bg) ©Sean Davey/Aurora Photos/Corbis; (inset) ©Jon Sparks/Corbis

Big Idea

The oceans are a connected system of water in motion that transports matter and energy around Earth's surface.

Ocean waves carry a tremendous amount of energy, which surfers use to travel back to shore.

What do you think?

Day and night, ocean waves strike shorelines around the world. Is it possible to harvest the energy of ocean waves?

Waves crashing ashore can destroy structures and erode rock.

Unit 2
Oceanography

Immersion Learning

Immersion Learning, a science-education organization, provides middle-school students with year-round access to scientific exploration that is being conducted in oceans around the world. For example, research is being done about sharks and rays, dolphins and whales, seals, kelp forests, the ocean floor, and shipwrecks.

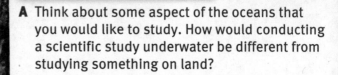

① Think About It

A Think about some aspect of the oceans that you would like to study. How would conducting a scientific study underwater be different from studying something on land?

_____

_____

_____

B What special skills or technology would help you to study something under the ocean?

_____

_____

_____

Remotely operated vehicles (ROVs) are used to study the ocean.

② Ask a Question

With your classmates, explore the program descriptions on the Immersion Learning web page. Then, answer this question: How would these programs help me to better understand Earth's oceans?

_____

_____

_____

_____

_____

③ Make a Plan

Pick one area of oceanography that you would most like to study. Make a plan for further study by listing some things you can do to learn more about that subject and about careers in oceanography.

_____

_____

_____

_____

Studying coral reefs is important because they serve as nurseries for fish and other sea life.

Take It Home

Visit a nearby aquarium or explore the web page of an aquarium, such as the Monterey Bay Aquarium in Monterey, California. See *ScienceSaurus*® for more information about ocean life.

Earth's Oceans
and the
Ocean Floor

ESSENTIAL QUESTION

What lies within and beneath Earth's oceans?

By the end of this lesson, you should be able to describe the properties and physical features of Earth's oceans.

Scientists use technology such as robot submersibles to explore the deepest depths of the ocean.

© Houghton Mifflin Harcourt Publishing Company • Image Credits: (bg) ©Randy Olson/National Geographic/Getty Images; ©HMH

✋ **Lesson Labs**

Quick Labs
• Evaporation Rates
• Ocean Density

Exploration Lab
• Measuring Salinity

 Engage Your Brain

1 Predict Look at this photo. How much of Earth do you think is covered by oceans?

_____

_____

2 Describe Write a word or phrase beginning with each letter of the word OCEAN that describes oceans.

O _____

C _____

E _____

A _____

N _____

✏️ **Active Reading**

3 Apply Use context clues to write your own definitions for the words *salinity* and *ocean trench*.

Example sentence
Adding salt to a solution increases the solution's salinity.

salinity:

_____

_____

Example sentence
The deepest parts of the ocean are the ocean trenches.

ocean trench:

_____

_____

Vocabulary Terms

• salinity   • deep-ocean basin
• thermocline   • mid-ocean ridge
• continental margin • ocean trench

4 Apply As you learn the definition of each vocabulary term in this lesson, make your own definition or sketch to help you remember the meaning of the term.

Feelin' Blue

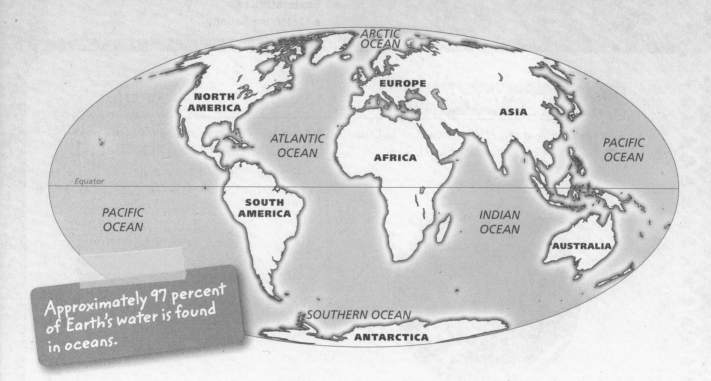

Approximately 97 percent of Earth's water is found in oceans.

What are Earth's five main oceans?

You can see on the map above that the continents are like huge islands surrounded by one vast, interconnected global ocean. Almost three-fourths of Earth is covered by ocean water. In places, the global ocean is more than 11 km deep.

Earth's global ocean is divided into five main oceans. The largest is the Pacific Ocean. It contains about half of Earth's water. The Atlantic Ocean is next in size. It stretches in a north-south direction. The third-largest ocean, the Indian Ocean, is found mainly in the Southern Hemisphere. The Southern Ocean is located near Antarctica. The smallest ocean, the Arctic Ocean, is nearly covered by ice much of the year.

What are some characteristics of ocean water?

 **Active Reading**

5 Identify As you read, underline characteristics of ocean water.

Like all matter, ocean water has both chemical and physical properties. Its chemical characteristics include **salinity**, or the amount and type of dissolved salts, and the amount and type of gases in the seawater. Its physical characteristics include temperature and density.

Salinity

On average, one kilogram of seawater contains about 35 g of dissolved salts. Thus, the overall salinity of seawater is about 3.5 percent.

Dissolved salts come from different sources. Water flowing on or under Earth's surface weathers rocks and carries calcium, magnesium, and sodium ions into the ocean. Underwater volcanoes and vents release solutions that are the source of chloride ions.

Over time, the salinity of seawater has remained relatively steady. However, it does vary from place to place. The salinity of water near the ocean's surface can be lower than average in areas where freshwater streams enter the ocean or where abundant precipitation falls into the ocean. Conversely, salinity can be higher than average in areas where rates of evaporation are high.

The white substance isn't snow. Above, a woman breaks apart salt that is left behind as water evaporates from these shallow, salty pools in Sri Lanka.

Temperature

Ocean water temperature varies by latitude, by depth, and by season. There are three distinct temperature layers by depth. The top layer, or surface zone, is the warmest layer. This layer is heated by the sun. The thermocline is the next zone. In the **thermocline**, water temperature drops with increased depth faster than it does in other layers. The deep zone is the deepest layer, and the coldest.

By latitude, the warmest surface water is near the equator. The coldest is near the poles. But the surface zone is generally warmer than deeper water regardless of latitude. Surface water is warmest in summer and coldest in winter. Driven by winds and density differences, both surface currents and deep currents travel through the global ocean, distributing energy in the form of heat.

Ocean water temperature varies by latitude (above) and depth (right).

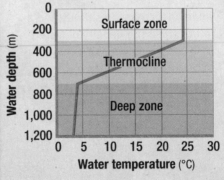

6 Identify At what latitude and depth is ocean water warmest?

_____

_____

Density

Recall that *density* is a measure of the mass of a substance divided by its volume. The density of ocean water depends on temperature and salinity. Salt water is denser than fresh water because salt water contains a large amount of dissolved solids.

Temperature also affects water density. As liquid ocean water becomes colder, its molecules move around less and pack closer together. Thus, cold ocean water is denser than warm ocean water.

Temperature affects the density of ocean water more than salinity does. So the densest ocean water is found near the poles, where the ocean surface is coldest. In the global ocean, differences in density drive the circulation of deep ocean currents, which distribute energy in the form of heat throughout the ocean.

Visualize It!

The yellow cups contain water that is dyed blue. The blue water is trickling out of holes poked in the bottoms of the yellow cups and into the beakers. The beakers contain fresh water at room temperature.

7 Infer One of the yellow cups contains water that is colder and saltier than the other. Which cup is it? Explain your answer.

_____

_____

_____

_____

Can you tell what the difference is between these two trials?

8 Summarize How would an increase in salinity and a decrease in temperature affect the density of water?

Increase in salinity	→	Effect on density
Decrease in temperature	→	

salt

Seeing the Sea

How is the ocean floor studied?

As you learned earlier in this lesson, the ocean is 11 km deep in some places. People cannot safely dive down to such extreme depths. So what lies at the deepest, darkest part of the ocean? How do scientists learn about the ocean floor? They use technology such as sonar, drills, underwater exploration vessels, and satellites.

Visualize It!

Differences in the times that sound waves take to return to the ship allow scientists to calculate the depth and shapes of ocean floor features.

9 Describe Draw arrows in the boxes to show the directions in which the sound waves are moving.

With Sonar

Sonar stands for *sound navigation and ranging.* This technology uses sound waves to measure distances. Scientists use sonar to determine the ocean's depth by sending sound pulses from a ship down into the ocean. The sound moves through the water, bounces off the ocean floor, and returns to the ship, where the sound waves are picked up by receivers. Computers on the ship calculate the time the sound takes to travel from the ship to the ocean floor and back again. The deeper the water is, the longer the round trip takes. Sonar data can be used to make maps of the ocean floor.

Features on the ocean floor can be mapped by using sonar.

10 Justify Which technologies would you use to explore the underwater landscape shown in this illustration? Explain why you chose these technologies.

_____

_____

_____

_____

_____

_____

_____

_____

With Satellites

Satellites can measure variations in the height of the ocean's surface. The features of the ocean floor can affect the height of the water above them. Scientists can use satellite data to make maps of the sea floor. Satellites can gather data from much larger areas than sonar can. Satellites can also measure other features, such as the ocean's surface temperature, with a high degree of accuracy.

In Underwater Vessels

Just as astronauts explore space by using rockets, scientists use underwater vessels to explore the oceans. Some vessels have pilots and can carry researchers. Other vessels are remotely operated. Remotely operated vehicles, or ROVs, are "flown" from the surface by remote control. ROVs can be used to explore the ocean at depths that are too dangerous for piloted vessels to explore.

With Deep-Sea Drilling

Scientists can collect cores, or long tubes of rock and sediment, from the sea floor. Cores are drilled using equipment on large ships. By studying the layers of rock and sediment in the cores, scientists learn about the history of Earth. For example, through drilling, scientists have found evidence of sea-floor spreading, which occurs where tectonic plates move apart.

In Deep Water

What are the two main regions of the ocean floor?

Picture yourself in a piloted research vessel deep below the ocean surface. What would you see on the ocean floor? The ocean floor is not all flat. It has features that include the world's longest mountain chain and deep canyons. The two main regions of the ocean floor are the continental margin and the deep-ocean basin.

The Continental Margin

The **continental margin** is the edge of the continent that is covered by the ocean. The continental margin is divided into the continental shelf, the continental slope, and the continental rise. These divisions are based on depth and changes in slope.

The continental shelf is a relatively flat underwater extension of the continent, which is the land that is above water. The shelf ends at a steeply sloping region, the continental slope. The ocean floor eventually becomes a more gently sloping terrain. This gently sloping area is the continental rise.

The Deep-Ocean Basin

The **deep-ocean basin** begins at the end of the continental margin. It extends under the deepest parts of the ocean. The deep-ocean basin includes narrow depressions and flat, smooth plains.

Active Reading 11 **Apply** Imagine the ocean is a giant swimming pool. Which region would be the shallow end, and which region would be the deep end?

_____

_____

_____

The continental margin has three parts.

Boston
New York
Washington, D.C.
Savannah

Continental Margin

Continental Shelf
Continental Slope
Continental Rise

Deep-Ocean Basin

ATLANTIC OCEAN

What are the features of the ocean floor?

You may know that the movement of tectonic plates forms features, such as mountains and volcanoes, on continents. These movements also form features on the ocean floor. As Earth's tectonic plates move, the plates slide past each other, collide with each other, or move away from each other. As a result, mid-ocean ridges, trenches, and seamounts form.

 **Visualize It!**

12 Label On the drawing, label the continental shelf and slope.

B Continental _____

A Continental _____

 **Active Reading**

13 Identify As you read, underline how mid-ocean ridges form.

Mid-Ocean Ridge: Diverging Plates

A long, undersea mountain chain that forms along the floor of the ocean is called a **mid-ocean ridge**. Mid-ocean ridges occur at the boundaries of Earth's tectonic plates, where plates move apart from each other. This motion creates a crack in the ocean floor called a rift, and allows hot magma to move upward. The magma rises through the rift and cools to form new rock. The ridges, like the ocean crust, are made of this rock. The world's longest mountain chain is a mid-ocean ridge that stretches about 65,000 km along the global ocean floor.

Abyssal Plains: Very Flat Regions of Earth

The large, flat, almost level area of the deep-ocean basin is called the *abyssal plain*. This area is covered with layers of fine sediment. Some of these sediments are carried here by wind and ocean currents. Other sediment is made of the remains of organisms that settle to the ocean floor when the organisms die.

Think Outside the Book (Inquiry)

14 **Hypothesize** Select a feature of the ocean floor. Write a research question about this feature. Then write two possible hypotheses.

Ocean Trenches: Subducting Plates

A long, narrow depression in the deep-ocean basin is called an **ocean trench**. The Mariana Trench, in the Pacific Ocean, is the deepest place in Earth's crust. Ocean trenches form where one tectonic plate subducts, or moves under, another plate.

As the plates move, the subducting plate releases fluids into surrounding rock. The surrounding rock melts, forming magma, which may rise to the surface to form volcanoes. Earthquakes are also common in and along subduction zones.

Volcanic islands like this one can form over a tectonic plate boundary or a hot spot.

Seamounts and Volcanic Islands: Where Magma Rises

Submerged volcanic mountains on the ocean floor are called seamounts. They may form at tectonic plate boundaries. Seamounts can also form far from plate boundaries over places called hot spots. At a hot spot, magma breaks through the overlying plate. The resulting volcano may grow into a seamount.

If a seamount grows above sea level, it becomes a *volcanic island*. The Hawaiian Islands are volcanic islands that formed over a hot spot.

Visual Summary

To complete this summary, circle the correct word. Then, use the key below to check your answers. You can use this page to review the main concepts of the lesson.

Earth's Oceans and the Ocean Floor

About three-fourths of Earth is covered by oceans.

15 The Pacific Ocean is the smallest / **largest** ocean.

16 Sonar uses **sound** / light waves to measure distance to the ocean floor.

The properties of ocean water include salinity, temperature, and density.

17 The temperature of ocean water varies with depth, usually forming two / **three** distinct layers.

The two main regions of the ocean floor are the continental margin and the deep-ocean basin.

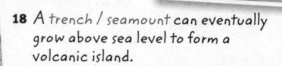

18 A trench / **seamount** can eventually grow above sea level to form a volcanic island.

Answers: 15 largest; 16 sound; 17 three; 18 seamount

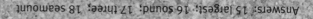

19 **Model** Design a way to model the features of the ocean floor.

Lesson Review

Vocabulary

Draw a line to connect the following terms to their definitions.

1 continental margin

2 deep-ocean basin

3 mid-ocean ridge

4 ocean trench

5 salinity

6 thermocline

A a water layer with great temperature changes

B a long, narrow underwater depression

C the measure of the amount of dissolved salts in a given amount of liquid

D a long, underwater mountain chain

E the edge of the continent covered by ocean water

F the part of the ocean that begins at the end of the continental margin

Key Concepts

7 **Sequence** In order from largest to smallest, what are Earth's five main oceans?

_____

_____

_____

8 **List** What are the three main temperature layers in the ocean?

_____

_____

9 **Identify** What two properties affect the density of ocean water?

_____

_____

_____

_____

Critical Thinking

Use the graph to answer the questions that follow.

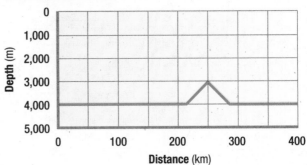

Ocean Floor Profile

10 **Infer** What major region does this profile most likely represent?

_____

11 **Analyze** What types of features are evident on the profile?

_____

_____

12 **Infer** Suppose the salinity of surface ocean water is high in a particular place. What might you infer about the area's rates of evaporation?

_____

_____

13 **Assess** How is exploring oceans similar to exploring space?

_____

_____

_____

_____

_____

_____

My Notes

Understanding a Bathymetric Map

Topographic maps are contour maps that illustrate the mountains, valleys, and hills on land. Bathymetric maps are contour maps that illustrate similar features on the ocean floor.

Tutorial

A bathymetric map uses curved contour lines that each represent a specific depth. Colors are also often used to show different depths. Because sea level is at 0 meters, increasing depths are shown by negative numbers. The bathymetric map below shows a part of the Mariana Trench, the deepest known part of the world's ocean.

Bathymetric Map

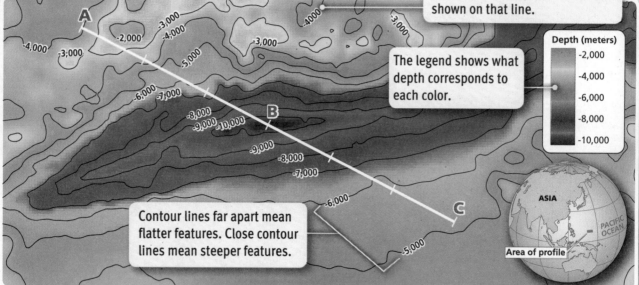

Every point along a contour line is at the same depth, the number shown on that line.

The legend shows what depth corresponds to each color.

Contour lines far apart mean flatter features. Close contour lines mean steeper features.

Bathymetric Profile

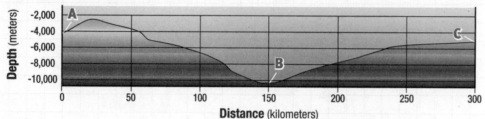

A bathymetric profile shows the change in depth across any chosen reference line on a bathymetric map. This profile details the change in depth across the line ABC shown on the map above. To see how the profile was made, move your finger along the line ABC on the map. Every time you cross a contour line, check that the profile crosses the same depth line on the grid.

You Try It!

Now follow the steps below to draw the profile for this bathymetric map of a region near Monterey Bay, California.

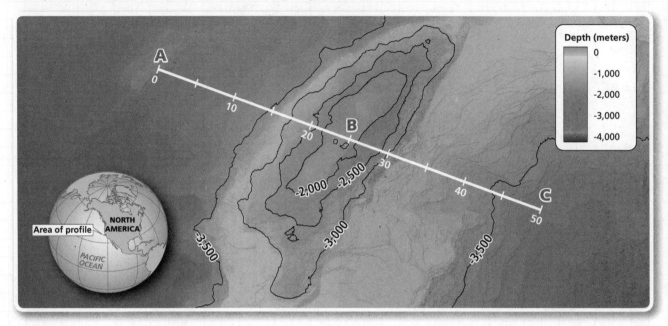

Profile Grid

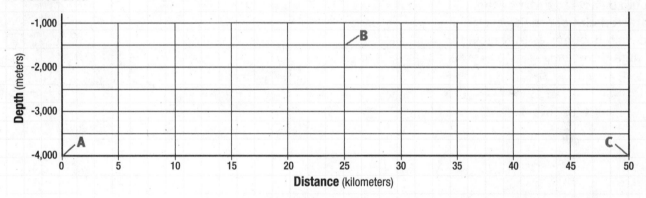

1 List Use the color legend to estimate the depths at points A, B, and C. Record this data in the table below.

Point	Color	Depth
A		
B		
C		

2 Distinguish For each tick mark on the line ABC, place a dot on the corresponding profile grid line at the correct depth.

3 Graph Move your finger along the ABC line on the map and place a dot on the profile grid at the correct depth for each contour line you cross.

4 Draw To complete the profile, connect the dots you plotted.

5 Evaluate Describe the ocean floor feature that you just plotted.

_____

_____

_____

_____

_____

_____

Ocean Waves

ESSENTIAL QUESTION

How does an ocean wave form and move?

By the end of this lesson, you should be able to describe the characteristics of ocean waves and what happens as they move through the ocean.

You've probably seen an ocean wave before, but did you know not all ocean waves are the same? In this lesson, you'll find out how ocean waves form and how they move.

Lesson Labs

Quick Labs
- Making Waves
- Factors in Wave Formation

Exploration Lab
- Wave Movement

Engage Your Brain

1 Identify Read the following vocabulary terms. In the spaces provided, place a + if you know the term well, a ~ if you have heard the term but are not sure what it means, and a ? if you are unfamiliar with the term. Then write a sentence that includes one of the words you are most familiar with.

_____ **wave**

_____ **crest**

_____ **tsunami**

Sentence using known word:

_____

_____

2 Describe Imagine you are a photographer who is taking a set of photos for a lesson about ocean waves. Describe the photos you will take. Be specific.

_____

_____

_____

_____

_____

_____

_____

_____

Active Reading

3 Synthesize You can often define an unknown word if you know the meaning of its word parts. Use the word parts and sentences below to make an educated guess about the meaning of the term *wave period*.

Word part	Meaning
wave	a periodic disturbance
period	an interval of time

Example sentence

Edward watched waves travel under his boat. It took about two seconds for each wave to pass, so he knew the <u>wave period</u> was two seconds.

wave period:

_____

_____

_____

Vocabulary Terms

- **wave**
- **ocean wave**
- **crest**
- **trough**
- **wavelength**
- **wave period**
- **mechanical wave**
- **tsunami**

4 Apply As you learn the definition of each vocabulary term in this lesson, create your own definition or sketch to help you remember the meaning of the term.

Catch the Wave

What are some properties of a wave?

Have you ever seen a surfer riding waves? Or have you jumped in a pool and made waves? A **wave** is any disturbance that transfers energy through matter or empty space. An **ocean wave** is a disturbance that transfers energy through ocean water.

Size

Waves are made up of two main parts—crests and troughs. A **crest** is the highest point of a wave. A **trough** is the lowest point of a wave. The top of a rise on a roller-coaster track is similar to the crest of a wave. The bottom of a dip in the track resembles the trough of a wave. The distance between two adjacent wave crests or wave troughs is a **wavelength**. Wave *amplitude* is half the distance between the crest and the trough. The diagram below shows the parts of a wave.

👁 **Visualize It!**

5 Describe Use a ruler to find the amplitude of this wave.

_____

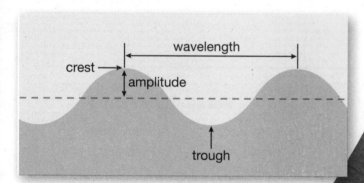

6 Apply Use a ruler to draw a wave with a wavelength of 3 cm.

This wave is transferring energy.

Frequency and Wave Period

Wavelength and amplitude are not the only properties used to describe a wave. Waves also vary in frequency and wave period. These two properties are related, but different.

Frequency is the number of waves produced in a given amount of time. You can measure the frequency of an ocean wave by counting how many waves pass a fixed point in a certain amount of time. If you see five waves pass the point in ten seconds, then the frequency is 5 waves per 10 seconds, or 0.5 waves/second.

Wave period, in contrast, is a measurement of how much time it takes for a wave to pass the fixed point. In other words, it is the inverse of frequency. Frequency is measured in waves/time while wave period is measured in time/wave.

Wave Speed

Waves come in many different sizes and travel at different speeds. *Wave speed* is how fast a wave travels. To calculate wave speed, you can multiply the wave's wavelength by its frequency, as shown below. For any given wave, an increase in either the frequency of the wave or the wavelength will cause an increase in wave speed.

wave speed (v) = wavelength (λ) × frequency (*f*)

Wave speed is measured in distance/time.

 **Do the Math**

Imagine you are in a boat on the open ocean. You count 5 waves passing under your boat in 10 seconds. You estimate the wavelength to be 2 m.

Sample Problem

A What do you know?

wave frequency and wavelength

B What do you want to find out?

wave speed

C Write the formula:

wave speed (v) = wavelength (λ) × frequency (*f*)

D Substitute into the formula:

$v = 2\ m/wave \times 0.5\ waves/s$

E Calculate and check your units:

$2\ m/wave \times 0.5\ waves/s = 1\ m/s$

Answer: 1 m/s

You Try It!

7 Calculate You count 2 waves traveling right under your boat in 10 seconds. You estimate the wavelength to be 3 m. What is the wave speed?

Identify

A What do you know?

B What do you want to find out?

Plan

C Write the formula:

D Substitute into the formula:

Solve

E Calculate and check your units:

Answer:

Surf's UP!

What causes ocean waves?

Waves carry energy. Ocean waves are a type of wave known as a **mechanical wave**. Mechanical waves carry energy through matter, such as water. Ocean waves form when energy is transferred from a source such as wind to the ocean water.

Active Reading 8 **Identify** As you read, underline the source of energy that causes each wave to form.

Wind

Most ocean waves form when energy in the atmosphere is transferred to the ocean's surface. Wind blows across the water's surface and transfers energy to the water. The energy is then carried by the wave, usually all the way to the ocean shore.

Have you ever wondered why ocean waves are different sizes? When wind begins to blow over water, small waves, or ripples, form. If the wind keeps blowing, more energy is transferred to the ripples. They grow into larger waves. The longer the wind blows in the same direction across the water, the more energy is transferred from the wind to the water, and the larger the waves become.

These waves were caused by wind blowing across the water.

Visualize It!

9 **Infer** Look at the boats in the photo. Which direction is the wind blowing? Explain how you know.

_____

_____

_____

Earthquakes

Waves can also form from other sources of energy. For example, underwater earthquakes can cause waves to form in the ocean. You could model this process by using a thin aluminum pan filled with water. Pushing up on the bottom of the pan will cause water in the tray to move.

Volcanoes

Underwater volcanoes are another source of energy that can cause waves to form. Underwater volcanoes cause waves in a very similar way to how underwater earthquakes form waves. As the volcano erupts, the surrounding water is displaced, sending out a wave in all directions.

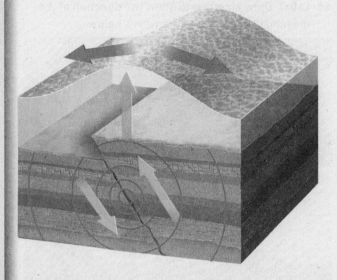

Landslides

Underwater landslides can also displace water and cause waves. The ocean floor is made up of many features, including towering cliffs and the world's longest mountain chains. Landslides along these landforms push the surrounding water. The energy is then transferred outward, lifting the sea surface above the landslide.

Meteorites and Asteroids

Meteorites and asteroids are rocky bodies from space that can collide with Earth. If a meteorite or asteroid lands in the ocean, it can displace enough water to cause large waves. If a large asteroid landed in the Atlantic Ocean, for example, the resulting wave could flood much of the east coast of the United States.

Doing the Wave

What happens when a wave moves through the water?

If you have watched ocean waves, you may have noticed that water seems to move across the ocean's surface. But this movement is only an illusion. Actually, waves don't move water. Instead, they transfer energy through the water.

Energy Travels

As you learned on the previous pages, most waves form when winds blow. Wind transfers energy to the water. As the energy moves through the water, so do the waves. But the water itself does not travel with the energy.

Water Rises and Falls But Stays in the Same Place

Notice in the illustration that the floating seagull remains in approximately the same spot as the wave travels from left to right. The water and the seagull do not move with the wave, but only rise and fall in circular movements. This circular movement of water is generally the greatest at the ocean surface. Wave energy affects surface water to a depth of about half a wavelength. Deeper water is not affected by the energy of surface waves.

Active Reading 10 **Compare** How does the movement of water compare to the movement of energy in a wave?

_____

_____

_____

11 **Label** Draw an arrow to show the direction of the movement of energy in the waves below.

Like the bird in this illustration, water remains in the same place as waves travel through it.

Watts from Waves

Every minute of every day, waves are crashing against the coastline of the United States. That's a lot of energy being delivered directly to our doorstep! In fact, the Department of Energy estimates that about 7% of our electrical energy needs could be met by capturing the wave energy along our coastlines.

This is the Pelamis Wave Energy Converter

Anchor

Power cable

The up-and-down motion of Pelamis is converted by a generator into electrical energy.

Electrical energy is transferred to the power cable.

The power cable carries energy back to shore.

Extend

Inquiry

12 Explain What are some advantages to using wave energy instead of fossil fuels to generate electricity?

13 Identify Research some disadvantages, such as the impact on marine life, to installing wave power generators along a coastline.

14 Model Build a model of a wave power generator. Include labels to show how the wave energy is transformed into electrical energy.

Totally Turbulent

What happens when a wave reaches the shore?

Ocean waves can transfer energy over very long distances. In fact, waves can travel thousands of miles across the ocean's surface. The energy is carried all the way to the shore.

Energy Decreases with Depth

Why do waves crash on shore? The figure below shows how changes in the depth of water cause waves to crash. When waves reach water shallower than one-half their wavelength, they begin to interact with the ocean floor. As waves touch the ocean floor, the waves transfer energy to the ocean floor. As a result, the water at the bottom of the wave slows down.

It Breaks in Shallow Water

As water depth decreases, wave height increases, because more water is forced between wave crests. The top of the wave travels faster than the bottom of the wave, which is dragging on the ocean floor. Eventually, gravity pulls the wave crests down, and they crash onto the shore. These waves that crash onto shore are called breakers.

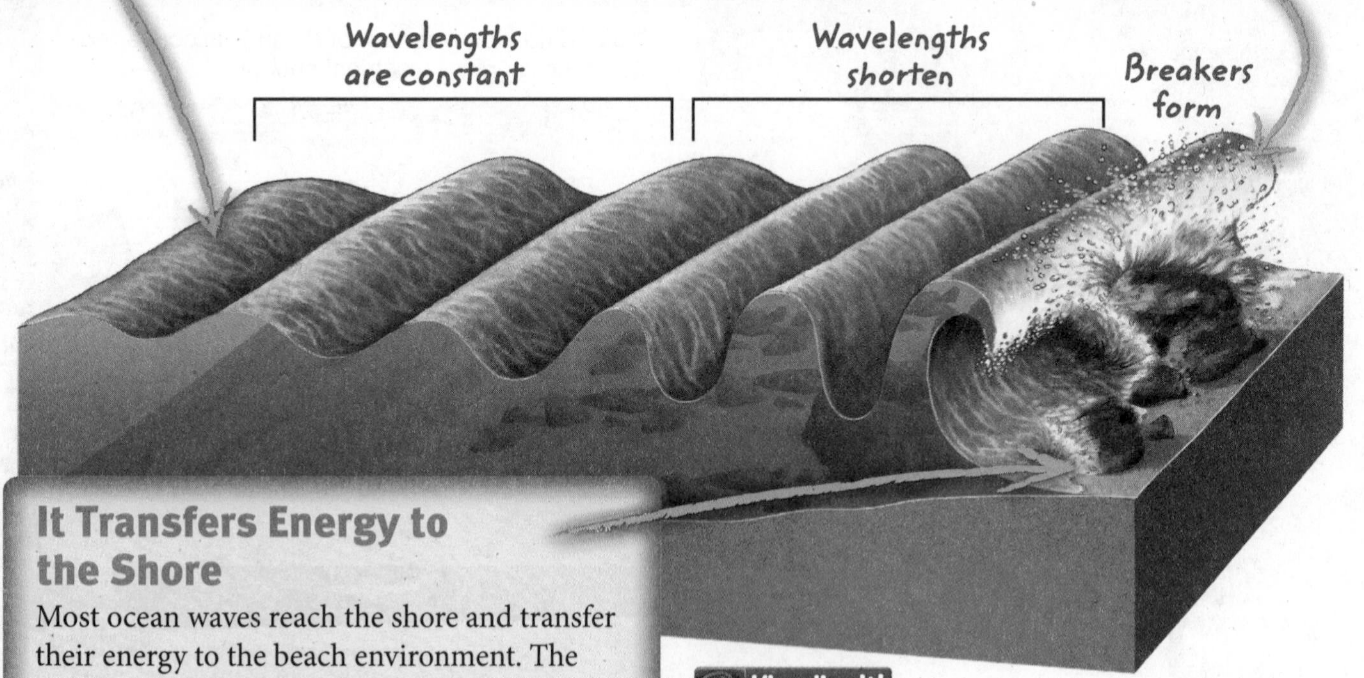

Wavelengths are constant

Wavelengths shorten

Breakers form

It Transfers Energy to the Shore

Most ocean waves reach the shore and transfer their energy to the beach environment. The energy of the wave and the angle at which the wave hits the shore determine how much energy is transferred. High-energy waves can quickly erode beaches. Strong waves can even throw boulders and other debris up on the beach, particularly during storms.

Visualize It!

15 **Explain** Why do waves break as they reach the shore?

_____

_____

_____

What is a tsunami?

Surfers can go to Hawaii to catch some of the highest waves in the world. But even the best surfers would not be able to handle a tsunami. A **tsunami** [tsoo•NAH•mee] is a series of waves that form when a large volume of ocean water is suddenly moved up or down. This movement can be caused by earthquakes, volcanic eruptions, landslides, or the impact of a meteorite or asteroid. The illustration below shows how an underwater earthquake can cause a tsunami.

Most tsunamis occur in the Pacific Ocean, because many earthquakes occur in that region. When a tsunami approaches land, the waves slow down and get taller as they interact with the ocean floor. Tsunamis can reach more than 30 m in height as they slam into the coast, destroying almost everything in their path. The huge volume of water that crashes onto shore then rushes back into the ocean. This powerful flow of water, called an undertow, can be as destructive as the tsunami itself.

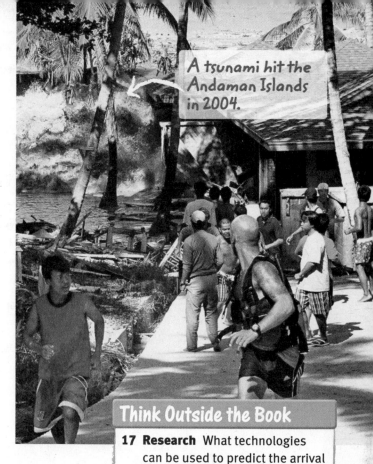

A tsunami hit the Andaman Islands in 2004.

Think Outside the Book

17 Research What technologies can be used to predict the arrival of a tsunami? Select two, and describe the opportunities and drawbacks of each.

Visualize It!

16 Explain Review the illustration. Then describe the sequence of events in the illustration by writing a caption for each event.

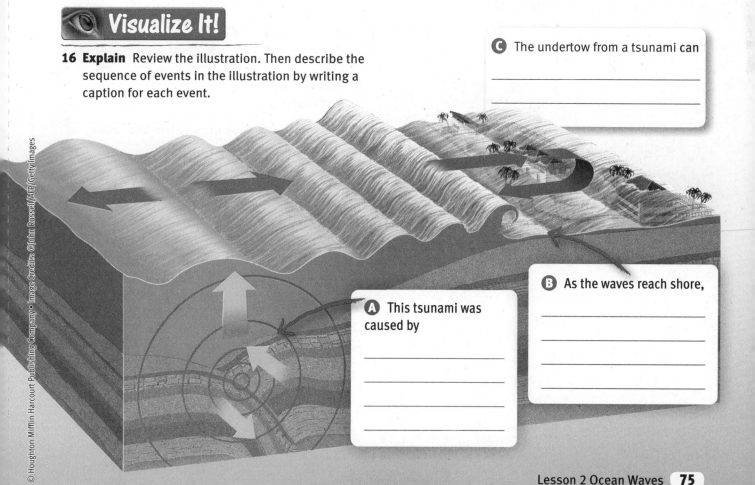

C The undertow from a tsunami can
_____
_____

A This tsunami was caused by
_____
_____
_____

B As the waves reach shore,
_____
_____
_____
_____

Visual Summary

To complete this summary, fill in the blanks and circle the correct term. Then use the key below to check your answers. You can use this page to review the main concepts of the lesson.

Ocean Waves

Waves vary in size, frequency, wave period, and speed.

18 A wave's speed is equal to its _____ multiplied by its _____

Ocean waves form as energy is transferred to the water.

19 Waves form when energy is transferred to ocean water by:

- _____
- earthquakes and volcanoes
- _____
- meteorite and asteroid impacts

Wave energy is carried all the way to shore.

20 Waves transfer _____, not matter.

21 When a wave approaches the shoreline, it slows down/speeds up.

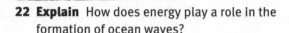

Answers: 18 wavelength, frequency; 19 wind, landslides; 20 energy; 21. slows down

22 Explain How does energy play a role in the formation of ocean waves?

_____

Lesson Review

Vocabulary

Define Fill in the blank with the correct term.

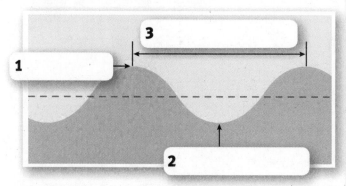

Define For each pair of terms, explain how the meanings of the terms differ.

4 *wave* and *tsunami*

_____

_____

_____

5 *wave period* and *wave speed*

_____

_____

_____

Key Concepts

6 Summarize How do most ocean waves form?

_____

_____

7 Describe What happens to the energy in an ocean wave as the wave reaches the shore?

_____

_____

_____

_____

8 Calculate A scientist determines that an ocean wave has a wavelength of 4.3 m and a frequency of 0.2 waves/second. What is the wave's speed?

_____

_____

Critical Thinking

Use the table to answer the following question.

Wave	Time wave passes Buoy 1	Time wave passes Buoy 2
A	8:15 a.m.	8:21 a.m.
B	1:24 p.m.	1:36 p.m.
C	6:58 p.m.	7:02 p.m.

9 Calculate Which wave has the smallest wave period? What is its period?

_____

_____

_____

10 Synthesize Which property of a wave do you think changes the most as the wave approaches the shore? Explain your answer.

_____

_____

_____

_____

_____

_____

11 Infer Suppose a person sailing a ship saw breaking waves 1 kilometer offshore. Should the person try to sail the ship through the area or steer around it? Explain.

_____

_____

_____

_____

_____

_____

_____

My Notes

Evan B. Forde

OCEANOGRAPHER

Pillow lava on the ocean floor, seen from *Alvin*

Evan B. Forde is an oceanographer at the Atlantic Oceanographic and Meteorological Laboratory in Miami, Florida. His main areas of study have included looking at the different processes occurring in the U.S. east coast submarine canyons. To study these canyons, Evan became the first African American to participate in research dives in underwater submersibles—machines that can take a human being under water safely—such as *Alvin*. He is currently studying how conditions in the atmosphere relate to the formation of hurricanes.

Evan graduated with degrees in Geology and Marine Geology and Geophysics from Columbia University in New York City. Along with his scientific research, he is committed to science education. He has developed and taught courses on Tropical Meteorology at the University of Miami. Keeping younger students in mind, he created an oceanography course for middle-school students through the Miami-Dade Public Libraries. Evan speaks often to students about oceanography and the sciences, and is involved with many community youth projects.

Social Studies Connection

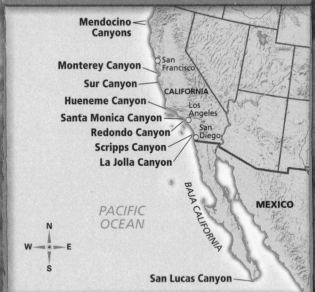

Mendocino Canyons
Monterey Canyon — San Francisco
Sur Canyon — CALIFORNIA
Hueneme Canyon — Los Angeles
Santa Monica Canyon — San Diego
Redondo Canyon
Scripps Canyon
La Jolla Canyon

BAJA CALIFORNIA

PACIFIC OCEAN

MEXICO

San Lucas Canyon

Research the Monterey Submarine Canyon shown on the map. Find out its size and if it is still considered one of the largest canyons off the Pacific Coast. Research the kind of organisms that can live there.

Evan B. Forde

JOB BOARD

Wind Turbine Technician

What You'll Do: Operate and maintain wind turbine units, including doing repairs and preventative maintenance.

Where You Might Work: You will need to travel often to the different wind farms that have wind turbines. Some technicians may have the chance to travel to wind farms in different countries to complete repairs on wind turbines.

Education: Typically, technicians will graduate from a wind energy program. Technicians should have a solid understanding of math, meteorology, computer, and problem solving skills.

Other Job Requirements: To do these tasks, you will need to climb wind towers as high as 125 meters, so it is helpful if you do not have a fear of heights.

Environmental Engineering Technician

What You'll Do: Help environmental engineers and scientists prevent, control, and get rid of environmental hazards. Inspect, test, decontaminate, and operate equipment used to control and help fix environmental pollution.

Where You Might Work: Offices, laboratories, or industrial plants. Most technicians have to complete field work, so they do spend time working outdoors in all types of weather.

Education: You will need an associate's degree in environmental engineering technology, environmental technology, or hazardous materials information systems technology.

Wind turbine

Ocean Currents

ESSENTIAL QUESTION

How does water move in the ocean?

By the end of this lesson, you should be able to describe the movement of ocean water, explain what factors influence this movement, and explain why ocean circulation is important in the Earth system.

This iceberg off the coast of Newfoundland broke off an Arctic ice sheet and drifted south on ocean surface currents.

Lesson Labs

Quick Labs
• Modeling the Coriolis Effect
• The Formation of Deep Currents
• Can Messages Travel on Ocean Water?

Engage Your Brain

1 Predict Check T or F to show whether you think each statement is true or false.

T	F	
☐	☐	Ocean currents are always cold.
☐	☐	Continents affect the directions of currents.
☐	☐	Currents only flow near the surface of the ocean.
☐	☐	Wind affects currents.
☐	☐	The sun affects currents near the surface of the ocean.

2 Analyze What can you learn about ocean currents from this image?

_____

_____

_____

_____

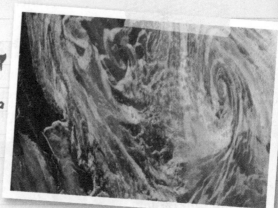

This image shows sea ice caught in ocean currents.

Active Reading

3 Synthesize You can often define an unknown word if you know the meaning of its word parts. Use the word parts and sentence below to make an educated guess about the meaning of the word *upwelling*.

Word part	Meaning
up-	from beneath the ground or water
well	to rise

Example Sentence

In areas where <u>upwelling</u> occurs, plankton feed on nutrients from deep in the ocean.

upwelling:

_____

_____

Vocabulary Terms

• ocean current
• surface current
• Coriolis effect
• deep current
• convection current
• upwelling

4 Apply As you learn the definition of each vocabulary term in this lesson, create your own definition or sketch to help you remember the meaning of the term.

Going with the Flow

What are ocean currents?

The oceans contain streamlike movements of water called **ocean currents**. Ocean currents that occur at or near the surface of the ocean, caused by wind, are called **surface currents**. Most surface currents reach depths of about 100 m, but some go deeper. Surface currents also reach lengths of several thousand kilometers and can stretch across oceans. An example of a surface current is the Gulf Stream. The Gulf Stream is one of the strongest surface currents on Earth. The Gulf Stream transports, or moves, more water each year than is transported by all the rivers in the world combined.

Infrared cameras on satellites provide images that show differences in temperature. Scientists add color to the images afterward to highlight the different temperatures, as shown below.

What affects surface currents?

Surface currents are affected by three factors: continental deflections, the Coriolis effect, and global winds. These factors keep surface currents flowing in distinct patterns around Earth.

Active Reading

5 Identify As you read, underline three factors that affect surface currents.

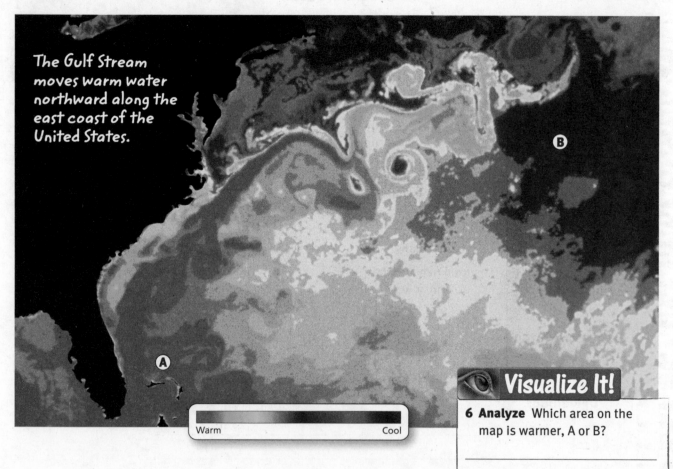

The Gulf Stream moves warm water northward along the east coast of the United States.

Warm — Cool

Visualize It!

6 Analyze Which area on the map is warmer, A or B?

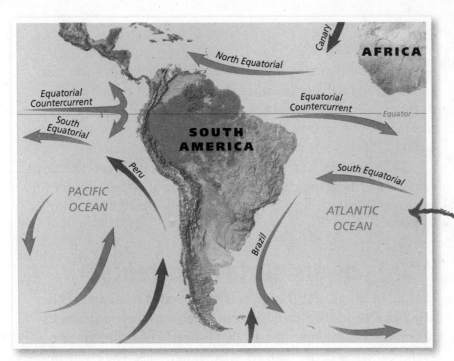

7 Identify Circle areas on the map where ocean currents have been deflected by a land mass.

Currents change direction when they meet continents.

Continental Deflections

If Earth's surface were covered only with water, surface currents would simply travel continually in one direction. However, water does not cover the entire surface of Earth. Continents rise above sea level over about one-third of Earth's surface. When surface currents meet continents, the currents are deflected and change direction. For example, the South Equatorial Current turns southward as it meets the coast of South America.

The Coriolis Effect

Earth's rotation causes all wind and ocean currents, except on the equator, to be deflected from the paths they would take if Earth did not rotate. The deflection of moving objects from a straight path due to Earth's rotation is called the **Coriolis effect** (kawr•ee•OH•lis ih•FEKT). Earth is spherical, so Earth's circumference at latitudes above and below the equator is shorter than the circumference at the equator. But the period of rotation is always 24 hours. Therefore, points on Earth near the equator travel faster than points closer to the poles.

The difference in speed of rotation causes the Coriolis effect. For example, wind and water traveling south from the North Pole actually go toward the southwest instead of straight south. Wind and water deflect to the right because the wind and water move east more slowly than Earth rotates beneath them. In the Northern Hemisphere, currents are deflected to the right. In the Southern Hemisphere, currents are deflected to the left.

The Coriolis effect is most noticeable for objects that travel over long distances, without any interruptions. Over short distances, the difference in Earth's rotational speed from one point to another point is not great enough to cause noticeable deflection.

In the Northern Hemisphere, currents are deflected to the right.

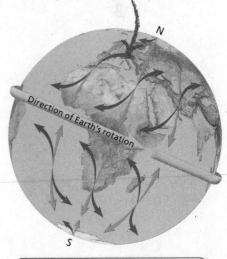

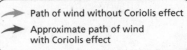

→ Path of wind without Coriolis effect
→ Approximate path of wind with Coriolis effect

Global Winds

Have you ever blown gently on a cup of hot chocolate? You may have noticed that your breath makes ripples that push the hot chocolate across the surface of the liquid. Similarly, winds that blow across the surface of Earth's oceans push water across Earth's surface. This process causes surface currents in the ocean.

Different winds cause currents to flow in different directions. For example, near the equator, the winds blow east to west for the most part. Most surface currents in the same area follow a similar pattern.

What powers surface currents?

The sun heats air near the equator more than it heats air at other latitudes. Pressure differences form because of these differences in heating. For example, the air that is heated near the equator is warmer and less dense than air at other latitudes. The rising of warm air creates an area of low pressure near the equator. Pressure differences in the atmosphere cause the wind to form. So, the sun causes winds to form, and winds cause surface currents to form. Therefore, the major source of the energy that powers surface currents is the sun.

8 Analyze Fill in the cause-and-effect chart to show how the sun's energy powers surface ocean currents.

The sun heats the atmosphere.

Global Surface Winds

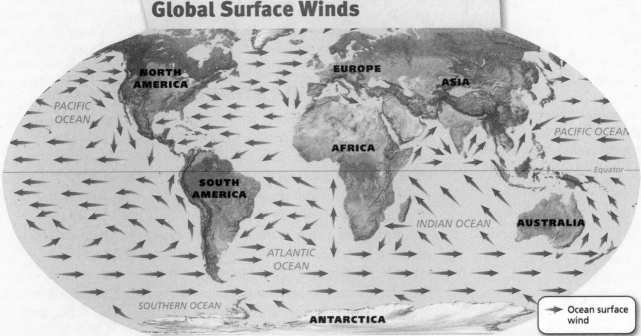

Ocean surface wind

Global Surface Currents

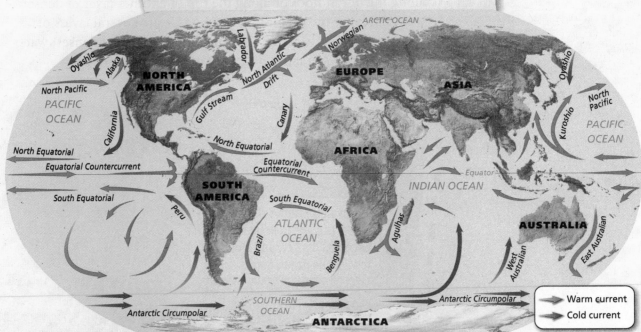

Warm current
Cold current

Visualize It!

9 Analyze Circle the same area on each map. Describe what you observe about these two areas.

_____

_____

_____

Current Events

How do deep currents form?

Movements of ocean water far below the surface are called **deep currents**. Deep currents are caused by differences in water density. *Density* is the amount of matter in a given space or volume. The density of ocean water is affected by salinity (suh•LIN•ih•tee) and temperature. *Salinity* is a measure of the amount of dissolved salts or solids in a liquid. Water with high salinity is denser than water with low salinity. And cold water is denser than warm water. When water cools, it contracts and the water molecules move closer together. This contraction makes the water denser. When water warms, it expands and the water molecules move farther apart. The warm water is less dense, so it rises above the cold water.

When ocean water at the surface becomes denser than water below it, the denser water sinks. The water moves from the surface to the deep ocean, forming deep currents. Deep currents flow along the ocean floor or along the top of another layer of denser water. Because the ocean is so deep, there are several layers of water at any location in the ocean. The deepest and densest water in the ocean is Antarctic Bottom Water, near Antarctica.

10 Identify As you read, underline the cause of deep currents.

Polar region

Convection current

B — Warm water from surface currents cools in polar regions, becomes denser, and sinks toward the ocean floor.

C — Deep currents carry colder, denser water in the deep ocean from polar regions to other parts of Earth.

Visualize It!

11 Illustrate Complete the drawing at part B on the diagram.

What are convection currents?

As you read about convection currents, refer to the illustration below. Surface currents and deep currents are linked in the ocean. Together they form convection currents. In the ocean, a **convection current** is a movement of water that results from density differences. Convection currents can be vertical, circular, or cyclical. Think of convection currents in the ocean as a conveyor belt. Surface currents make up the top part of the belt. Deep currents make up the bottom part of the belt. Water from a surface current may become a deep current in areas where water density increases. Deep current water then rises up to the surface in areas where the surface current is carrying low-density water away.

How do convection currents transfer energy?

Convection currents transfer energy. Water at the ocean's surface absorbs energy from the sun. Surface currents carry this energy to colder regions. The warm water loses energy to its surroundings and cools. As the water cools, it becomes denser and it sinks. The cold water travels along the ocean bottom. Then, the cold water rises to the surface as warm surface water moves away. The cold water absorbs energy from the sun, and the cycle continues.

© Houghton Mifflin Harcourt Publishing Company • Image Credits: (inset) ©Dominique Vorillon/Botanica/Getty Images

Surface currents carry warmer, less dense water from warm equatorial regions to polar areas.

A

D

Equatorial region

Water from deep currents rises to replace water that leaves in surface currents.

Earth

Note: Drawing is not to scale.

Think Outside the Book · Inquiry

12 Apply Write an interview with a water molecule following a convection current. Be sure to include questions and answers. Can you imagine the temperature changes the molecule would experience?

Inquiry

13 Inquire How are convection currents important in the Earth system?

_____

_____

That's Swell!

What is upwelling?

At times, winds blow toward the equator along the northwest coast of South America and the west coast of North America. These winds cause surface currents to move away from the shore. The warm surface water is then replaced by cold, nutrient-rich water from the deep ocean in a process called **upwelling**. The deep water contains nutrients, such as iron and nitrate.

Upwelling is extremely important to ocean life. The nutrients that are brought to the surface of the ocean support the growth of phytoplankton (fy•toh•PLANGK•tuhn) and zooplankton. These tiny plants and animals are food for other organisms, such as fish and seabirds. Many fisheries are located in areas of upwelling because ocean animals thrive there. Some weather conditions can interrupt the process of upwelling. When upwelling is reduced, the richness of the ocean life at the surface is also reduced.

© Houghton Mifflin Harcourt Publishing Company • Image Credits: (tl) ©Staffan Widstrand/Corbis; (tr) ©Bruce Hall/Alamy

Active Reading

14 Identify As you read, underline the steps that occur in upwelling.

15 Predict What might happen to the fisheries if upwelling stopped?

_____
_____
_____
_____
_____
_____

The livelihood of these Peruvian fishermen depends on upwelling.

On the coast of California, upwelling sustains large kelp forests.

Wind

Warm surface water

During upwelling, cold, nutrient-rich water from the deep ocean rises to the surface.

Why It Matters

Hitching a Ride!

What do coconuts, plankton, and sea turtles have in common? They get free rides on ocean currents.

Sprouting Coconuts!
This sprouting coconut may be transported by ocean currents to a beach. This transport explains why coconut trees can grow in several areas.

World Travel
When baby sea turtles are hatched on a beach, they head for the ocean. They can then pick up ocean currents to travel. Some travel from Australia to South America on currents.

Fast Food
Diatoms are a kind of phytoplankton. They are tiny, one-celled plants that form the basis of the food chain. Diatoms ride surface currents throughout the world.

Extend

16 Identify List three organisms transported by ocean currents.

17 Research Investigate the Sargasso Sea. State why a lot of plastic collects in this sea. Find out whether any plastic collects on the shoreline nearest you.

18 Explain Describe how plastic and other debris can collect in the ocean by doing one of the following:
- make a poster
- write a song
- write a poem
- write a short story

Traveling the World

What do ocean currents transport?

Ocean water circulates through all of Earth's ocean basins. The paths are like the main highway on which ocean water flows. If you could follow a water molecule on this path, you would find that the molecule takes more than 1,000 years to return to its starting point! Along with water, ocean currents also transport dissolved solids, dissolved gases, and energy around Earth.

Active Reading

19 Identify As you read, underline the description of how energy reaches the poles.

20 Describe Choose a location on the map. Using your finger, follow the route you would take if you could ride a current. Describe your route. Include the direction you go and the landmasses you pass.

_____

_____

_____

_____

Antarctica is not shown on this map, but the currents at the bottom of the map circulate around Antarctica.

Ocean Currents Transport Energy

Global ocean circulation is very important in the transport of energy in the form of heat. Remember that ocean currents flow in huge convection currents that can be thousands of kilometers long. These convection currents carry about 40% of the energy that is transported around Earth's surface.

Near the equator, the ocean absorbs a large amount of solar energy. The ocean also absorbs energy from the atmosphere. Ocean currents carry this energy from the equator toward the poles. When the warm water travels to cooler areas, the energy is released back into the atmosphere. Therefore, ocean circulation has an important influence on Earth's climate.

In the Pacific Ocean, surface currents transport energy from the tropics to latitudes above and below the equator.

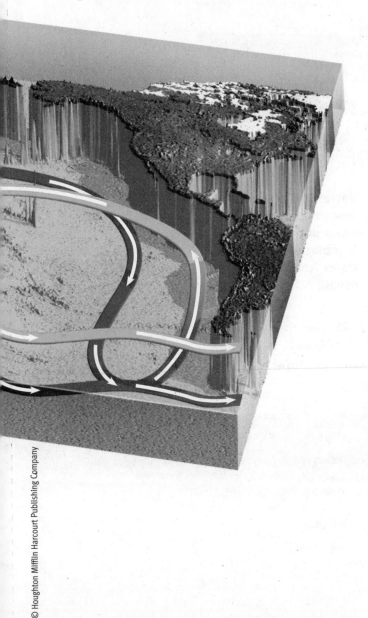

Ocean Currents Transport Matter

Besides water, ocean currents transport whatever is in the water. The most familiar dissolved solid in ocean water is sodium chloride, or table salt. Other dissolved solids are important to marine life. Ocean water contains many nutrients—such as nitrogen and phosphorus—that are important for plant and animal growth.

Ocean water also transports gases. Gases in the atmosphere are absorbed by ocean water at the ocean surface. As a result, the most abundant gases in the atmosphere—nitrogen, oxygen, argon, and carbon dioxide—are also abundant in the ocean. Dissolved oxygen and carbon dioxide are necessary for the survival of many marine organisms.

21 List Write three examples of matter besides water that are transported by ocean currents.

_____

_____

_____

_____

_____

Visual Summary

To complete this summary, draw an arrow to show each type of ocean current. Fill in the blanks with the correct word. Then use the key below to check your answers. You can use this page to review the main concepts of the lesson.

Surface currents are streamlike movements of water at or near the surface of the ocean.

22 The direction of a surface current is affected by

_____ ,

_____ ,

and _____

Deep currents are streamlike movements of ocean water located far below the surface.

23 Deep currents form where the

_____

of ocean water increases.

Ocean Currents

A convection current in the ocean is any movement of matter that results from differences in density.

24 A convection current in the ocean transports matter and

_____

Upwelling is the process in which warm surface water is replaced by cold water from the deep ocean.

25 The cold water from deep in the ocean contains

_____

Answers: 22 continental deflections, the Coriolis effect, global winds; 23 density; 24 energy; 25 nutrients

26 **Describe** State the two general patterns of global ocean circulation.

_____

Lesson Review

Vocabulary

Fill in the blanks with the terms that best complete the following sentences.

1 _____ are streamlike movements of water in the ocean.

2 The _____ causes currents in open water to move in a curved path rather than a straight path.

3 _____ causes cold, nutrient-rich waters to move up to the ocean's surface.

Key Concepts

4 Explain List the steps that show how the sun provides the energy for surface ocean currents.

_____

_____

_____

_____

_____

5 Explain State how a deep current forms.

_____

_____

_____

_____

_____

6 Describe Explain how a convection current transports energy around the globe.

_____

_____

_____

7 List Write the three factors that affect surface ocean currents.

_____

_____

_____

_____

Critical Thinking

Use this diagram to answer the following questions.

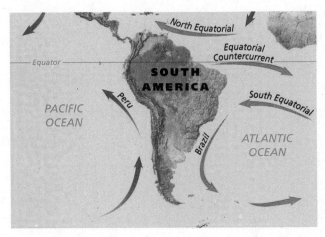

8 Apply Explain why the direction of the South Equatorial current changes.

_____

_____

_____

_____

9 Apply If South America were not there, explain how the direction of the South Equatorial current would be different.

_____

_____

_____

_____

_____

10 Apply Describe how surface currents would be affected if Earth did not rotate.

_____

_____

_____

_____

_____

_____

_____

My Notes

Unit 2

Lesson 1

ESSENTIAL QUESTION
What lies within and beneath Earth's oceans?

Describe the properties and physical features of Earth's oceans.

Lesson 2

ESSENTIAL QUESTION
How does an ocean wave form and move?

Describe the characteristics of ocean waves and what happens as they move through the ocean.

Lesson 3

ESSENTIAL QUESTION
How does water move in the ocean?

Describe the movement of ocean water, explain what factors influence this movement, and explain why ocean circulation is important in the Earth system.

Connect ESSENTIAL QUESTIONS
Lessons 1 and 3

1 Synthesize Name two factors that contribute to the density of ocean water. How does density influence the movement of ocean water?

_____

_____

_____

_____

_____

_____

Think Outside the Book

2 Synthesize Choose one of these activities to help synthesize what you have learned in this unit.

☐ Using what you learned in lessons 1 and 2, make a flipbook that shows how an earthquake along a fault near a subducting plate might affect the ocean water above it.

☐ Using what you learned in lessons 1 and 3, make a poster presentation describing how the temperature of ocean water is important to distributing energy as heat around the global ocean.

Unit 2 Review

Name _____

Vocabulary

Check the box to show whether each statement is true or false.

T	F	
☐	☐	**1** A <u>mid-ocean ridge</u> is a long, narrow depression located in a deep-ocean basin.
☐	☐	**2** An ocean layer in which the temperature drops with depth faster than in other layers is called a <u>thermocline</u>.
☐	☐	**3** A wave that requires a medium such as air or water through which to travel is called a <u>mechanical wave</u>.
☐	☐	**4** A <u>tsunami</u> is a large ocean wave caused by severe winds.
☐	☐	**5** A <u>convection current</u> is any movement of matter that results from differences in density.

Key Concepts

Read each question below, and circle the best answer.

6 A scientist measured the salinity of the ocean water at the surface every 100 meters along a coastline. The measurements are displayed in the line graph below.

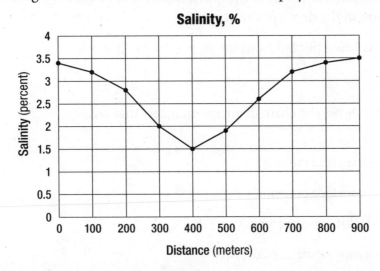

What best describes the dip in salinity centered at 400 meters along the shore?

A A factory dumps wastewater with 10% salinity into that area of the ocean.

B More sunlight reaches that area of the coastline causing more evaporation.

C The instruments must be faulty, since ocean water does not vary in salinity.

D A river's mouth at around 400 meters carries freshwater into the ocean.

7 The picture below shows a method of studying the ocean.

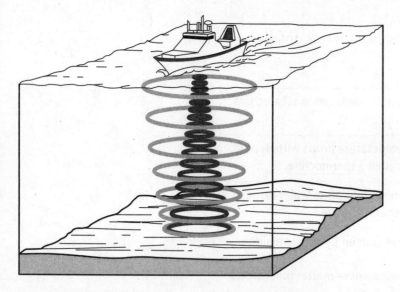

Which of the following best explains this method of studying the ocean?

A A bright beam of white light is being shone down through the ocean to illuminate the ocean floor.

B Sound waves are being sent down through the ocean, and the variation in time taken for the sound waves to return tells how the depth varies.

C A satellite is being used to measure variations in the gravitational field of the Earth, which tells the variation in the depth of the ocean.

D A remotely operated vehicle is being piloted from the ship to take pictures of the ocean floor.

8 Which of the following correctly shows the chain of energy transfers that create surface currents on the ocean?

A solar energy → wind energy → surface currents

B wind energy → solar energy → surface currents

C tidal energy → wind energy → surface currents

D geothermal energy → wind energy → surface currents

9 Looking at a pole at the end of a pier, Maria counted 20 wave crests pass the pole in 10 seconds. She also estimated that the wavelength was 8 pole widths. If the pole is 0.5 meters wide, what was the approximate wave speed?

A 2 m/s

B 4 m/s

C 8 m/s

D 16 m/s

Name _____

10 The dashed lines on this map indicate the path of a 2004 tsunami.

December 2004 Tsunami

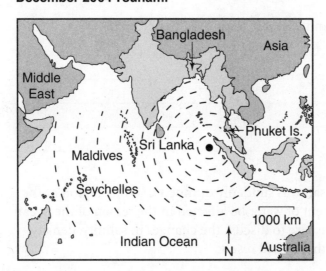

Would an observer standing on a beach on the southeast shore of Sri Lanka have known that a tsunami was coming?

A Yes, because the water would have rushed away from shore.

B No, because the observer was not in the path of the tsunami.

C Yes, because storm clouds would have formed offshore to the southeast.

D No, because the winds that caused the tsunami were from the northeast.

11 Which type of current occurs when the ocean's surface water becomes denser than the water below it and sinks?

A Coriolis current   **C** surface current

B deep current   **D** upwelling

12 The drawing below shows a snapshot of a wave.

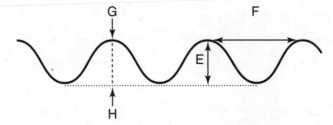

What does the measurement labeled E equal?

A The wave's period   **C** The wave's amplitude

B The wave's wavelength   **D** Twice the wave's amplitude

Critical Thinking

Answer the following questions in the space provided.

13 Explain what an upwelling is and why it is important to ocean life.

_____

_____

_____

_____

_____

14 Suppose a massive amount of salt was suddenly dumped into one region of the ocean. How would the movement of water be affected in the region of the ocean where the salt was dumped? Be sure to discuss the changes in salinity, density, and the type of ocean current that would result.

_____

_____

_____

_____

_____

Connect ESSENTIAL QUESTIONS
Lessons 1, 2, and 3

Answer the following question in the space provided.

15 Most of the energy that powers ocean waves and ocean currents ultimately comes from the sun. Using what you learned in Lessons 1, 2, and 3, describe how ocean waves and ocean currents transfer solar energy around the globe.

_____

_____

_____

_____

_____

_____

_____

Earth's Atmosphere

Big Idea

Earth's atmosphere is a mixture of gases that interacts with solar energy.

Earth's atmosphere is divided into different layers. These clouds have formed in the troposphere, the lowest layer of the atmosphere where most weather occurs.

Wind is the movement of air caused by differences in air pressure.

What do you think?

Like other parts of the Earth system, energy is transferred through Earth's atmosphere. What are the three processes by which energy is transferred through the atmosphere?

Unit 3
Earth's Atmosphere

CITIZEN SCIENCE

Clearing the Air

In some areas, there are many vehicles on the roads every day. Some of the gases from vehicle exhausts react with sunlight to form ozone. There are days when the concentration of ozone is so high that it becomes a health hazard. Those days are especially difficult for people who have problems breathing. What can you do to reduce gas emissions?

① Think About It

A How do you get to school every day?

_____

_____

_____

B How many of the students in your class come to school by car?

_____

Gas emissions are high during rush-hour traffic.

Ride a bicycle to school.

② Ask A Question

How can you reduce the number of vehicles students use to get to school one day each month?

With your teacher and classmates, brainstorm different ways in which you can reduce the number of vehicles students use to get to school.

Check off the points below as you use them to design your plan.

☐ how far a student lives from school

☐ the kinds of transportation students may have available to them

③ Make A Plan

A Write down different ways that you can reduce the number of vehicles that bring students to school.

_____

_____

_____

_____

_____

_____

_____

C In the space below, design a sign-up sheet that your classmates will use to choose how they will come to school on the designated day.

B Create a short presentation for your principal that outlines how the whole school could become involved in your vehicle-reduction plan. Write down the points of your presentation in the space below.

_____

_____

_____

_____

_____

_____

_____

_____

_____

Take It Home

Give your presentation to an adult. Then, have the adult brainstorm ways to reduce their daily gas emissions. See *ScienceSaurus®* for more information about conservation of energy.

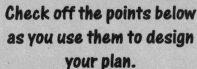

The Atmosphere

ESSENTIAL QUESTION

What is the atmosphere?

By the end of this lesson, you should be able to describe the composition and structure of the atmosphere and explain how the atmosphere protects life and insulates Earth.

The atmosphere is a very thin layer compared to the whole Earth. However, it is essential for life on our planet.

✋ Lesson Labs

Quick Labs
- Modeling Air Pressure
- Modeling Air Pressure Changes with Altitude

Field Lab
- Measuring Oxygen in the Air

Engage Your Brain

1 Predict Check T or F to show whether you think each statement is true or false.

T	F	
☐	☐	Oxygen is in the air we breathe.
☐	☐	Pressure is not a property of air.
☐	☐	The air around you is part of the atmosphere.
☐	☐	As you climb up a mountain, the temperature usually gets warmer.

2 Explain Does the air in this balloon have mass? Why or why not?

_____

_____

_____

_____

Active Reading

3 Synthesize Many English words have their roots in other languages. Use the ancient Greek words below to make an educated guess about the meanings of the words *atmosphere* and *mesosphere*.

Greek word	Meaning
atmos	vapor
mesos	middle
sphaira	ball

Vocabulary Terms

- atmosphere
- air pressure
- thermosphere
- mesosphere
- stratosphere
- troposphere
- ozone layer
- greenhouse effect

4 Apply As you learn the definition of each vocabulary term in this lesson, create your own definition or sketch to help you remember the meaning of the term.

atmosphere:

_____

_____

mesosphere:

_____

_____

Up and Away!

What is Earth's atmosphere?

The mixture of gases that surrounds Earth is the **atmosphere**. This mixture is most often referred to as air. The atmosphere has many important functions. It protects you from the sun's damaging rays and also helps to maintain the right temperature range for life on Earth. For example, the temperature range on Earth allows us to have an abundant amount of liquid water. Many of the components of the atmosphere are essential for life, such as the oxygen you breathe.

A Mixture of Gases and Small Particles

As shown below, the atmosphere is made mostly of nitrogen gas (78%) and oxygen gas (21%). The other 1% is other gases. The atmosphere also contains small particles such as dust, volcanic ash, sea salt, and smoke. There are even small pieces of skin, bacteria, and pollen floating in the atmosphere!

Water is also found in the atmosphere. Liquid water, as water droplets, and solid water, as snow and ice crystals, are found in clouds. But most water in the atmosphere exists as an invisible gas called water vapor. Under certain conditions, water vapor can change into solid or liquid water. Then, snow or rain might fall from the sky.

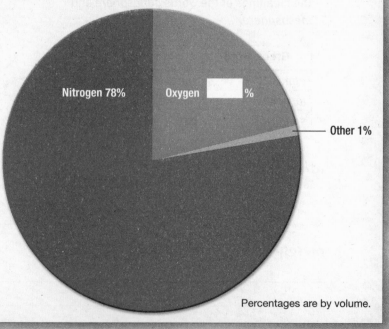

Visualize It!

5 Identify Fill in the missing percentage for oxygen.

Nitrogen is the most abundant gas in the atmosphere.

Oxygen is the second most abundant gas in the atmosphere.

The remaining 1% of the atmosphere is made up of argon, carbon dioxide, water vapor, and other gases.

Composition of the Atmosphere

Nitrogen 78%

Oxygen ____ %

Other 1%

Percentages are by volume.

How do pressure and temperature change in the atmosphere?

6 Identify As you read, underline what happens to temperature and to pressure as altitude increases.

The atmosphere is held around Earth by gravity. Gravity pulls gas molecules in the atmosphere toward Earth's surface, causing air pressure. **Air pressure** is the measure of the force with which air molecules push on an area of a surface. At sea level, air pressure is over 1 lb for every square centimeter of your body. That is like carrying a 1-liter bottle of water on the tip of your finger!

However, air pressure is not the same throughout the atmosphere. Although there are many gas molecules that surround you on Earth, there are fewer and fewer gas molecules in the air as you move away from Earth's surface. So, as altitude increases, air pressure decreases.

As altitude increases, air temperature also changes. These changes are mainly due to the way solar energy is absorbed in the atmosphere. Some parts of the atmosphere are warmer because they contain a high percentage of gases that absorb solar energy. Other parts of the atmosphere contain less of these gases and are cooler.

Inquiry

7 Explain Why does a mountain climber need an oxygen supply at very high altitudes, even though the air still contains 21% oxygen?

_____

_____

_____

At high altitudes such as the top of Mount Everest, air pressure and temperature are lower than they are at sea level.

Look Way Up

What are the layers of the atmosphere?

Earth's atmosphere is divided into four layers, based on temperature and other properties. As shown at the right, these layers are the troposphere (TROH•puh•sfir), stratosphere (STRAT•uh•sfir), mesosphere (MEZ•uh•sfir), and thermosphere (THER•muh•sfir). Although these names sound complicated, they give you clues about the layers' features. *Tropo-* means "turning" or "change," and the troposphere is the layer where gases turn and mix. *Strato-* means "layer," and the stratosphere is where gases are layered and do not mix very much. *Meso-* means "middle," and the mesosphere is the middle layer. Finally, *thermo-* means "heat," and the thermosphere is the layer where temperatures are highest.

Think Outside the Book

8 Describe Research the part of the thermosphere called the ionosphere. Describe what the aurora borealis is.

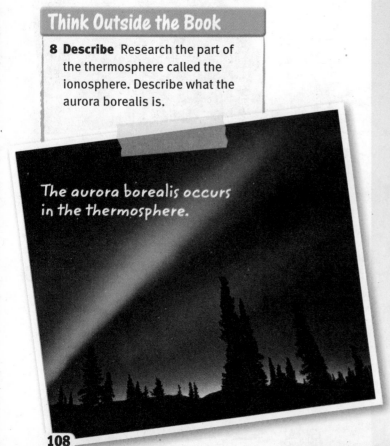

The aurora borealis occurs in the thermosphere.

Thermosphere

The **thermosphere** is the uppermost layer of the atmosphere. The temperature increases as altitude increases because gases in the thermosphere absorb high-energy solar radiation. Temperatures in the thermosphere can be 1,500 °C or higher. However, the thermosphere feels cold. The density of particles in the thermosphere is very low. Too few gas particles collide with your body to transfer heat energy to your skin.

Mesosphere

The **mesosphere** is between the thermosphere and stratosphere. In this layer, the temperature decreases as altitude increases. Temperatures can be as low as –120 °C at the top of the mesosphere. Meteoroids begin to burn up in the mesosphere.

Stratosphere

The **stratosphere** is between the mesosphere and troposphere. In this layer, temperatures generally increase as altitude increases. Ozone in the stratosphere absorbs ultraviolet radiation from the sun, which warms the air. An ozone molecule is made of three atoms of oxygen. Gases in the stratosphere are layered and do not mix very much.

Troposphere

The **troposphere** is the lowest layer of the atmosphere. Although temperatures near Earth's surface vary greatly, generally, temperature decreases as altitude increases. This layer contains almost 80% of the atmosphere's total mass, making it the densest layer. Almost all of Earth's carbon dioxide, water vapor, clouds, air pollution, weather, and life forms are in the troposphere.

In the graph, the green line shows pressure change with altitude.
The red line shows temperature change with altitude.

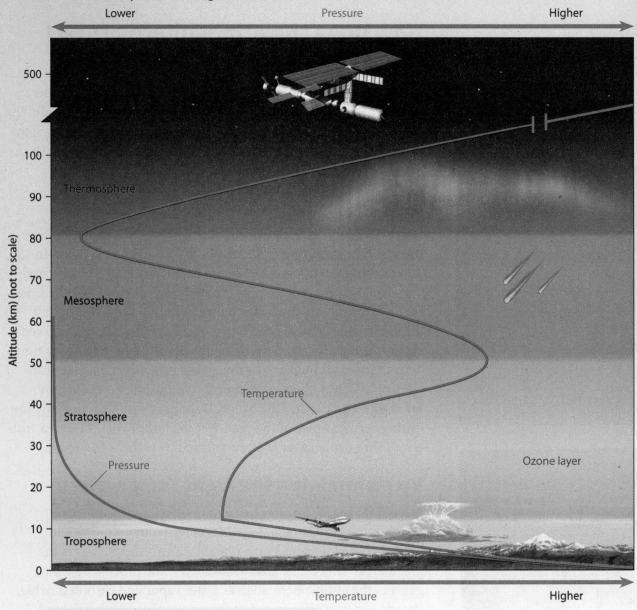

The layers of the atmosphere are defined by changes in temperature.

9 Analyze Using the graph and descriptions provided, indicate if air pressure and temperature increase or decrease with increased altitude in each layer of the atmosphere. One answer has been provided for you.

Layer	Air pressure	Temperature
Thermosphere	decreases	
Mesosphere		
Stratosphere		
Troposphere		

Visualize It!

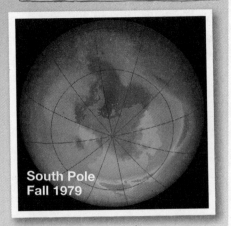

South Pole
Fall 1979

Less ozone   More ozone

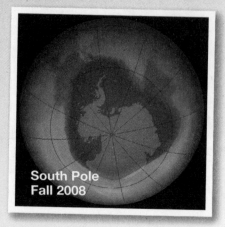

South Pole
Fall 2008

10 Compare How did the ozone layer over the South Pole change between 1979 and 2008?

_____

_____

_____

How does the atmosphere protect life on Earth?

The atmosphere surrounds and protects Earth. The atmosphere provides the air we breathe. It also protects Earth from harmful solar radiation and from space debris that enters the Earth system. In addition, the atmosphere controls the temperature on Earth.

By Absorbing or Reflecting Harmful Radiation

Earth's atmosphere reflects or absorbs most of the radiation from the sun. The **ozone layer** is an area in the stratosphere, 15 km to 40 km above Earth's surface, where ozone is highly concentrated. The ozone layer absorbs most of the solar radiation. The thickness of the ozone layer can change between seasons and at different locations. However, as shown at the left, scientists have observed a steady decrease in the overall volume of the ozone layer over time. This change is thought to be due to the use of certain chemicals by people. These chemicals enter the stratosphere, where they react with and destroy the ozone. Ozone levels are particularly low during certain times of the year over the South Pole. The area with a very thin ozone layer is often referred to as the "ozone hole."

By Maintaining the Right Temperature Range

Without the atmosphere, Earth's average temperature would be very low. How does Earth remain warm? The answer is the greenhouse effect. The **greenhouse effect** is the process by which gases in the atmosphere, such as water vapor and carbon dioxide, absorb and give off infrared radiation. Radiation from the sun warms Earth's surface, and Earth's surface gives off infrared radiation. Greenhouse gases in the atmosphere absorb some of this infrared radiation and then reradiate it. Some of this energy is absorbed again by Earth's surface, while some energy goes out into space. Because greenhouse gases keep energy in the Earth system longer, Earth's average surface temperature is kept at around 15°C (59°F). In time, all the energy ends up back in outer space.

Active Reading **11 List** Name two examples of greenhouse gases.

_____

_____

the Sun ...

The Greenhouse Effect

Greenhouse gas molecules absorb and emit infrared radiation.

Atmosphere without Greenhouse Gases

Without greenhouse gases in Earth's atmosphere, radiation from Earth's surface is lost directly to space.
Average Temperature: -18°C

Atmosphere with Greenhouse Gases

With greenhouse gases in Earth's atmosphere, radiation from Earth's surface is lost to space more slowly, which makes Earth's surface warmer.
Average Temperature: 15°C

━━━ sunlight   ━━━ infrared radiation

The atmosphere is much thinner than shown here.

 **Visualize It!**

12 Illustrate Draw your own version of how greenhouse gases keep Earth warm.

Visual Summary

To complete this summary, fill in the blanks with the correct word or phrase. Then, use the key below to check your answers. You can use this page to review the main concepts of the lesson.

The Atmosphere

Both air pressure and temperature change within the atmosphere.

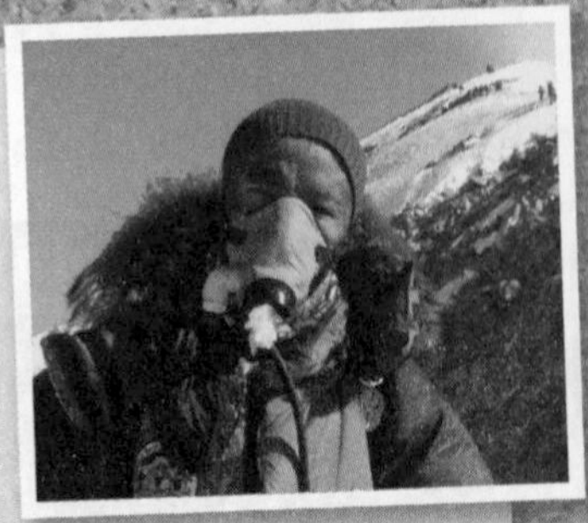

13 *As altitude increases, air pressure*

____

The atmosphere protects Earth from harmful radiation and helps to maintain a temperature range that supports life.

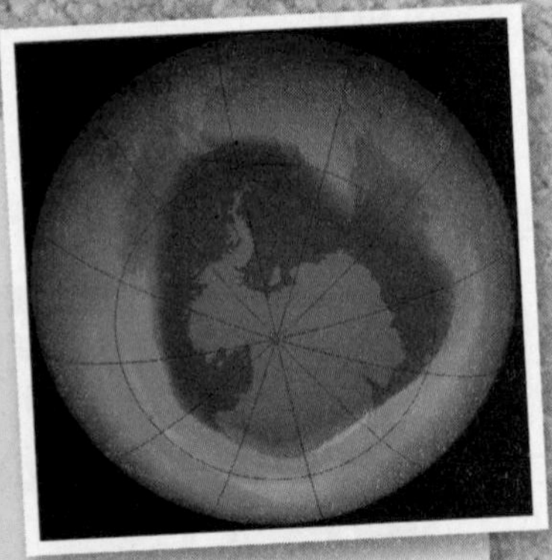

14 *Earth is protected from harmful solar radiation by the*

____

The atmosphere is divided into four layers, according to temperature and other properties.

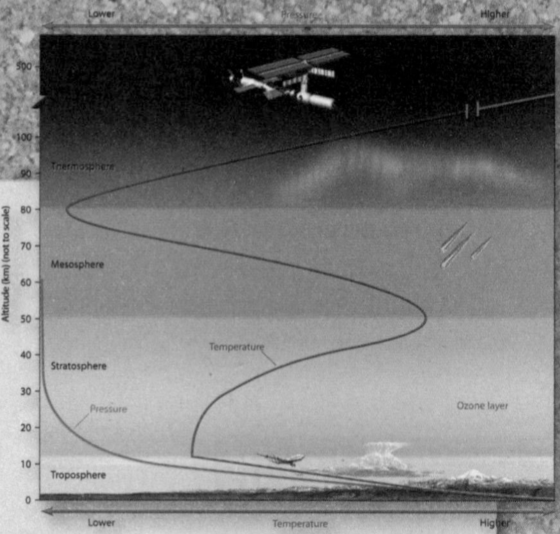

15 *The four layers of the atmosphere are the*

____

____

____

____

Answers: 13 decreases; 14 ozone layer; 15 troposphere, stratosphere, mesosphere, thermosphere

16 Hypothesize What do you think Earth's surface would be like if Earth did not have an atmosphere?

Lesson Review

Vocabulary

Fill in the blanks with the terms that best complete the following sentences.

1 The _____ is a mixture of gases that surrounds Earth.

2 The measure of the force with which air molecules push on a surface is called _____ .

3 The _____ is the process by which gases in the atmosphere absorb and reradiate heat.

Key Concepts

4 List Name three gases in the atmosphere.

_____

_____

5 Identify What layer of the atmosphere contains the ozone layer?

_____

6 Identify What layer of the atmosphere contains almost 80% of the atmosphere's total mass?

_____

7 Describe How and why does air pressure change with altitude in the atmosphere?

_____

_____

_____

8 Explain What is the name of the uppermost layer of the atmosphere? Why does it feel cold there, even though the temperature can be very high?

_____

_____

_____

_____

Critical Thinking

9 Hypothesize What would happen to life on Earth if the ozone layer was not present?

_____

_____

_____

10 Criticize A friend says that temperature increases as altitude increases because you're moving closer to the sun. Is this true? Explain.

_____

_____

_____

11 Predict Why would increased levels of greenhouse gases contribute to higher temperatures on Earth?

_____

_____

_____

Use this graph to answer the following questions.

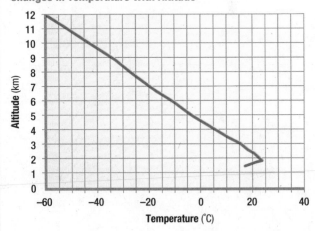

Changes in Temperature with Altitude

Source: National Weather Service. Data taken at Riverton, Wyoming, 2001

12 Analyze The top of Mount Everest is at about 8,850 m. What would the approximate air temperature be at that altitude? _____

13 Analyze What is the total temperature change between 3 km and 7 km above Earth's surface? _____

My Notes

Lesson 2

Energy Transfer

ESSENTIAL QUESTION

How does energy move through Earth's system?

By the end of this lesson, you should be able to summarize the three mechanisms by which energy is transferred through Earth's system.

Ice absorbs energy from the sun. This can cause ice to melt—even these icicles in Antarctica.

Lesson Labs

Quick Labs
• The Sun's Angle and Temperature
• How Does Color Affect Temperature?
• Modeling Convection

S.T.E.M. Lab
• Heat from the Sun

Engage Your Brain

1 Describe Fill in the blank with the word or phrase that you think correctly completes the following sentences.

An example of something hot is

_____

An example of something cold is

_____

The sun provides us with

_____

A thermometer is used to measure

_____

2 Explain If you placed your hands around this mug of hot chocolate, what would happen to the temperature of your hands? Why do you think this would happen?

_____

_____

_____

_____

_____

_____

_____

Active Reading

3 Apply Many scientific words, such as *heat*, are used to convey different meanings. Use context clues to write your own definition for each meaning of the word *heat*.

The student won the first <u>heat</u> of the race.

heat:

_____

_____

The man wondered if his rent included <u>heat</u>.

heat:

_____

_____

Energy in the form of <u>heat</u> was transferred from the hot pan to the cold counter.

heat:

_____

_____

Vocabulary Terms

• temperature	• radiation
• thermal energy	• convection
• thermal expansion	• conduction
• heat	

4 Identify This list contains the vocabulary terms you'll learn in this lesson. As you read, circle the definition of each term.

Hot and Cold

How are energy and temperature related?

All matter is made up of moving particles, such as atoms or molecules. When particles are in motion, they have kinetic energy. Because particles move at different speeds, each has a different amount of kinetic energy.

Temperature (TEMM•per•uh•choor) is a measure of the average kinetic energy of particles. The faster a particle moves, the more kinetic energy it has. As shown below, the more kinetic energy the particles of an object have, the higher the temperature of the object. Temperature does not depend on the number of particles. A teapot holds more tea than a cup. If the particles of tea in both containers have the same average kinetic energy, the tea in both containers is at the same temperature.

Thermal energy is the total kinetic energy of particles. A teapot full of tea at a high temperature has more thermal energy than a teapot full of tea at a lower temperature. Thermal energy also depends on the number of particles. The more particles there are in an object, the greater the object's thermal energy. The tea in a teapot and a cup may be at the same temperature, but the tea in the pot has more thermal energy because there is more of it.

Visualize It!

5 Analyze Which container holds particles with the higher average kinetic energy?

_____

_____

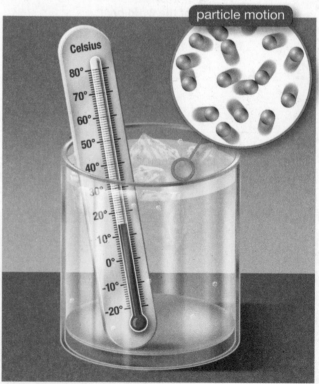

What is thermal expansion?

When the temperature of a substance increases, the substance's particles have more kinetic energy. Therefore, the particles move faster and move apart. As the space between the particles increases, the substance expands. The increase in volume that results from an increase in temperature is called **thermal expansion**. Most substances on Earth expand when they become warmer and contract when they become cooler. Water is an exception. Cold water expands as it gets colder and then freezes to form ice.

Thermal expansion causes a change in the density of a substance. *Density* is the mass per unit volume of a substance. When a substance expands, its mass stays the same but its volume increases. As a result, density decreases. Differences in density that are caused by thermal expansion can cause movement of matter. For example, air inside a hot-air balloon is warmed, as shown below. The air expands as its particles move faster and farther apart. As the air expands, it becomes less dense than the air outside the balloon. The less-dense air inside the balloon is forced upward by the colder, denser air outside the balloon. This same principle affects air movement in the atmosphere, water movement in the oceans, and rock movement in the geosphere.

7 Apply Why would an increase in the temperature of the oceans contribute to a rise in sea level?

_____

_____

_____

_____

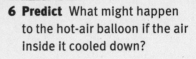

6 Predict What might happen to the hot-air balloon if the air inside it cooled down?

_____

_____

When the air in this balloon becomes hotter, it becomes less dense than the surrounding air. So, the balloon goes up, up, and away!

Getting Warm

What is heat?

Active Reading

8 Identify As you read, underline the direction of energy transfer between objects that are at different temperatures.

You might think of the word *heat* when you imagine something that feels hot. But heat also has to do with things that feel cold. In fact, heat is what causes objects to feel hot or cold. You may often use the word *heat* to mean different things. However, in this lesson, the word *heat* has only one meaning. **Heat** is the energy that is transferred between objects that are at different temperatures.

Energy Transferred Between Objects

When objects that have different temperatures come into contact, energy will be transferred between them until both objects reach the same temperature. The direction of this energy transfer is always from the object with the higher temperature to the object with the lower temperature. When you touch something cold, energy is transferred from your body to that object. When you touch something hot, like the pan shown below, energy is transferred from that object to your body.

Visualize It!

9 Predict Draw an arrow to show the direction in which energy is transferred between the pan and the oven mitts.

This pan is being removed from the oven and is very hot.

Why can the temperatures of land, air, and water differ?

When the same amount of energy is being transferred, some materials will get warmer or cooler at a faster rate than other materials. Suppose you are walking along a beach on a sunny day. You may notice that the land feels warmer than the air and the water, even though they are all exposed to the same amount of energy from the sun. This is because the land warms up at a faster rate than the water and air do.

Specific Heat

The different rates at which materials become warmer or cooler are due to a property called *specific heat*. A substance that has a high specific heat requires a lot of energy to show an increase in temperature. A substance with a lower specific heat requires less energy to show the same increase in temperature. Water has a higher specific heat than land. So, water warms up more slowly than land does. Water also cools down more slowly than land does.

10 Predict Air has a lower specific heat than water. Once the sun goes down, will the air or the water cool off faster? Why?

_____

_____

_____

The temperatures of land, water, and air may differ— even when they are exposed to the same amount of energy from the sun.

Heat

How is energy transferred by radiation?

On a summer day, you can feel warmth from the sun on your skin. But how did that energy reach you from the sun? The sun transfers energy to Earth by radiation. **Radiation** is the transfer of energy as electromagnetic (ee•LEK•troh•mag•NEH•tik) waves. Radiation can transfer energy between objects that are not in direct contact with each other. Many objects other than the sun also radiate energy as light and heat. These include a hot burner on a stove and a campfire, shown below.

Electromagnetic Waves

Energy from the sun is called *electromagnetic radiation*. This energy travels in waves. You are probably familiar with one form of radiation called *visible light*. You can see the visible light that comes from the sun. Electromagnetic radiation includes other forms of energy, which you cannot see. Most of the warmth that you feel from the sun is infrared radiation. This energy has a longer wavelength and lower energy than visible light. Higher-energy radiation includes x-rays and ultraviolet light.

Visualize It!

11 Analyze Write a caption for the campfire photo on the right. Make sure the caption relates the image to radiation.

_____

_____

_____

Energy from this hot burner is being transferred by radiation.

Energy from the sun is transferred through space.

Where does radiation occur on Earth?

We live almost 150 million km from the sun. Yet almost all of the energy on Earth is transmitted from the sun by radiation. The sun is the major source of energy for processes at Earth's surface. Receiving that energy is absolutely vital for life on Earth. The electromagnetic waves from the sun also provide energy that drives the water cycle.

When solar radiation reaches Earth, some of the energy is reflected and scattered by Earth's atmosphere. But much of the energy passes through Earth's atmosphere and reaches Earth's surface. Some of the energy that Earth receives from the sun is absorbed by the atmosphere, geosphere, and hydrosphere. Then, the energy is changed into thermal energy. This thermal energy may be reradiated into the Earth system or into space. Much of the energy is transferred through Earth's systems by the two other ways—convection and conduction.

12 Summarize Give two examples of what happens when energy from the sun reaches Earth.

_____

_____

_____

_____

© Houghton Mifflin Harcourt Publishing Company

Heating Up

How is energy transferred by convection?

Have you ever watched a pot of boiling water, such as the one below? If so, you have seen convection. **Convection** (kun•VECK•shuhn) is the transfer of energy due to the movement of matter. As water warms up at the bottom of the pot, some of the hot water rises. At the same time, cooler water from other parts of the pot sink and replace the rising water. This water is then warmed and the cycle continues.

Convection Currents

Convection involves the movement of matter due to differences in density. Convection occurs because most matter becomes less dense when it gets warmer. When most matter becomes warmer, it undergoes thermal expansion and a decrease in density. This less-dense matter is forced upward by the surrounding colder, denser matter that is sinking. As the hot matter rises, it cools and becomes more dense. This causes it to sink back down. This cycling of matter is called a *convection current*. Convection most often occurs in fluids, such as water and air. But convection can also happen in solids.

wax

convection current

energy sources

Visualize It! Inquiry

14 Apply How is convection related to the rise and fall of wax in lava lamps?

_____

_____

_____

_____

_____

Where does convection occur on Earth?

If Earth's surface is warmer than the air, energy will be transferred from the ground to the air. As the air becomes warmer, it becomes less dense. This air is pushed upward and out of the way by cooler, denser air that is sinking. As the warm air rises, it cools and becomes denser and begins to sink back toward Earth's surface. This cycle moves energy through the atmosphere.

Convection currents also occur in the ocean because of differences in the density of ocean water. More dense water sinks to the ocean floor, and less dense water moves toward the surface. The density of ocean water is influenced by temperature and the amount of salt in the water. Cold water is denser than warmer water. Water that contains a lot of salt is more dense than less-salty water.

Energy produced deep inside Earth heats rock in the mantle. The heated rock becomes less dense and is pushed up toward Earth's surface by the cooler, denser surrounding rock. Once cooled near the surface, the rock sinks. These convection currents transfer energy from Earth's core toward Earth's surface. These currents also cause the movement of tectonic plates.

Active Reading **15 Name** What are three of Earth's spheres in which energy is transferred by convection?

_____

_____

Visualize It!

16 Apply Draw the convection current that could occur in the body of water in this image.

Convection currents occur throughout the Earth system.

Ouch!

How is energy transferred by conduction?

Have you ever touched an ice cube and wondered why it feels cold? An ice cube has only a small amount of energy, compared to your hand. Energy is transferred to the ice cube from your hand through the process of conduction. **Conduction** (kun•DUHK•shuhn) is the transfer of energy from one object to another object through direct contact.

Direct Contact

Remember that the atoms or molecules in a substance are constantly moving. Even a solid block of ice has particles in constant motion. When objects at different temperatures touch, their particles interact. Conduction involves the faster-moving particles of the warmer object transferring energy to the slower-moving particles in the cooler object. The greater the difference in energy of the particles, the faster the transfer of energy by conduction occurs.

Active Reading **17 Apply** Name two examples of conduction that you experience every day.

_____

_____

_____

_____

These desert sands would feel hot because of conduction.

Where does conduction occur on Earth?

Energy can be transferred between the geosphere and the atmosphere by conduction. When cooler air molecules come into direct contact with the warm ground, energy is passed to the air by conduction. Conduction between the ground and the air happens only within a few centimeters of Earth's surface.

Conduction also happens between particles of air and particles of water. For example, if air transfers enough energy to liquid water, the water may evaporate. If water vapor transfers energy to the air, the kinetic energy of the water decreases. As a result, the water vapor may condense to form liquid water droplets.

Inside Earth, energy transfers between rock particles by conduction. However, rock is a poor conductor of heat, so this process happens very slowly.

Visualize It!

18 Compare Does conduction also occur in a city like the one shown below? Explain.

_____

_____

_____

_____

_____

19 Summarize Complete the following spider map by describing the three types of energy transfer. One answer has been started for you.

Radiation
Transfer of energy as
_____
_____

_____
_____
_____

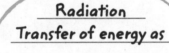
Types of Energy Transfer

_____
_____
_____

Visual Summary

To complete this summary, fill in the blanks with the correct word or phrase. Then, use the key below to check your answers. You can use this page to review the main concepts of the lesson.

Energy Transfer

Heat is the energy that is transferred between objects that are at different temperatures.

20 The particles in a hot pan have _____ kinetic energy than the particles in a cool oven mitt.

Energy can be transferred in different ways.

21 The three ways that energy can be transferred are labeled in the image as

A: _____

B: _____

C: _____

Answers: 20 more; 21 A: radiation, B: conduction, C: convection

22 Apply What type of energy transfer is responsible for making you feel cold when you are swimming in cool water? Explain your answer.

Lesson Review

Vocabulary

In your own words, define the following terms.

1 radiation

_____

_____

2 convection

_____

_____

3 conduction

_____

_____

_____

Key Concepts

4 Compare What is the difference between temperature, thermal energy, and heat?

_____

_____

_____

_____

_____

5 Describe What is happening to a substance undergoing thermal expansion?

_____

_____

_____

6 Explain What is the main source of energy for most processes at Earth's surface?

_____

7 Summarize What happens when two objects at different temperatures touch? Name one place where it occurs in Earth's system.

_____

_____

_____

8 Identify What is an example of convection in Earth's system?

Critical Thinking

9 Apply Why can metal utensils get too hot to touch when you are cooking with them?

_____

_____

_____

10 Predict You are doing an experiment outside on a sunny day. You find the temperature of some sand is 28°C. You also find the temperature of some water is 25°C. Explain the difference in temperatures.

_____

_____

_____

_____

Use this image to answer the following questions.

11 Analyze Name one example of where energy transfer by radiation is occurring.

_____

12 Analyze Name one example of where energy transfer by conduction is occurring.

_____

13 Analyze Name one example of where energy transfer by convection is occurring.

_____

My Notes

Engineering Design Process

Skills
Identify a need
Conduct research
✔ Brainstorm solutions
✔ Select a solution
Design a prototype
✔ Build a prototype
✔ Test and evaluate
✔ Redesign to improve
✔ Communicate results

Objectives

- Explain how a need for clean energy has driven a technological solution.
- Describe two examples of wind-powered generators.
- Design a technological solution to a problem.
- Test and modify a prototype to achieve the desired result.

Building a Wind Turbine

During the Industrial Revolution, machines began to replace human and animal power for doing work. From agriculture and manufacturing to transportation, machines made work faster and easier. However, these machines needed fuel. Fossil fuels, such as coal, oil, and gasoline, powered the Industrial Revolution and are still used today. But burning fossil fuels produces waste products that harm the environment. In addition, fossil fuels will eventually run out. As a result, we need to better understand alternative, renewable sources of energy.

Brainstorming Solutions

There are many sources of energy besides fossil fuels. One of the most abundant renewable sources is wind. A wind turbine is a device that uses energy from the wind to turn an axle. The turning axle can be attached to other equipment to do jobs such as pumping water, cutting lumber, or generating electricity. To generate electricity, the axle spins magnets around a coiled wire. This causes electrons to flow in the wire. Flowing electrons produce an electric current. Electric current is used to power homes and businesses or electrical energy can be stored in a battery.

1 Brainstorm What are other possible sources of renewable energy that could be used to power a generator?

_____

_____

_____

_____

_____

_____

_____

HAWTs must be pointed into the wind to work. A motor turns the turbine to keep it facing the wind. HAWT blades are angled so that wind strikes the front of the blades, and then pushes the blades as it flows over them. Because wind flows over the blades fairly evenly, there is little vibration. So HAWTs are relatively quiet, and the turbines last a long time.

Wind direction

Blade moves counterclockwise

The Modern Design

There are two general types of modern wind turbines. A horizontal-axis wind turbine (HAWT) has a main axle that is horizontal, and a generator at the top of a tall tower. A vertical-axis wind turbine (VAWT) has a main axle that is vertical, and a generator at ground level. The blades are often white or light gray, to blend with the clouds. Blades can be more than 40 meters (130 ft) long, supported by towers more than 90 meters (300 ft) tall. The blade tips can travel more than 320 kilometers (200 mi) per hour!

2 Infer What problems may have been encountered as prototypes for modern wind turbines were tested?

_____

_____

_____

VAWTs do not need to be pointed into the wind to work. The blades are made so that one blade is pushed by the wind while the other returns against the wind. But because each blade moves against the wind for part of its rotation, VAWTs are less efficient than HAWTs. They also tend to vibrate more and, as a result, make more noise.

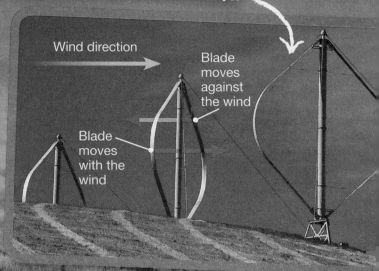

Wind direction

Blade moves against the wind

Blade moves with the wind

👋 You Try It!

Now it's your turn to design a wind turbine that will generate electricity and light a small bulb.

 You Try It!

Now it's your turn to design an efficient wind turbine that will generate enough electricity to light a small bulb.

Materials

✔ assorted wind turbine parts

✔ fan

✔ gears

✔ small bulb

✔ small motor

✔ socket

1 Brainstorm solutions

Brainstorm ideas for a wind turbine that will turn an axle on a small motor. The blades must turn fast enough so that the motor generates enough electricity to light a small bulb. Fill in the table below with as many ideas as you can for each part of your wind turbine. Circle each idea you decide to try.

Type of axis	Shape of turbine	Attaching axis to motor	Control speed

2 Select a solution

From the table above, choose the features for the turbine you will build. In the space below, draw a model of your wind turbine idea. Include all the parts and show how they will be connected.

③ Build a prototype

Now build your wind turbine. As you built your turbine, were there some parts of your design that could not be assembled as you had predicted? What parts did you have to revise as you were building the prototype?

_____
_____
_____
_____

④ Test and evaluate

Point a fan at your wind turbine and see what happens. Did the bulb light? If not, what parts of your turbine could you revise?

_____
_____
_____
_____

⑤ Redesign to improve

Choose one part to revise. Modify your design and then test again. Repeat this process until your turbine lights up the light bulb.

_____
_____
_____
_____

⑥ Communicate results

Which part of the turbine seemed to have the greatest effect on the brightness of the light bulb?

_____
_____
_____
_____

Wind in the Atmosphere

ESSENTIAL QUESTION

What is wind?

By the end of this lesson, you should be able to explain how energy provided by the sun causes atmospheric movement, called wind.

Although you cannot see wind, you can see how it affects things like these kites.

Engage Your Brain

1 Predict Check T or F to show whether you think each statement is true or false.

T	F	
☐	☐	The atmosphere is often referred to as air.
☐	☐	Wind does not have direction.
☐	☐	During the day, there is often a wind blowing toward shore from the ocean or a large lake.
☐	☐	Cold air rises and warm air sinks.

2 Explain If you opened the valve on this bicycle tire, what would happen to the air inside of the tire? Why do you think that would happen?

_____

_____

_____

 Active Reading

3 Synthesize You can often define an unknown phrase if you know the meaning of its word parts. Use the word parts below to make an educated guess about the meanings of the phrases *local wind* and *global wind*.

Word part	Meaning
wind	movement of air due to differences in air pressure
local	involving a particular area
global	involving the entire Earth

Vocabulary Terms

• wind
• Coriolis effect
• global wind
• jet stream
• local wind

4 Identify This list contains the vocabulary terms you'll learn in this lesson. As you read, circle the definition of each term.

local wind:

_____

_____

global wind:

_____

_____

Blow It Out!

What causes wind?

The next time you feel the wind blowing, you can thank the sun! The sun does not warm the whole surface of the Earth in a uniform manner. This uneven heating causes the air above Earth's surface to be at different temperatures. Cold air is more dense than warmer air is. Colder, denser air sinks. When denser air sinks, it places greater pressure on the surface of Earth than warmer, less-dense air does. This results in areas of higher air pressure. Air moves from areas of higher pressure toward areas of lower pressure. The movement of air caused by differences in air pressure is called **wind**. The greater the differences in air pressure, the faster the air moves.

Areas of High and Low Pressure

Cold, dense air at the poles creates areas of high pressure at the poles. Warm, less-dense air at the equator forms an area of lower pressure. This pressure gradient results in global movement of air. However, instead of moving in one circle between the equator and the poles, air moves in smaller circular patterns called *convection cells*, shown below. As air moves from the equator, it cools and becomes more dense. At about 30°N and 30°S latitudes, a high-pressure belt results from the sinking of air. Near the poles, cold air warms as it moves away from the poles. At around 60°N and 60°S latitudes, a low-pressure belt forms as the warmed air is pushed upward.

Visualize It!

5 Identify In the white oval area on the map, draw the convection cell that was left out. Use a pencil to indicate warm air and a pen to indicate cool air.

The warming and cooling of air produces pressure belts every 30° of latitude.

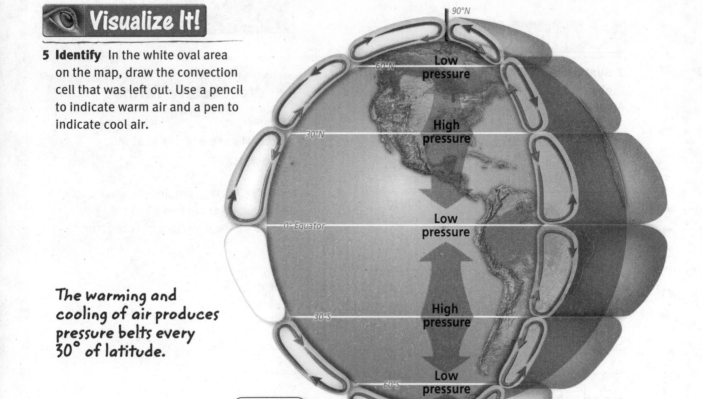

Cool air
Warm air

How does Earth's rotation affect wind?

Pressure differences cause air to move between the equator and the poles. If Earth was not rotating, winds would blow in a straight line. However, winds are deflected, or curved, due to Earth's rotation, as shown below. The apparent curving of the path of a moving object from an otherwise straight path due to Earth's rotation is called the **Coriolis effect** (kawr•ee•OH•lis ih•FEKT). This effect is most noticeable over long distances.

Because each point on Earth makes one complete rotation every day, points closer to the equator must travel farther and, therefore, faster than points closer to the poles do. When air moves from the equator toward the North Pole, it maintains its initial speed and direction. If the air travels far enough north, it will have traveled farther east than a point on the ground beneath it. As a result, the air appears to follow a curved path toward the east. Air moving from the North Pole to the equator appears to curve to the west because the air moves east more slowly than a point on the ground beneath it does. Therefore, in the Northern Hemisphere, air moving to the north curves to the east and air moving to the south curves to the west.

Active Reading

6 Identify As you read, underline how air movement in the Northern Hemisphere is influenced by the Coriolis effect.

Visualize It!

7 Label In the white ovals on the map, draw the direction and path of the winds that would occur at those locations on Earth.

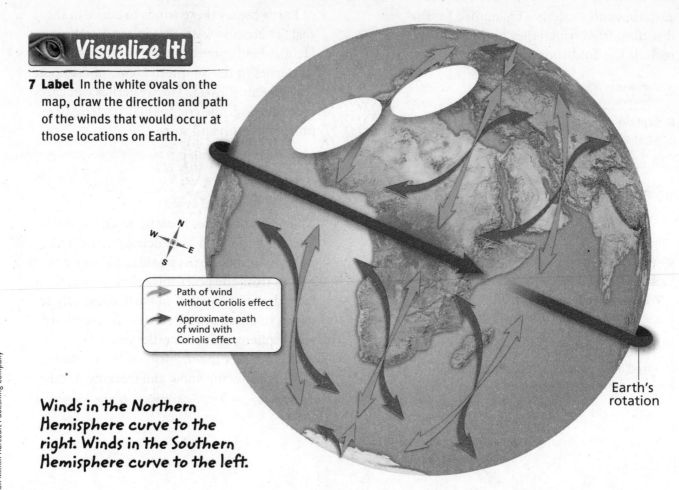

Path of wind without Coriolis effect

Approximate path of wind with Coriolis effect

Earth's rotation

Winds in the Northern Hemisphere curve to the right. Winds in the Southern Hemisphere curve to the left.

Blowin' Around

What are examples of global winds?

Recall that air travels in circular patterns called convection cells that cover approximately 30° of latitude. Pressure belts at every 30° of latitude and the Coriolis effect produce patterns of calm areas and wind systems. These wind systems occur at or near Earth's surface and are called **global winds**. As shown at the right, the major global wind systems are the *polar easterlies* (EE•ster•leez), the *westerlies* (WES•ter•leez), and the *trade winds*. Winds such as polar easterlies and westerlies are named for the direction from which they blow. Calm areas include the doldrums and the horse latitudes.

Active Reading

8 Explain If something is being carried by westerlies, what direction is it moving toward?

_____

_____

Think Outside the Book Inquiry

9 Model Winds are described according to their direction and speed. Research wind vanes and what they are used for. Design and build your own wind vane.

Trade Winds

The trade winds blow between 30° latitude and the equator in both hemispheres. The rotation of Earth causes the trade winds to curve to the west. Therefore, trade winds in the Northern Hemisphere come from the northeast, and trade winds in the Southern Hemisphere come from the southeast. These winds became known as the trade winds because sailors relied on them to sail from Europe to the Americas.

Westerlies

The westerlies blow between 30° and 60° latitudes in both hemispheres. The rotation of Earth causes these winds to curve to the east. Therefore, westerlies in the Northern Hemisphere come from the southwest, and westerlies in the Southern Hemisphere come from the northwest. The westerlies can carry moist air over the continental United States, producing rain and snow.

Polar Easterlies

The polar easterlies blow between the poles and 60° latitude in both hemispheres. The polar easterlies form as cold, sinking air moves from the poles toward 60°N and 60°S latitudes. The rotation of Earth causes these winds to curve to the west. In the Northern Hemisphere, polar easterlies can carry cold Arctic air over the majority of the United States, producing snow and freezing weather.

The major global wind systems

10 Identify Label the polar easterlies, the westerlies, and the trade winds in the white boxes on the map.

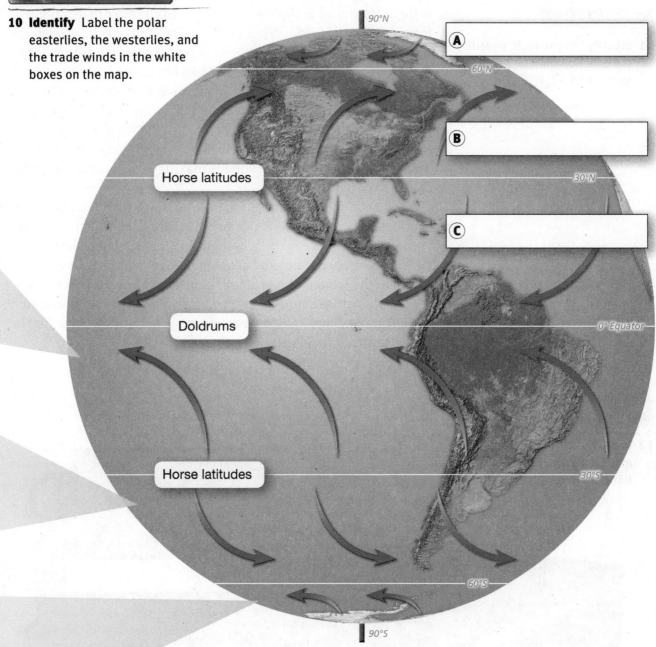

The Doldrums and Horse Latitudes

The trade winds of both hemispheres meet in a calm area around the equator called the *doldrums* (DOHL•druhmz). Very little wind blows in the doldrums because the warm, less-dense air results in an area of low pressure. The name doldrums means "dull" or "sluggish." At about 30° latitude in both hemispheres, air stops moving and sinks. This forms calm areas called the *horse latitudes*. This name was given to these areas when sailing ships carried horses from Europe to the Americas. When ships were stalled in these areas, horses were sometimes thrown overboard to save water.

The Jet Streams

A flight from Seattle to Boston can be 30 min faster than a flight from Boston to Seattle. Why? Pilots can take advantage of a jet stream. **Jet streams** are narrow belts of high-speed winds that blow from west to east, between 7 km and 16 km above Earth's surface. Airplanes traveling in the same direction as a jet stream go faster than those traveling in the opposite direction of a jet stream. When an airplane is traveling "with" a jet stream, the wind is helping the airplane move forward. However, when an airplane is traveling "against" the jet stream, the wind is making it more difficult for the plane to move forward.

The two main jet streams are the polar jet stream and the subtropical (suhb•TRAHP•i•kuhl) jet stream, shown below. Each of the hemispheres experiences these jet streams. Jet streams follow boundaries between hot and cold air and can shift north and south. In the winter, as Northern Hemisphere temperatures cool, the polar jet stream moves south. This shift brings cold Arctic air to the United States. When temperatures rise in the spring, this jet stream shifts to the north.

Active Reading

11 Identify As you read, underline the direction that the jet streams travel.

Visualize It!

12 Identify Label the polar jet stream and the subtropical jet stream in the Northern Hemisphere.

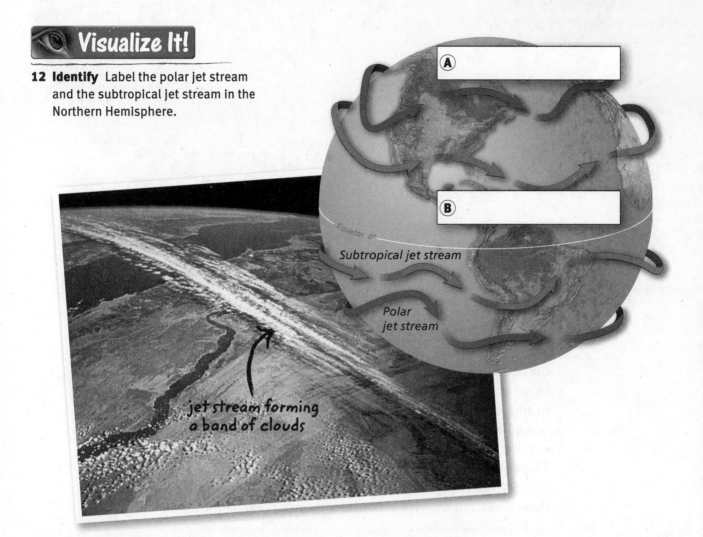

A

B

Equator 0°

Subtropical jet stream

Polar jet stream

jet stream forming a band of clouds

Why It Matters

Desert Trades

How does some of the Sahara end up in the Americas? Global winds carry it.

Trade Wind Carriers
Trade winds can carry Saharan dust across the Atlantic Ocean to Florida and the Caribbean.

Africa

Florida Meets the Sahara
This hazy skyline in Miami is the result of a dust storm. Where did the dust come from? It all started in the Sahara.

The Sahara
The Sahara is the world's largest hot desert. Sand and dust storms that produce skies like this are very common in this desert.

Extend

Inquiry

13 Explain Look at a map and explain how trade winds carry dust from the Sahara to the Caribbean.

14 Relate Investigate the winds that blow in your community. Where do they usually come from? Identify the wind system that could be involved.

15 Apply Investigate how winds played a role in distributing radioactive waste that was released after an explosion at the Chernobyl Nuclear Power Plant in Ukraine. Present your findings as a map illustration or in a poster.

Feelin' Breezy

What are examples of local winds?

Local geographic features, such as a body of water or a mountain, can produce temperature and pressure differences that cause local winds. Unlike global winds, **local winds** are the movement of air over short distances. They can blow from any direction, depending on the features of the area.

Sea and Land Breezes

Have you ever felt a cool breeze coming off the ocean or a lake? If so, you were experiencing a sea breeze. Large bodies of water take longer to warm up than land does. During the day, air above land becomes warmer than air above water. The colder, denser air over water flows toward the land and pushes the warm air on the land upward. While water takes longer to warm than land does, land cools faster than water does. At night, cooler air on land causes a higher-pressure zone over the land. So, a wind blows from the land toward the water. This type of local wind is called a land breeze.

sea breeze

B _____ pressure

A _____ pressure

land breeze

D _____ pressure

C _____ pressure

Valley and Mountain Breezes

Areas that have mountains and valleys experience local winds called mountain and valley breezes. During the day, the sun warms the air along the mountain slopes faster than the air in the valleys. This uneven heating results in areas of lower pressure near the mountain tops. This pressure difference causes a valley breeze, which flows from the valley up the slopes of the mountains. Many birds float on valley breezes to conserve energy. At nightfall, the air along the mountain slopes cools and moves down into the valley. This local wind is called a mountain breeze.

Visualize It!

18 Analyze Label the areas of high pressure and low pressure.

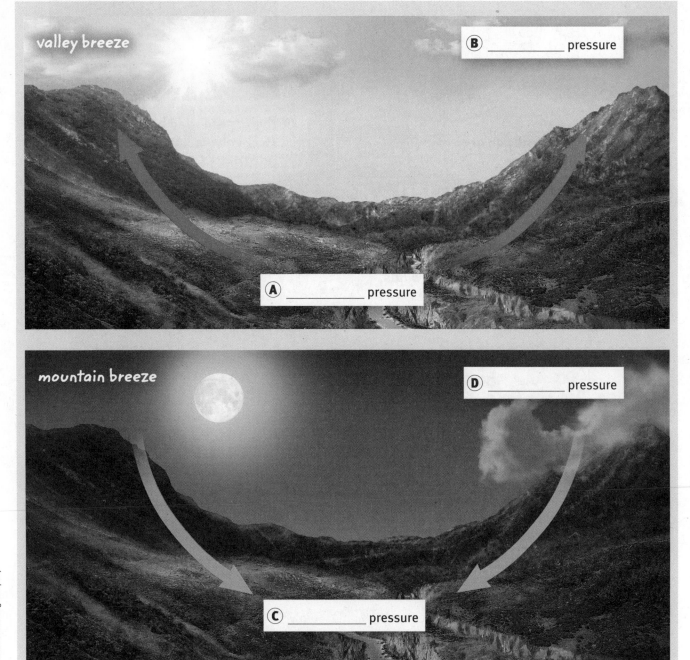

valley breeze

Ⓑ _____ pressure

Ⓐ _____ pressure

mountain breeze

Ⓓ _____ pressure

Ⓒ _____ pressure

Visual Summary

To complete this summary, circle the correct word or phrases. Then use the key below to check your answers. You can use this page to review the main concepts of the lesson.

Wind is the movement of air from areas of higher pressure to areas of lower pressure.

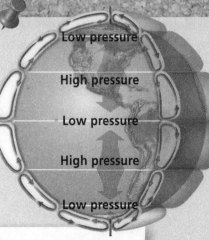

Low pressure

High pressure

Low pressure

High pressure

Low pressure

19 Cool air sinks, causing an area of high / low air pressure.

Global wind systems occur on Earth.

20 High-speed wind between 7 km and 16 km above Earth's surface is a jet stream / mountain breeze.

Wind in the Atmosphere

Geographic features can produce local winds.

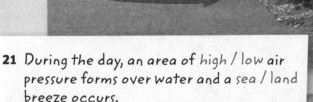

21 During the day, an area of high / low air pressure forms over water and a sea / land breeze occurs.

Answers: 19 high; 20 jet stream; 21 high, sea

22 Explain Would there be winds if the air above Earth's surface was the same temperature everywhere? Explain your answer.

Lesson Review

Vocabulary

Fill in the blanks with the term that best completes the following sentences.

1 Another term for air movement caused by differences in air pressure is

_____

2 Pilots often take advantage of the
_____ , which are
high-speed winds between 7 km and 16 km
above Earth's surface.

3 The apparent curving of winds due to Earth's
rotation is the _____

Key Concepts

4 Explain How does the sun cause wind?

_____
_____
_____
_____

5 Predict If Earth did not rotate, what would
happen to the global winds? Why?

_____
_____
_____
_____

6 Explain How do convection cells in Earth's
atmosphere cause high- and low-pressure belts?

_____
_____
_____
_____

7 Describe What factors contribute to global
winds? Identify areas where winds are weak.

_____
_____
_____
_____

8 Identify Name a latitude where each of the
following occurs: polar easterlies, westerlies,
and trade winds.

_____
_____

Critical Thinking

9 Predict How would local winds be affected if
water and land absorbed and released heat at
the same rate? Explain your answer.

_____
_____
_____
_____

10 Compare How is a land breeze similar to a
sea breeze? How do they differ?

_____
_____
_____
_____

Use this image to answer the following questions.

11 Analyze What type of local wind would you
experience if you were standing in the valley?
Explain your answer.

_____
_____
_____

12 Infer Would the local wind change if it was
nighttime? Explain.

_____
_____
_____
_____

My Notes

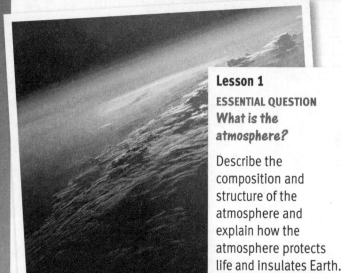

Lesson 1

ESSENTIAL QUESTION
What is the atmosphere?

Describe the composition and structure of the atmosphere and explain how the atmosphere protects life and insulates Earth.

Lesson 2

ESSENTIAL QUESTION
How does energy move through Earth's system?

Summarize the three mechanisms by which energy is transferred through Earth's system.

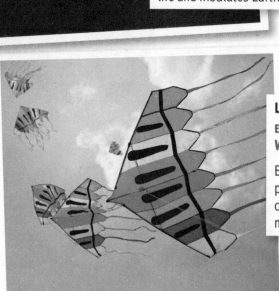

Lesson 3

ESSENTIAL QUESTION
What is wind?

Explain how energy provided by the sun causes atmospheric movement, called wind.

Think Outside the Book

2 Synthesize Choose one of these activities to help synthesize what you have learned in this unit.

☐ Using what you learned in lessons 2 and 3, make a poster presentation explaining the role that radiation, conduction, and convection play in the transfer of energy in Earth's atmosphere.

☐ Using what you learned in lessons 1 and 2, explain how solar radiation contributes to the greenhouse effect. Include the terms *radiation* and *reradiation* in your explanation.

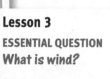 **Connect** **ESSENTIAL QUESTIONS**
Lessons 2 and 3

1 Synthesize Explain how the uneven warming of Earth causes air to move.

_____

_____

_____

_____

Unit 3 Review

Name _____

Vocabulary

Check the box to show whether each statement is true or false.

T	F	
☐	☐	**1** <u>Radiation</u> is a measure of the average kinetic energy of the particles in an object.
☐	☐	**2** <u>Thermal expansion</u> is the increase in volume that results from an increase in temperature.
☐	☐	**3** The <u>stratosphere</u> is the top layer of Earth's atmosphere.
☐	☐	**4** A <u>jet stream</u> is a wide band of low-speed winds that flow in the middle atmosphere.
☐	☐	**5** The curving of the path of a moving object as a result of Earth's rotation is called the <u>Coriolis effect</u>.

Key Concepts

Read each question below, and circle the best answer.

6 The picture below shows all three methods of energy transfer.

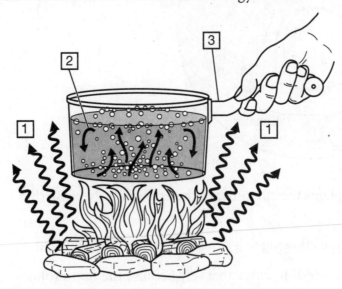

Which of these correctly identifies the three methods of energy transfer?

A 1: convection   2: radiation   3: conduction

B 1: radiation   2: conduction   3: convection

C 1: conduction   2: convection   3: radiation

D 1: radiation   2: convection   3: conduction

7 Which of these is not a way in which energy is transferred to Earth from the sun?

A conduction

C visible light

B infrared radiation

D x-rays

8 A plastic spoon that has a temperature of 78° F is placed into a bowl of soup that has a temperature of 84° F. Which of these correctly describes what will happen?

A Energy as heat moves from the spoon to the soup.

B Energy as heat does not move, because the spoon is plastic.

C Energy as heat moves from the soup to the spoon.

D Energy as heat does not move, because the temperature difference is too small.

9 Refer to the diagram of winds and currents below to answer the question.

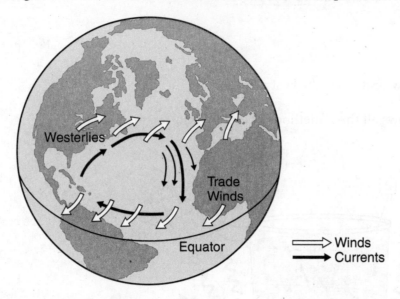

Which of the following best explains the curvature of the arrows for the westerlies and the trade winds?

A The ocean currents create winds flowing in a similar direction to the current.

B The Coriolis effect causes the winds to curve that way because the Earth rotates from left to right.

C The Coriolis effect causes the winds to curve that way because the Earth rotates from right to left.

D The sun is shining and warming the air from the right side of this diagram.

10 An astronomer studying planets outside our solar system has analyzed the atmospheres of four planets. Which of these planets' atmospheres would be most able to support a colony of humans?

A Planet A: 76% Nitrogen, 23% Oxygen, 1% Other

B Planet B: 82% Nitrogen, 11% Oxygen, 7% Other

C Planet C: 78% Nitrogen, 1% Oxygen, 21% Other

D Planet D: 27% Nitrogen, 3% Oxygen, 70% Other

11 Refer to the picture below to answer the question.

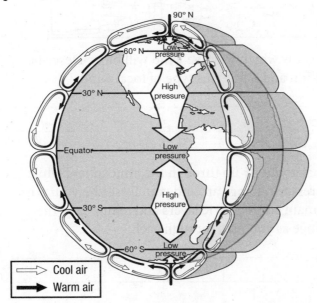

Which of the following is most responsible for the moving bands of air around Earth that are shown in the picture above?

A conduction

B convection

C Coriolis effect

D greenhouse effect

12 Which of the following describes the general pattern of winds near the equator?

A Winds are generally weak because the equator is a region where low and high air pressure atmospheric bands come together.

B Winds are generally strong because the equator is a region where low and high air pressure atmospheric bands come together.

C Winds are generally strong because the equator is a region of mostly high air pressure.

D Winds are generally weak because the equator is a region of mostly low air pressure.

Critical Thinking

Answer the following questions in the space provided.

13 The picture below shows a situation that causes local winds.

Draw an arrow on the picture to show which way the wind will blow. Describe why the wind blows in that direction and name this type of local wind.

_____

_____

14 Suppose you were a superhero that could fly up through the atmosphere while feeling the temperature and air pressure change around you. Describe your trip in a paragraph, naming the four main atmospheric layers and telling how the temperature and air pressure change as you pass through each.

_____

_____

_____

_____

_____

Connect ESSENTIAL QUESTIONS
Lessons 1, 2, and 3

Answer the following question in the space provided.

15 Explain how Earth gets energy from the sun and what the atmosphere does with that energy to help life survive on Earth.

_____

_____

_____

_____

Weather and Climate

Strong winds create huge waves that crash on shore.

Houghton Mifflin Harcourt Publishing Company • Image Credits: (bkgd) ©Burton McNeely/Stone/Getty Images; (br) ©Drake Fleege/Alamy

Big Idea

Air pressure, temperature, air movement, and humidity in the atmosphere affect both weather and climate.

Warning flags are used to show how safe this beach is.

What do you think?

The weather can change very quickly. In severe weather, people and pets can get hurt, and property can be damaged. Can you think of ways to keep people, pets, and property safe?

Unit 4
Weather and Climate

Exit Strategy

When there is an emergency, knowing what to do helps keep people as safe as possible. So what's the plan?

1 Think About It

A Do you know what to do if there were a weather emergency while you were in school?

_____

B What kinds of information might you need to stay safe? List them below.

_____

_____

_____

_____

_____

Floods can happen very quickly during a bad storm.

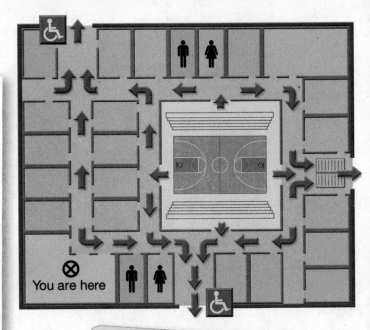

② Ask A Question

How well do you know your school's emergency evacuation plan? Obtain a copy of the school's emergency evacuation plan. Read through the plan and answer the following questions as a class.

A Is the emergency evacuation plan/map easy for students to understand?

_____

B How would you know which way to go?

_____

_____

C How often do you have practice drills?

_____

EMERGENCY EVACUATION ROUTE

③ Propose and Apply Improvements

A Using what you have learned about your school's emergency evacuation plan, list your ideas for improvements below.

_____
_____
_____
_____

B Develop and give a short oral presentation to your principal about your proposal on ways to improve the school's emergency evacuation plan. Write the main points of your presentation below.

_____
_____
_____
_____

C As a class, practice the newly improved emergency evacuation plan. Describe how well the improved emergency evacuation plan worked.

_____
_____
_____
_____
_____
_____

Take It Home

With an adult, create an emergency evacuation plan for your family or evaluate your family's emergency evacuation plan and propose improvements. See *ScienceSaurus*® for more information about weather.

Elements of Weather

ESSENTIAL QUESTION

What is weather and how can we describe different types of weather conditions?

By the end of this lesson, you should be able to describe elements of weather and explain how they are measured.

Weather stations placed all around the world allow scientists to measure the elements, or separate parts, of weather.

A researcher checks an automatic weather station on Alexander Island, Antarctica.

Lesson Labs

Quick Labs
- Investigate the Measurement of Rainfall
- Classifying Features of Different Types of Clouds

Field Lab
- Comparing Different Ways to Estimate Wind Speed

Engage Your Brain

1 Predict Check T or F to show whether you think each statement is true or false.

T	F	
☐	☐	Weather can change every day.
☐	☐	Temperature is measured by using a barometer.
☐	☐	Air pressure increases as you move higher in the atmosphere.
☐	☐	Visibility is a measurement of how far we can see.

2 Describe Use at least three words that might describe the weather on a day when the sky looks like the picture above.

_____

_____

_____

Active Reading

3 Distinguish The words *weather*, *whether*, and *wether* all sound alike but are spelled differently and mean entirely different things. You may have never heard of a wether—it is a neutered male sheep or ram.

Circle the correct use of the three words in the sentence below.

The farmer wondered *weather* / *whether* / *wether* the cold *weather* / *whether* / *wether* had affected his *weather* / *whether* / *wether*.

Vocabulary Terms

- weather
- humidity
- relative humidity
- dew point
- precipitation
- air pressure
- wind
- visibility

4 Apply As you learn the definition of each vocabulary term in this lesson, create your own definition or sketch to help you remember the meaning of the term.

Wonder about Weather?

What is weather?

Weather is the condition of Earth's atmosphere at a certain time and place. Different observations give you clues to the weather. If you see plants moving from side to side, you might infer that it is windy. If you see a gray sky and wet, shiny streets, you might decide to wear a raincoat. People talk about weather by describing factors such as temperature, humidity, precipitation, air pressure, wind, and *visibility* (viz•uh•BIL•i•tee).

What is temperature and how is it measured?

Temperature is a measure of how hot or cold something is. An instrument that measures and displays temperature is called a *thermometer*. A common type of thermometer uses a liquid such as alcohol or mercury to display the temperature. The liquid is sealed in a glass tube. When the air gets warmer, the liquid expands and rises in the tube. Cooler air causes the liquid to contract and fill less of the tube. A scale, often in Celsius (°C) or Fahrenheit (°F), is marked on the glass tube.

Another type of thermometer is an electrical thermometer. As the temperature becomes higher, electric current flow increases through the thermometer. The strength of the current is then translated into temperature readings.

Extreme Weather Facts

Earth's highest recorded temperature was in El Azizia, Libya, on September 1922 at 58 °C (136 °F).

Earth's lowest recorded temperature was in Vostok, Antarctica, on July 1983 at −89 °C (−128 °F).

Visualize It!

5 Identify Color in the liquid in the thermometer above to show Earth's average temperature in 2009 (58 °F). Write the Celsius temperature that equals 58 °F on the line below.

_____

What is humidity and how is it measured?

As water evaporates from oceans, lakes, and ponds, it becomes water vapor, or a gas that is in the air. The amount of water vapor in the air is called **humidity**. As more water evaporates and becomes water vapor, the humidity of the air increases.

Humidity is often described through relative humidity. **Relative humidity** is the amount of water vapor in the air compared to the amount of water vapor needed to reach saturation. As shown below, when air is saturated, the rates of evaporation and condensation are equal. Saturated air has a relative humidity of 100%. A psychrometer (sy•KRAHM•i•ter) is an instrument that is used to measure relative humidity.

Air can become saturated when evaporation adds water vapor to the air. Air can also become saturated when it cools to its dew point. The **dew point** is the temperature at which more condensation than evaporation occurs. When air temperature drops below the dew point, condensation forms. This can cause dew on surfaces cooler than the dew point. It also can form fog and clouds.

Active Reading

6 Identify Underline the name of the instrument used to measure relative humidity.

7 Sketch In the space provided, draw what happens in air that is below the dew point.

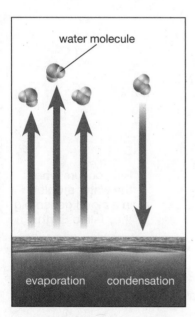

water molecule

evaporation   condensation

In unsaturated air, more water evaporates into the air than condenses back into the water.

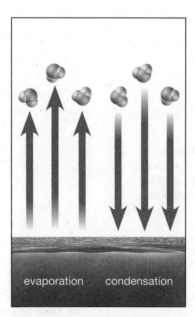

evaporation   condensation

In saturated air, the amount of water that evaporates equals the amount that condenses.

When air cools below its dew point, more water vapor condenses into water than evaporates.

8 Explain Why does dew form on grass overnight?

_____

_____

What is precipitation and how is it measured?

Water vapor in the air condenses not only on Earth's surfaces, but also on tiny particles in the air to form clouds. When this water from the air returns to Earth's surface, it falls as precipitation. **Precipitation** is any form of water that falls to Earth's surface from the clouds. The four main forms of precipitation are rain, snow, hail, and sleet.

Rain is the most common form of precipitation. Inside a cloud, the droplets formed by condensation collide and form larger droplets. They finally become heavy enough to fall as raindrops. Rain is measured with a rain gauge, as shown in the picture below. A funnel or wide opening at the top of the gauge allows rain to flow into a cylinder that is marked in centimeters.

Snow forms when air temperatures are so low that water vapor turns into a solid. When a lot of snow has fallen, it is measured with a ruler or meterstick. When balls or lumps of ice fall from clouds during thunderstorms it is called *hail*. Sleet forms when rain falls through a layer of freezing air, producing falling ice.

Visualize It! Inquiry

9 Synthesize What are two ways in which all types of precipitation are alike?

_____

_____

_____

Snow
Snow can fall as single ice crystals or ice crystals can join to form snowflakes.

Rain
Rain occurs when the water droplets in a cloud get so big they fall to Earth.

Sleet
Small ice pellets fall as sleet when rain falls through cold air.

Hail
Hailstones are layered lumps of ice that fall from clouds.

10 Measure How much rain has this rain gauge collected?

_____

© Houghton Mifflin Harcourt Publishing Company • Image Credits: (bl) ©Kent Knudson/PhotoLink/Photodisc/Getty Images; (bc) ©CamEl Creative/Workbook Stock/Getty Images; (br) ©Johner Images/Alamy

Watching Clouds

Cirrus Clouds

Cumulus Clouds

Stratus Clouds

As you can see above, cirrus (SIR•uhs) clouds appear feathery or wispy. Their name means "curl of hair." They are made of ice crystals. They form when the wind is strong.

Cumulus (KYOOM•yuh•luhs) means "heap" or "pile." Usually these clouds form in fair weather but if they keep growing taller, they can produce thunderstorms.

Stratus (STRAY•tuhs) means "spread out." Stratus clouds form in flat layers. Low, dark stratus clouds can block out the sun and produce steady drizzle or rain.

If you watch the sky over a period of time, you will probably observe different kinds of clouds. Clouds have different characteristics because they form under different conditions. The shapes and sizes of clouds are mainly determined by air movement. For example, puffy clouds form in air that rises sharply or moves straight up and down. Flat, smooth clouds covering large areas form in air that rises gradually.

Extend

Inquiry

11 Reflect Think about the last time you noticed the clouds. When are you most likely to notice what type of cloud is in the sky?

12 Research Word parts are used to tell more about clouds. Look up the word parts *-nimbus* and *alto-*. What are cumulonimbus and altostratus clouds?

The Air Out There

What is air pressure and how is it measured?

Scientists use an instrument called a *barometer* (buh•RAHM•i•ter) to measure air pressure. **Air pressure** is the force of air molecules pushing on an area. The air pressure at any area on Earth depends on the weight of the air above that area. Although air is pressing down on us, we don't feel the weight because air pushes in all directions. So, the pressure of air pushing down is balanced by the pressure of air pushing up.

Air pressure and density are related; they both decrease with altitude. Notice in the picture that the molecules at sea level are closer together than the molecules at the mountain peak. Because the molecules are closer together, the pressure is greater. The air at sea level is denser than air at high altitude.

Air pressure and density are lower at a high altitude.

Air pressure and density are higher at sea level.

© Houghton Mifflin Harcourt Publishing Company • Image Credits: (tl) ©Phillipe Giraud/Sygma/Corbis; (bl) ©David Buffington/Photographer's Choice/Getty Images

---

13 Identify Look at the photos below and write whether wind direction or wind speed is being measured.

Anemometer

An anemometer measures:

_____

Wind vane

A wind vane measures:

_____

What is wind and how is it measured?

Wind is air that moves horizontally, or parallel to the ground. Uneven heating of Earth's surface causes pressure differences from place to place. These pressure differences set air in motion. Over a short distance, wind moves directly from higher pressure toward lower pressure.

An anemometer (an•uh•MAHM•i•ter) is used to measure wind speed. It has three or four cups attached to a pole. The wind causes the cups to rotate, sending an electric current to a meter that displays the wind speed.

Wind direction is measured by using a wind vane or a windsock. A wind vane has an arrow with a large tail that is attached to a pole. The wind pushes harder on the arrow tail due to its larger surface area. This causes the wind vane to spin so that the arrow points into the wind. A windsock is a cone-shaped cloth bag open at both ends. The wind enters the wide end and the narrow end points in the opposite direction, showing the direction the wind is blowing.

What is visibility and how is it measured?

Visibility is a measure of the transparency of the atmosphere. Visibility is the way we describe how far we can see, and it is measured by using three or four known landmarks at different distances. Sometimes not all of the landmarks will be visible. Poor visibility can be the result of air pollution or fog.

Poor visibility can be dangerous for all types of travel, whether by air, water, or land. When visibility is very low, roads may be closed to traffic. In areas where low visibility is common, signs are often posted to warn travelers.

 **Active Reading**

14 Explain What are two factors that can affect visibility?

_____

_____

Fog forms as land cools overnight, causing water vapor in the air above the land to condense.

What are some ways to collect weather data?

Many forms of technology are used to gather weather data. The illustration below shows some ways weather information can be collected. Instruments within the atmosphere can make measurements of local weather conditions. Satellites can collect data from above the atmosphere.

 **Visualize It! Inquiry**

15 Infer What are the benefits of stationary weather collection? Moving weather collection?

_____

_____

_____

_____

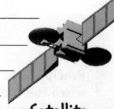
Satellite

Airplane

Ground station

Stationary
Some forms of technology provide measurements from set locations.

Moving
Some forms of technology report changing measurements along their paths.

Weather buoy

Ship

Lesson 1 Elements of Weather **161**

© Houghton Mifflin Harcourt Publishing Company • Image Credits: (t) ©Grant V. Faint/Photodisc/Getty Images

Visual Summary

To complete this summary, fill in the blanks with the correct word or phrase. Then use the key below to check your answers. You can use this page to review the main concepts of the lesson.

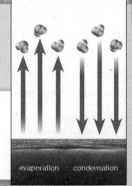

Elements of Weather

Weather is a condition of the atmosphere at a certain time and place.

16 Weather is often expressed by describing _____, humidity, precipitation, air pressure, wind, and visibility.

Humidity describes the amount of water vapor in the air.

17 The amount of moisture in the air is commonly expressed as _____ humidity.

Uneven heating of Earth's surface causes air pressure differences and wind.

18 Wind moves from areas of _____ pressure to areas of _____ pressure.

Visibility describes how far into the distance objects can be seen.

19 Visibility can be affected by air pollution and _____

Precipitation occurs when the water that condenses as clouds falls back to Earth in solid or liquid form.

20 The main types of precipitation are hail, snow, _____, and rain.

Answers: 16 temperature; 17 relative; 18 higher, lower; 19 fog; 20 sleet

21 Synthesize What instruments would you take along if you were going on a 3-month field study to measure how the weather on a mountaintop changes over the course of a season?

Lesson Review

Vocabulary

In your own words, define the following terms.

1 weather _____

_____

_____

2 humidity _____

_____

3 air pressure _____

_____

4 visibility _____

_____

_____

Key Concepts

Weather element	Instrument
5 Identify Measures temperature	
	6 Identify Is measured by using a barometer
7 Identify Measures relative humidity	
	8 Identify Is measured by using a rain gauge or meterstick
9 Identify Measures wind speed	

10 List What are four types of precipitation?

_____

_____

Critical Thinking

11 Apply Explain how wind is related to the uneven heating of Earth's surfaces by the sun.

_____

_____

_____

_____

12 Explain Why does air pressure decrease as altitude increases?

_____

_____

_____

13 Synthesize What is the relative humidity when the air temperature is at its dew point?

_____

The weather data below was recorded from 1989–2009 by an Antarctic weather station similar to the station in the photo at the beginning of this lesson. Use these data to answer the questions that follow.

	Jan.	Apr.	July	Oct.
Mean max. temp. (°C)	2.1	−7.4	−9.9	−8.1
Mean min. temp. (°C)	−2.6	−14.6	−18.1	−15.1
Mean precip. (mm)	9.0	18.04	28.5	16.5

14 Identify Which month had the lowest mean minimum and maximum temperatures?

_____

15 Infer The precipitation that fell at this location was most likely in what form?

_____

My Notes

Clouds and Cloud Formation

ESSENTIAL QUESTION

How do clouds form, and how are clouds classified?

By the end of this lesson, you should be able to describe the formation and classification of clouds.

These altocumulus clouds cover the sky like a bluish-gray blanket. Clouds take various shapes and appear at different altitudes in the lower atmosphere. Scientists classify clouds by both their shape and the altitude at which they form.

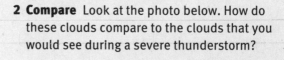

Lesson Labs

Quick Labs
- How Does a Cloud Form?
- Out of Thin Air

Engage Your Brain

1 Identify Read over the following vocabulary terms. In the spaces provided, place a + if you know the term well, a ~ if you have heard the term but are not sure what it means, and a ? if you are unfamiliar with the term. Then write a sentence that includes one of the words you are most familiar with.

_____ cloud

_____ dew point

_____ fog

Sentence using known word:

_____

_____

2 Compare Look at the photo below. How do these clouds compare to the clouds that you would see during a severe thunderstorm?

_____

_____

_____

_____

_____

Active Reading

3 Synthesize Many English words have their roots in other languages. Use the Latin words below to make an educated guess about the meaning of *cirrus cloud* and *cumulus cloud*.

Latin word	Meaning
cirrus	curl
cumulus	heap

Example sentence

Cirrus clouds are seen high in the sky.

cirrus cloud:

_____

_____

Example Sentence

Cumulus clouds change shape often.

cumulus cloud:

_____

_____

Vocabulary Terms

- cloud
- dew point
- stratus cloud
- cumulus cloud
- cirrus cloud
- fog

4 Apply As you learn the definition of each vocabulary term in this lesson, create your own definition or sketch to help you remember the meaning of the term.

Head in the Clouds

Storm clouds appear dark gray. They are so full of water droplets that little light can pass through them.

What are clouds?

When you look into the sky, you see the amazing shapes that clouds take and how quickly those shapes change. But, have you ever asked yourself what clouds are made of or how they form? And did you know that there are different types of clouds?

A **cloud** is a collection of small water droplets or ice crystals that are suspended in the air. Clouds are visible because water droplets and ice crystals reflect light. Clouds are most often associated with precipitation. However, the reality is that most cloud types do not produce precipitation.

How do clouds affect climate?

The precipitation that falls from clouds has a significant effect on local climate. In particular, the pattern of precipitation of an area will determine the climate of that area. For instance, a desert is an area that receives less than 25 cm of precipitation a year. But, a tropical rainforest may average 250 cm of precipitation a year.

Clouds also affect temperatures on Earth. About 25% of the sun's energy that reaches Earth is reflected back into space by clouds. Low-altitude clouds, which are thick and reflect more sunlight, help to cool Earth. On the other hand, thin, high-altitude clouds absorb some of the energy that radiates from Earth. Part of this energy is reradiated back to Earth's surface. This warms Earth, because this energy is not directly lost to space.

Active Reading 5 **Describe** What are two ways in which clouds affect Earth's climate?

_____

_____

_____

6 **Apply** Sketch a cloud, and write a caption that relates the drawing to the content on this page.

_____

_____

_____

_____

_____

How do clouds form?

Clouds form when water vapor condenses, or changes from a gas to a liquid. For water vapor to condense, two things must happen. Air must be cooled to its dew point, and there must be a solid surface on which water molecules can condense.

Air Cools to the Dew Point

As warm air rises in Earth's atmosphere, it expands and cools. If air rises high enough into the atmosphere, it cools to its dew point. **Dew point** is the temperature at which the rate of condensation equals the rate of evaporation. *Evaporation* is the change of state from a liquid to a gas that usually occurs at the surface of a liquid. Evaporation takes place at the surface of an ocean, lake, stream, or other body of water. Water vapor in the air can condense and form water droplets or ice crystals when the temperature is at or below the dew point.

Water Droplets or Ice Crystals Form on Nuclei

Water molecules condense much more rapidly when there is a solid surface on which to condense. In clouds, tiny solid particles called *cloud condensation nuclei* are the surfaces on which water droplets condense. Examples of cloud condensation nuclei include dust, salt, soil, and smoke.

Clouds are most commonly made of very large numbers of very small water droplets. However, at high altitudes, where temperatures are very cold, clouds are composed of ice crystals.

D Cloud formation takes place.

C Condensation takes place on nuclei.

condensation nucleus
0.0002 millimeter diameter

cloud droplet
0.05 millimeter diameter

B
_____
_____

A Warm air rises, expands, and cools.

7 Conclude Complete the flow chart by filling in the missing information.

What is the role of solar energy in cloud formation?

The water cycle is the movement of water between the atmosphere, land, and ocean. Solar energy drives the water cycle and, therefore, provides the energy for cloud formation.

About 50 percent of the sun's incoming energy is absorbed by land, by water on the land's surface, and by surface waters in the oceans. This absorbed energy causes liquid water at the water's surface to become water vapor, a gas. This process is called evaporation. The water vapor rises into the atmosphere with air that has been warmed near Earth's surface.

Solar energy does not warm the surface of Earth evenly. Unequal heating of Earth's surface causes areas of high pressure and low pressure to form in the atmosphere. Air flows horizontally from areas of high pressure to areas of low pressure. This horizontal movement of air is called *wind*. Wind causes clouds to move around Earth's surface. However, for air to be cooled to its dew point so that clouds can form, the air is pushed up, or is lifted, into the atmosphere.

What processes cool air enough to form clouds?

 **Active Reading** **8 Identify** As you read, underline the processes that can cool air enough to form clouds.

There are several ways in which air can be cooled to its dew point. These include frontal and orographic lifting (ohr•uh•GRAF•ik LIFT•ing). Frontal lifting can occur when a warm air mass rises over a cold air mass. Once the rising air cools to its dew point, condensation occurs and clouds form.

Frontal lifting can also occur when a mass of cold air slides under a mass of warm air, pushing the warm air upward. The rising air cools to the dew point. Clouds form that often develop into thunderstorms.

Orographic lifting occurs when an obstacle, such as a mountain range, forces a mass of air upward. Water vapor in the air cools to its dew point and condenses. The clouds that form release large amounts of precipitation as rain or snow as they rise up the mountain. The other side of the mountain receives little precipitation.

Visualize It!

9 Compare The images below show two processes by which clouds form when an air mass is lifted. In what ways are these two processes similar? In what ways are these two processes different?

_____

_____

_____

Frontal Lifting

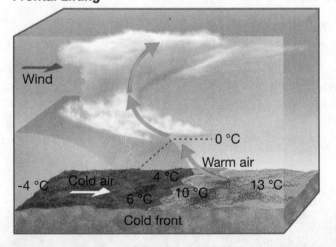

Orographic Lifting

What are three cloud shapes?

You have probably noticed the different shapes that clouds take as they move through the sky. Some clouds are thick and puffy. Other clouds are thin and wispy. Scientists use shape as a way to classify clouds. The three classes of clouds based on shape are stratus (STRAT•uhs) clouds, cumulus (KYOOM•yuh•luhs) clouds, and cirrus (SIR•uhs) clouds.

Stratus Clouds

The lowest clouds in the atmosphere are stratus clouds. **Stratus clouds** are thin and flat, and their edges are not clearly defined. *Stratus* is a Latin word that means "layer." Stratus clouds often merge into one another and may look like a single layer that covers the entire sky. Stratus clouds are often gray. Light mist or drizzle may fall from these clouds. Fog is a type of stratus cloud that forms at or near the ground.

Cumulus Clouds

Cumulus is a Latin word that means "heap." **Cumulus clouds** are thick and puffy on top and generally flat on the bottom. These clouds have well-defined edges and can change shape rapidly. Some may tower high into the atmosphere, where the top of the cloud sometimes flattens.

Fair-weather cumulus clouds are bright and white. But cumulus clouds can become dark as more and more water droplets or ice crystals are added to the cloud. Cumulus clouds can produce severe weather. Thunder, lightning, and heavy precipitation are associated with cumulus clouds.

Cirrus Clouds

Cirrus is a Latin word that means "curl." **Cirrus clouds** look feathery, and their ends curl. Cirrus clouds are white.

Cirrus clouds form high in the atmosphere. At the altitudes where cirrus clouds form, there is little water vapor, and temperatures are very cold. As a result, cirrus clouds are made of ice crystals rather than liquid water droplets. They do not produce precipitation that reaches Earth's surface.

 **Visualize It!**

10 Identify Name the three different clouds based on shape.

A _____

B _____

C _____

I've Looked at Clouds

Active Reading

11 Identify As you read the text, underline the prefixes associated with each class of cloud. If a class has no prefix, underline that information too.

What are the types of clouds based on altitude?

Scientists classify clouds by altitude as well as shape. The four classes of clouds based on altitude are low clouds, middle clouds, high clouds, and clouds of vertical development. These four classes are made up of 10 cloud types. Prefixes are used to name the clouds that belong to some of these classes.

Low Clouds

Low clouds form between Earth's surface and 2,000 m altitude. Water droplets commonly make up these clouds. The three types of low clouds are stratus, stratocumulus, and nimbostratus. There is no special prefix used to name low clouds. However, *nimbus* means "rain," so *nimbo*stratus clouds are rain clouds.

Middle Clouds

Middle clouds form between 2,000 m and 6,000 m altitude. They are most commonly made up of water droplets, but may be made up of ice crystals. The prefix *alto-* is used to name middle clouds. The two types of middle clouds are altocumulus and altostratus.

High Clouds

High clouds form above 6,000 m altitude. At these high altitudes, air temperature is below freezing. Therefore, high clouds are made up of ice crystals. The prefix *cirro-* is used to name high clouds. Cirrus, cirrocumulus, and cirrostratus are the types of high clouds.

Clouds of Vertical Development

Clouds of vertical development can rise high into the atmosphere. Although the cloud base is at low altitude, cloud tops can reach higher than 12,000 m. Clouds of vertical development are commonly formed by the rapid lifting of moist, warm air, which can result in strong vertical growth. There is no special prefix used to name clouds of vertical development. The two types of clouds of vertical development are cumulus and cumulonimbus.

Cumulonimbus clouds have the greatest vertical development of any cloud type. Air currents within these clouds can move upward at as much as 20 m/s. Cumulonimbus clouds are linked to severe weather and can produce rain, hail, lightning, tornadoes, and dangerous, rapidly sinking columns of air that strike Earth.

Think Outside the Book — Inquiry

12 Apply Research cumulonimbus clouds. When you complete your research, consider different materials that might be used to create a model of a cumulonimbus cloud. Then, use your materials to build a model that shows the structure of a cumulonimbus cloud.

from Both Sides Now

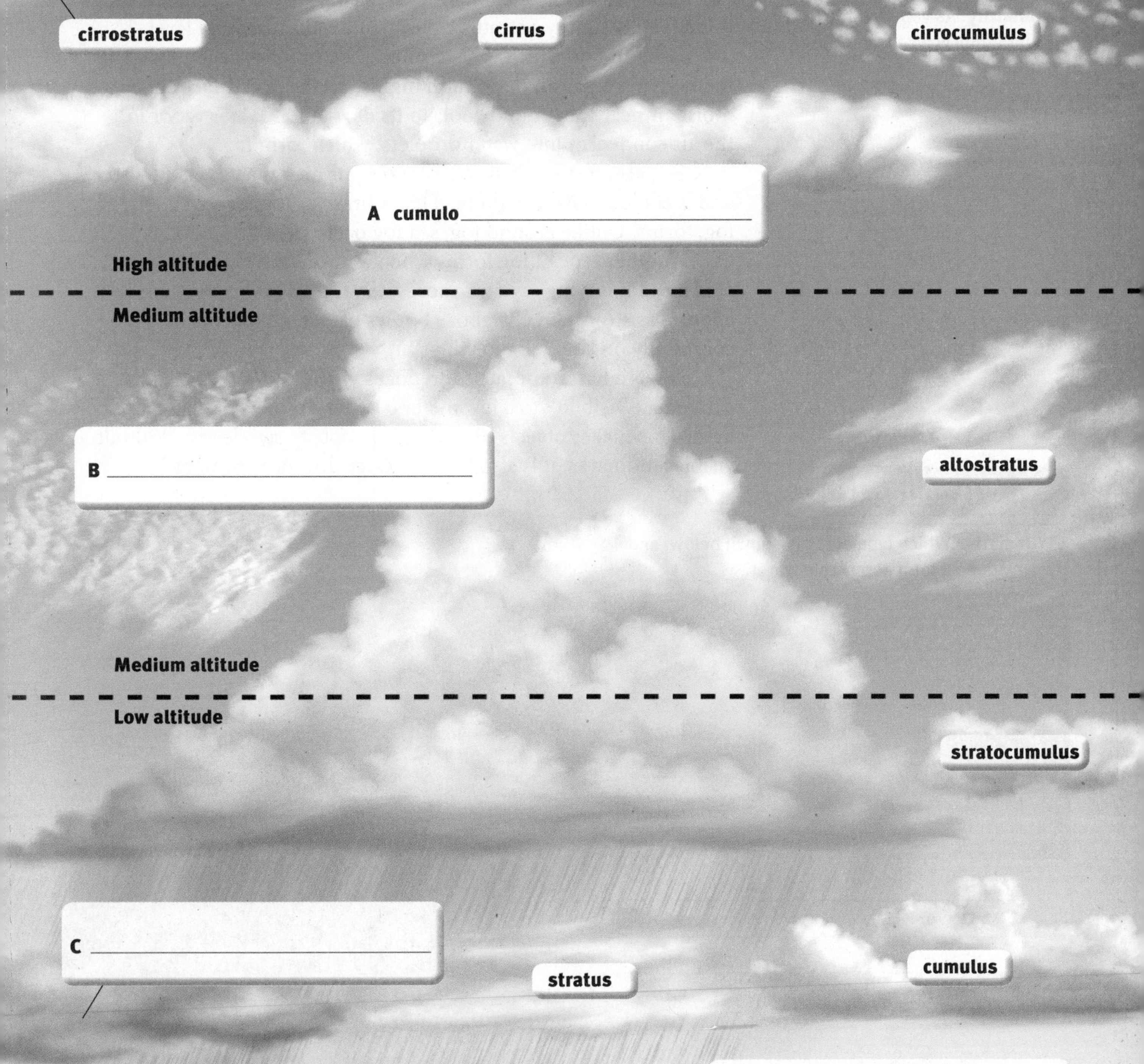

cirrostratus

cirrus

cirrocumulus

A cumulo _____

High altitude

- -

Medium altitude

B _____

altostratus

Medium altitude

- -

Low altitude

stratocumulus

C _____

stratus

cumulus

Visualize It!

13 Identify Meteorologists recognize 10 cloud types based on the altitude at which the clouds form. Using the illustration above, identify the names of the cloud types on the write-on lines provided.

Word Bank

cirrocumulus	cirrostratus
stratus	cumulus
altostratus	cirrus
stratocumulus	cumulonimbus
altocumulus	nimbostratus

How does fog form?

Water vapor that condenses very near Earth's surface is called **fog**. Fog forms when moist air at or near Earth's surface cools to its dew point. Fog is simply a stratus cloud that forms at ground level.

Ground fog, which is also called *radiation fog*, generally forms in low-lying areas on clear, calm nights. As Earth's surface cools, moist air near the ground cools to its dew point. Water vapor in the air condenses into water droplets, which form fog.

Fog also forms when warm, moist air moves across cold water and is cooled to its dew point. This is how sea fog, or advection fog, forms. Unlike ground fog, sea fog occurs at all times of day.

Another type of fog forms when evaporation takes place into cold air that is lying over warmer water. Called *steam fog*, this fog appears as steam directly above bodies of water. It occurs most commonly on cold fall mornings.

Fog is a hazard because it reduces visibility. Very dense fog can reduce visibility to a few meters. Water droplets in fog scatter light. This makes objects difficult for people to see clearly. Without visible landmarks, it is also hard to judge distance and speed.

14 Identify As you read the text, underline ways in which fog forms.

Visualize It!

15 Describe Which type of fog is shown below, and why does it form above cold water?

_____

_____

_____

Ground fog forms at night when Earth's surface cools. Moist air near the ground cools to its dew point, which causes water vapor to condense.

Clouds on Other Worlds

Like Earth, other bodies in the solar system have clouds in their atmosphere. There are clouds on Venus and Mars. Jupiter and Saturn both have deep atmospheres with clouds arranged in bands that circle the planet. Even Saturn's moon Titan has clouds in a thick, planet-like atmosphere.

Venus is surrounded by thick clouds of sulfur dioxide that reflect much of the sunlight that falls on them back into space.

Clouds and dust can be seen in the Martian atmosphere. Mars is covered in a red iron oxide dust. Dust particles act as condensation nuclei that can cause clouds to have a pinkish color.

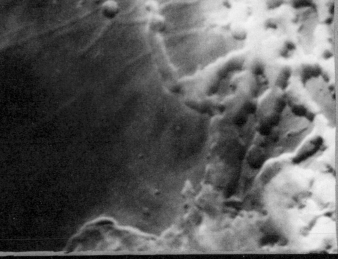

In 1976, *Viking Orbiter 1* took this photo of water-filled clouds that had formed over a large system of canyons just after the Martian sunrise.

Extend

Inquiry

16 Infer Can clouds form on all bodies in the solar system?

17 Apply Research clouds on another body in the solar system. Describe properties of clouds there.

18 Design Create a poster presentation or a slide presentation that examines the way in which clouds on the solar system body that you chose to research differ from clouds on Earth.

Visual Summary

To complete this summary, circle the correct word. Then, use the key below to check your answers. You can use this page to review the main concepts of the lesson.

Clouds and Cloud Formation

Clouds form when rising air cools to the dew point and condensation occurs.

19 Warm air that is forced upward by a cold front is an example of frontal/orographic lifting.

Clouds can be classified by altitude.

20 Clouds that are made up entirely of ice crystals are middle/high clouds.

Clouds can be classified by shape.

21 Thin, wispy clouds that do not produce precipitation are cirrus/cumulus clouds.

Fog is a cloud that has formed very near Earth's surface.

22 Ground/Sea fog generally forms in low-lying areas, such as valleys.

Answers: 19 frontal; 20 high; 21 cirrus; 22 Ground

23 **Synthesis** How can clouds be used to help predict the weather?

Lesson Review

Vocabulary

Fill in the blank with the term that best completes the following sentences.

1 A _____ cloud is thin, wispy, and made of ice crystals.

2 The temperature at which water vapor condenses is the _____

3 _____ is condensed water vapor that forms very close to Earth's surface.

Key Concepts

4 Compare What are two differences between stratus clouds and cirrus clouds?

_____

_____

_____

5 List What are the four classes of clouds based on altitude?

_____

_____

_____

6 Describe What are three ways in which clouds affect climate?

_____

_____

_____

_____

7 Explain What part do tiny, solid particles in the atmosphere play in cloud formation?

_____

_____

_____

Critical Thinking

Use this diagram to answer the following questions.

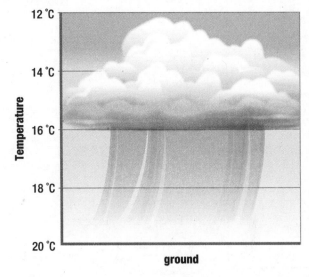

8 Analyze What is the dew-point temperature at which cloud formation began?

_____

_____

9 Explain Why doesn't cloud formation take place until the dew-point temperature is reached?

_____

_____

_____

_____

_____

10 Apply What kind of clouds would you expect to form at the leading edge of a cold front, where warm air is gradually being pushed above cold air?

_____

_____

_____

My Notes

Evaluating Technological Systems

Skills
✔ Identify inputs
✔ Identify outputs
✔ Identify system processes
Evaluate system feedback
Apply system controls
✔ Communicate results

Objectives
• Analyze weather forecasting as a system.
• Identify the inputs and outputs of a forecasting system.
• Interpret weather data to generate a weather map.

Using Data in Systems

A system is a group of interacting parts that work together to do a job. Technological systems process inputs and generate outputs. An input is any matter, energy, or information that goes into a system. Outputs are matter, energy, or information that come out of the system. When you use a computer, the data set that is entered is the input. The computer delivers your output on the monitor or the printer.

Weather Data Go Into a System

What do you do if you have an outdoor activity planned tomorrow? You probably check the weather forecast to help you decide what to wear. Meteorologists are scientists who use data from different sources to find out what is happening in the atmosphere. Weather data are the input. The data set is processed by computers that perform complex calculations to generate weather models. Weather forecast systems combine 72 hours of data from weather stations, weather balloons, radar, aircraft, and weather satellites to show what is happening in Earth's atmosphere now and to predict what will happen in the future.

1 Explain How is a television weather forecast part of a technological system?

_____

_____

_____

The atmosphere is a system that can have dramatic outputs. Those outputs are inputs into a weather forecasting system.

Forecast Data Come Out of the System

Weather maps are one type of output from a weather forecasting system. On a weather map you can find information about atmospheric pressure, and about the direction and temperature of moving air. The numbered lines on a weather map are called *isobars*. Isobars connect areas that have the same atmospheric pressure. Isobars center around areas of high and low pressure. An area of high pressure (H) indicates a place where cool, dense air is falling. An area of low pressure (L) indicates a place where warm, less dense air is rising. Pressure differences cause air to move. The leading edge of a cool air mass is called a *cold front*. The leading edge of a warm air mass is called a *warm front*. On a weather map, blue lines with triangles show cold fronts and red lines with half circles show warm fronts.

The direction of the triangles or half circles on a map shows which way a front is moving. Wind direction is described in terms of the direction from which the wind is blowing. A west wind is blowing from west to east.

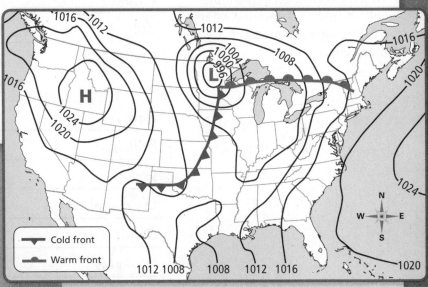

Cold front
Warm front

2 Analysis How would you describe the wind direction behind the warm and cold fronts shown on the map?

_____

_____

_____

Anemometer (wind speed)

Wind vane (wind direction)

Barometer (air pressure) & Rain gauge (precipitation)

Thermometer (temperature) & Hygrometer (humidity)

Weather instruments constantly measure conditions in the atmosphere and deliver data.

 You Try It! ⟶

Now it's your turn to use weather data to make a forecast.

Evaluating Technological Systems

✋ You Try It!

Now it's your turn to become part of the weather forecasting system. The table and map on these pages show some weather data for several cities in the United States. You will use those data to analyze weather and make predictions.

① Identify Inputs

Which information in the table will you use to determine where the high and low pressure areas may be located?

_____

_____

City	Barometric pressure (mbar)	Wind direction	Temperature (°F)
Atlanta	1009	S	63
Chicago	1012	W	36
Cleveland	1006	S	35
Denver	1021	S	34
New York	990	S	58
Billings	1012	SW	28
Spokane	1009	SW	27
Los Angeles	1009	W	68
Dallas	1012	NW	50
Memphis	1012	NW	45
Orlando	1006	S	78
Raleigh	998	S	60

② Identify Outputs

What outputs from weather stations are included on a weather map?

_____

_____

③ Identify System Processes

How will you process the information in the table and on the map to make predictions? Describe how you will use the inputs to develop an output.

_____

_____

_____

_____

(4) Communicate Results

Use data from the table and the map to answer the questions below.

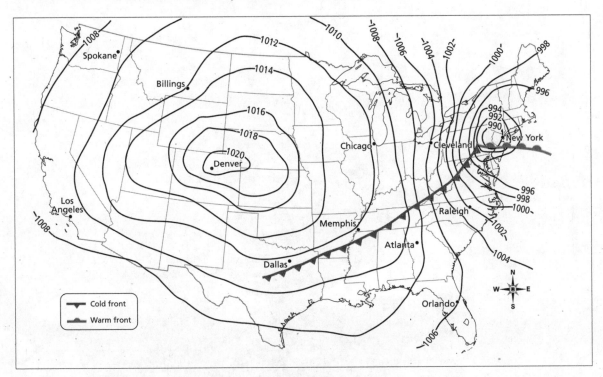

A According to the data in the table, where are the centers of the high and low pressure systems at this time? Mark them on the map using an H or an L.

B Add the temperature listed in the table for each city to the map.

C Imagine that you are a meteorologist in Atlanta and this is the current map. What temperature change would you predict over the next few hours, and why?

_____

_____

_____

D What pressure change would you predict for Denver over the next few days, and why?

_____

_____

_____

_____

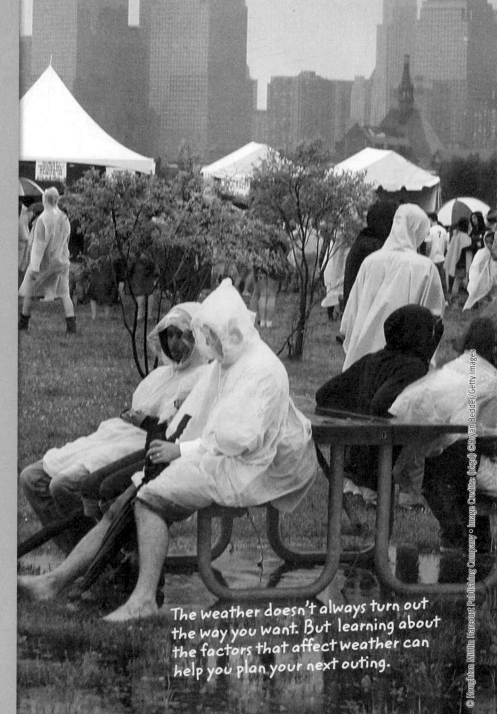

What Influences Weather?

ESSENTIAL QUESTION

How do the water cycle and other global patterns affect local weather?

By the end of this lesson, you should be able to explain how global patterns in Earth's system influence weather.

The weather doesn't always turn out the way you want. But learning about the factors that affect weather can help you plan your next outing.

✋ Lesson Labs

Quick Labs
• Analyze Weather Patterns
• Coastal Climate Model

Exploration Lab
• Modeling El Niño

 ## Engage Your Brain

1 Predict Check T or F to show whether you think each statement is true or false.

T   F

☐   ☐   The water cycle affects weather.

☐   ☐   Air can be warmed or cooled by the surface below it.

☐   ☐   Warm air sinks, cool air rises.

☐   ☐   Winds can bring different weather to a region.

2 Explain How can air temperatures along this coastline be affected by the large body of water that is nearby?

_____

_____

_____

 ## Active Reading

3 Infer A military front is a contested armed frontier between opposing forces. A *weather front* occurs between two air masses, or bodies of air. What kind of weather do you think usually happens at a weather front?

_____

_____

_____

_____

_____

_____

Vocabulary Terms

• air mass
• front
• jet stream

4 Apply As you learn the definition of each vocabulary term in this lesson, create your own definition or sketch to help you remember the meaning of the term.

Water, Water

How does the water cycle affect weather?

Weather is the short-term state of the atmosphere, including temperature, humidity, precipitation, air pressure, wind, and visibility. These elements are affected by the energy received from the sun and the amount of water in the air. To understand what influences weather, then, you need to understand the water cycle.

The *water cycle* is the continuous movement of water between the atmosphere, the land, the oceans, and living things. In the water cycle, shown to the right, water is constantly being recycled between liquid, solid, and gaseous states. The water cycle involves the processes of evaporation, condensation, and precipitation.

Evaporation occurs when liquid water changes into water vapor, which is a gas. Condensation occurs when water vapor cools and changes from a gas to a liquid. A change in the amount of water vapor in the air affects humidity. Clouds and fog form through condensation of water vapor, so condensation also affects visibility. Precipitation occurs when rain, snow, sleet, or hail falls from the clouds onto Earth's surface.

Active Reading

5 List Name at least 5 elements of weather.

_____

_____

_____

Visualize It!

6 Summarize Describe how the water cycle influences weather by completing the sentences on the picture.

Ⓐ Evaporation **affects weather by** _____

_____

_____

Everywhere . . .

B Condensation **affects weather by** _____
_____
_____

C Precipitation **affects weather by** _____
_____
_____

Runoff

👁 Visualize It! Inquiry

7 Identify What elements of weather are different on the two mountaintops? Explain why.

_____
_____
_____
_____
_____

Putting Up a **Front**

How do air masses affect weather?

Active Reading

8 Identify As you read, underline how air masses form.

You have probably experienced the effects of air masses—one day is hot and humid, and the next day is cool and pleasant. The weather changes when a new air mass moves into your area. An **air mass** is a large volume of air in which temperature and moisture content are nearly the same throughout. An air mass forms when the air over a large region of Earth stays in one area for many days. The air gradually takes on the temperature and humidity of the land or water below it. When an air mass moves, it can bring these characteristics to new locations. Air masses can change temperature and humidity as they move to a new area.

Where do fronts form?

When two air masses meet, density differences usually keep them from mixing. A cool air mass is more dense than a warm air mass. A boundary, called a **front**, forms between the air masses. For a front to form, one air mass must run into another air mass. The kind of front that forms depends on how these air masses move relative to each other, and on their relative temperature and moisture content. Fronts result in a change in weather as they pass. They usually affect weather in the middle latitudes of Earth. Fronts do not often occur near the equator because air masses there do not have big temperature differences.

The boundary between air masses, or front, cannot be seen, but is shown here to illustrate how air masses can take on the characteristics of the surface below them.

Air masses that form above water are moist.

Air masses that form above land are dry.

Cold Fronts Form Where Cold Air Moves under Warm Air

Warm air is less dense than cold air is. So, a cold air mass that is moving can quickly push up a warm air mass. If the warm air is moist, clouds will form. Storms that form along a cold front are usually short-lived but can move quickly and bring heavy rain or snow. Cooler weather follows a cold front.

9 Apply If you hear that a cold front is headed for your area, what type of weather might you expect?

_____

_____

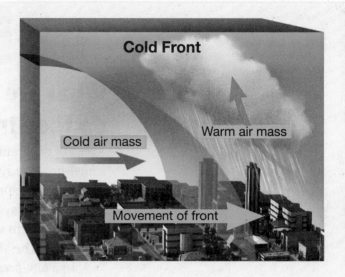

Cold Front

Warm air mass

Cold air mass

Movement of front

Warm Fronts Form Where Warm Air Moves over Cold Air

A warm front forms when a warm air mass follows a retreating cold air mass. The warm air rises over the cold air, and its moisture condenses into clouds. Warm fronts often bring drizzly rain and are followed by warm, clear weather.

10 Identify The rainy weather at the edge of a warm front is a result of

☐   the cold air mass that is leaving.

☐   the warm air rising over the cold air.

☐   the warm air mass following the front.

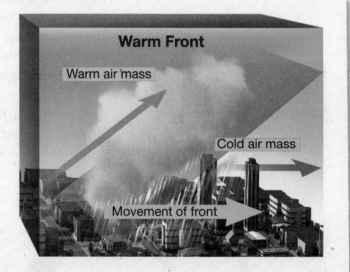

Warm Front

Warm air mass

Cold air mass

Movement of front

Stationary Fronts Form Where Cold and Warm Air Stop Moving

In a stationary front, there is not enough wind for either the cold air mass or the warm air mass to keep moving. So, the two air masses remain in one place. A stationary front can cause many days of unchanging weather, usually clear.

11 Infer When could a stationary front become a warm or cold front?

_____

_____

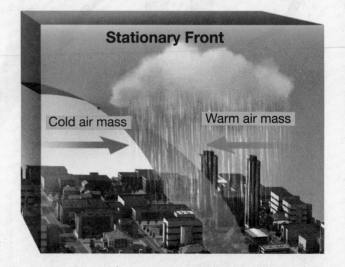

Stationary Front

Cold air mass

Warm air mass

Feeling the Pressure!

What are pressure systems, and how do they interact?

Areas of different air pressure cause changes in the weather. In a *high-pressure system*, air sinks slowly down. As the air nears the ground, it spreads out toward areas of lower pressure. Most high-pressure systems are large and change slowly. When a high-pressure system stays in one location for a long time, an air mass may form. The air mass can be warm or cold, humid or dry.

In a *low-pressure system*, air rises and so has a lower air pressure than the areas around it. As the air in the center of a low-pressure system rises, the air cools.

The diagram below shows how a high-pressure system can form a low-pressure system. Surface air, shown by the black arrows, moves out and away from high-pressure centers. Air above the surface sinks and warms. The green arrows show how air swirls from a high-pressure system into a low-pressure system. In a low-pressure system, the air rises and cools.

12 Identify Choose the correct answer for each of the pressure systems shown below.

A high-pressure system can spiral into a low-pressure system, as illustrated by the green arrows below. In the Northern Hemisphere, air circles in the directions shown.

(A) In a high-pressure system, air

☐ rises and cools.

☐ sinks and warms.

(B) in a low-pressure system, air

☐ rises and cools.

☐ sinks and warms.

How do different pressure systems affect us?

When air pressure differences are small, air doesn't move very much. If the air remains in one place or moves slowly, the air takes on the temperature and humidity of the land or water beneath it. Each type of pressure system has it own unique weather pattern. By keeping track of high- and low-pressure systems, scientists can predict the weather.

High-Pressure Systems Produce Clear Weather

High-pressure systems are areas where air sinks and moves outward. The sinking air is denser than the surrounding air, and the pressure is higher. Cooler, denser air moves out of the center of these high-pressure areas toward areas of lower pressure. As the air sinks, it gets warmer and absorbs moisture. Water droplets evaporate, relative humidity decreases, and clouds often disappear. A high-pressure system generally brings clear skies and calm air or gentle breezes.

Low-Pressure Systems Produce Rainy Weather

Low-pressure systems have lower pressure than the surrounding areas. Air in a low-pressure system comes together, or converges, and rises. As the air in the center of a low-pressure system rises, it cools and forms clouds and rain. The rising air in a low-pressure system causes stormy weather.

A low-pressure system can develop wherever there is a center of low pressure. One place this often happens is along a boundary between a warm air mass and a cold air mass. Rain often occurs at these boundaries, or fronts.

 **Visualize It!**

13 Match Label each picture as a result of a high- or low-pressure system. Then, draw a line from each photo to its matching air-pressure diagram.

(A)

(B)

Warm air rises

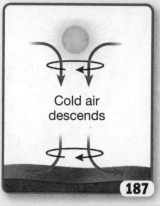
Cold air descends

Windy Weather

How do global wind patterns affect local weather?

Winds are caused by unequal heating of Earth's surface—which causes air pressure differences—and can occur on a global or on a local scale. On a local scale, air-pressure differences affect both wind speed and wind direction at a location. On a global level, there is an overall movement of surface air from the poles toward the equator. The heated air at the equator rises and forms a low-pressure belt. Cold air near the poles sinks and creates high-pressure centers. Because air moves from areas of high pressure to areas of low pressure, it moves from the poles to the equator. At high altitudes, the warmed air circles back toward the poles.

Temperature and pressure differences on Earth's surface also create regional wind belts. Winds in these belts curve to the east or the west as they blow, due to Earth's rotation. This curving of winds is called the *Coriolis effect* (kawr•ee•OH•lis eff•EKT). Winds would flow in straight lines if Earth did not rotate. Winds bring air masses of different temperatures and moisture content to a region.

Visualize It!

14 Apply Trade winds bring

☐ cool air to the warmer equatorial regions.

☐ warm air to the cooler, higher latitudes.

Belts of global winds circle Earth. The winds in these belts curve to the east or west. Between the global wind belts are calm areas.

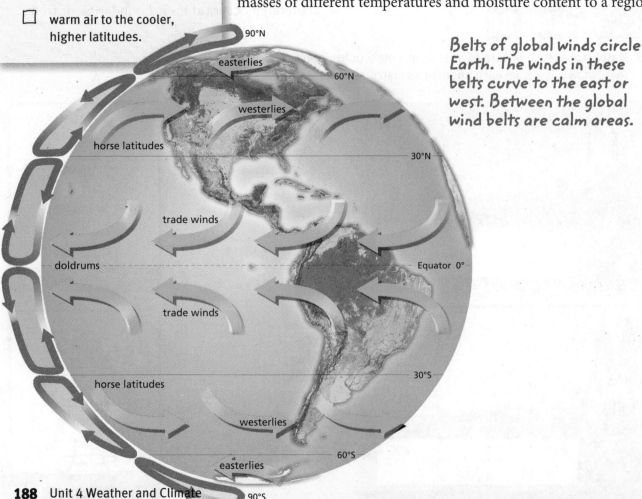

© Houghton Mifflin Harcourt Publishing Company

How do jet streams affect weather?

Long-distance winds that travel above global winds for thousands of kilometers are called **jet streams**. Air moves in jet streams with speeds that are at least 92 kilometers per hour and are often greater than 180 kilometers per hour. Like global and local winds, jet streams form because Earth's surface is heated unevenly. They flow in a wavy pattern from west to east.

Each hemisphere usually has two main jet streams, a polar jet stream and a subtropical jet stream. The polar jet streams flow closer to the poles in summer than in winter. Jet streams can affect temperatures. For example, a polar jet stream can pull cold air down from Canada into the United States and pull warm air up toward Canada. Jet streams also affect precipitation patterns. Strong storms tend to form along jet streams. Scientists must know where a jet stream is flowing to make accurate weather predictions.

Active Reading **15 Identify** What are two ways jet streams affect weather?

_____
_____
_____
_____

In winter months, the polar jet stream flows across much of the United States.

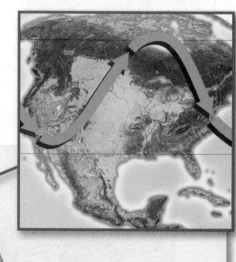

Polar jet stream

Subtropical jet streams

Polar jet stream

Visualize It!

16 Infer How does the polar jet stream influence the weather on the southern tip of South America?

_____
_____
_____
_____

Ocean Effects

How do ocean currents influence weather?

The same global winds that blow across the surface of Earth also push water across Earth's oceans, causing surface currents. Different winds cause currents to flow in different directions. The flow of surface currents moves energy as heat from one part of Earth to another. As the map below shows, both warm-water and cold-water currents flow from one ocean to another. Water near the equator carries energy from the sun to other parts of the ocean. The energy from the warm currents is transferred to colder water or to the atmosphere, changing local temperatures and humidity.

Oceans also have an effect on weather in the form of hurricanes and monsoons. Warm ocean water fuels hurricanes. Monsoons are winds that change direction with the seasons. During summer, the land becomes much warmer than the sea in some areas of the world. Moist wind flows inland, often bringing heavy rains.

Warm current
Cold current

Surface currents are caused by winds. They distribute energy across Earth's surface, changing local temperature and humidity.

Cool Ocean Currents Lower Coastal Air Temperatures

As currents flow, they warm or cool the atmosphere above, affecting local temperatures. The California current is a cold-water current that keeps the average summer high temperatures of coastal cities such as San Diego around 26 °C (78 °F). Cities that lie inland at the same latitude have warmer averages. The graph below shows average monthly temperatures for San Diego and El Centro, California.

👁 Visualize It!

18 Explain Why are temperatures in San Diego, California, usually cooler than they are in El Centro, California?

_____

_____

_____

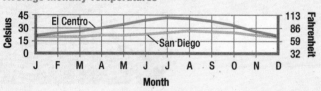

Average Monthly Temperatures

Source: weather.com

Warm Ocean Currents Raise Coastal Air Temperatures

In areas where warm ocean currents flow, coastal cities have warmer winter temperatures than inland cities at similar latitudes. For example, temperatures vary considerably from the coastal regions to the inland areas of Norway due to the warmth of the North Atlantic Current. Coastal cities such as Bergen have relatively mild winters. Inland cities such as Lillehammer have colder winters but temperatures similar to the coastal cities in summer.

👁 Visualize It!

19 Identify Circle the city that is represented by each color in the graph.

- ▮ Lillehammer/Bergen
- ▮ Lillehammer/Bergen

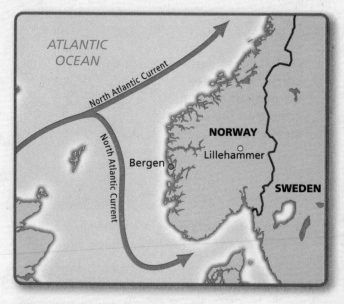

Average Monthly High Temperatures

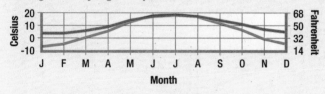

Source: worldweather.org

Visual Summary

To complete this summary, circle the correct word. Then, use the key below to check your answers. You can use this page to review the main concepts of the lesson.

Influences of Weather

Understanding the water cycle is key to understanding weather.

20 Weather is affected by the amount of oxygen / water in the air.

A front forms where two air masses meet.

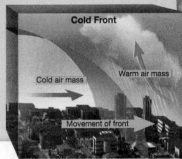

Cold Front

Cold air mass   Warm air mass

Movement of front

21 When a warm air mass and a cool air mass meet, the warm / cool air mass usually moves upward.

Low-pressure systems bring stormy weather, and high-pressure systems bring dry, clear weather.

Warm air rises

22 In a low-pressure system, air moves upward / downward.

Pressure differences from the uneven heating of Earth's surface cause predictable patterns of wind.

23 Global wind patterns occur as, due to temperature differences, air rises / sinks at the poles and rises / sinks at the equator.

Global ocean surface currents can have warming or cooling effects on the air masses above them.

24 Warm currents have a warming / cooling effect on the air masses above them.

Answers: 20 water; 21 warm; 22 upward; 23 sinks; rises; 24 warming

25 **Synthesize** How do air masses cause weather changes?

Lesson Review

Vocabulary

For each pair of terms, explain how the meanings of the terms differ.

1 *front* and *air mass*

_____

_____

_____

2 *high-pressure system* and *low-pressure system*

_____

_____

_____

3 *jet streams* and *global wind belts*

_____

_____

_____

Key Concepts

4 Apply If the weather becomes stormy for a short time and then becomes colder, which type of front has most likely passed?

_____

5 Describe Explain how an ocean current can affect the temperature and the amount of moisture of the air mass above the current and above nearby coastlines.

_____

_____

_____

_____

6 Synthesize How does the water cycle affect weather?

_____

_____

_____

_____

_____

Critical Thinking

Use the diagram below to answer the following question.

Cool air descends   Warm air rises

7 Interpret How does the movement of air affect the type of weather that forms from high-pressure and low-pressure systems?

_____

_____

_____

_____

_____

8 Explain How does the polar jet stream affect temperature and precipitation in North America?

_____

_____

_____

_____

_____

9 Describe Explain how changes in weather are caused by the interaction of air masses.

_____

_____

_____

_____

_____

_____

My Notes

Severe Weather and Weather Safety

ESSENTIAL QUESTION

How can humans protect themselves from hazardous weather?

By the end of this lesson, you should be able to describe the major types of hazardous weather and the ways human beings can protect themselves from hazardous weather and from sun exposure.

Lightning is often the most dangerous part of a thunderstorm. Thunderstorms are one type of severe weather that can cause a lot of damage.

Lesson Labs

Quick Labs
- Create your Own Lightning
- Sun Protection

Exploration Lab
- Preparing for Severe Weather

Engage Your Brain

1 Describe Fill in the blanks with the word or phrase that you think correctly completes the following sentences.

A _____ forms a funnel cloud and has high winds.

A flash or bolt of light across the sky during a storm is called _____

_____ is the sound that follows lightning during a storm.

One way to protect yourself from the sun's rays is to wear _____

2 Identify Name the weather event that is occurring in the photo. What conditions can occur when this event happens in an area?

_____

_____

_____

_____

Active Reading

3 Synthesize Use the sentence below to help you make an educated guess about what the term *storm surge* means. Write the meaning below.

Example sentence
Flooding causes tremendous damage to property and lives when a storm surge moves onto shore.

storm surge:

_____

_____

_____

_____

Vocabulary Terms

- thunderstorm
- lightning
- thunder
- hurricane
- storm surge
- tornado

4 Apply As you learn the definition of each vocabulary term in this lesson, create your own definition or sketch to help you remember the meaning of the term.

☑ Take Cover!

What do we know about thunderstorms?

SPLAAAAAT! BOOOOM! The loud, sharp noise of thunder might surprise you, and maybe even make you jump. The thunder may have been joined by lightning, wind, and rain. A **thunderstorm** is an intense local storm that forms strong winds, heavy rain, lightning, thunder, and sometimes hail. A thunderstorm is an example of severe weather. Severe weather is weather that can cause property damage and sometimes death.

Thunderstorms Form from Rising Air

Thunderstorms get their energy from humid air. When warm, humid air near the ground mixes with cooler air above, the warm air creates an updraft that can build a thunderstorm quickly. Cold downdrafts bring precipitation and eventually end the storm by preventing more warm air from rising.

Step 1
In the first stage, warm air rises and forms a cumulus cloud. The water vapor releases energy when it condenses into cloud droplets. This energy increases the air motion. The cloud continues building up.

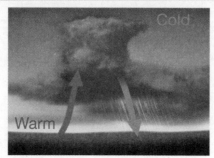

Step 2
Ice particles may form in the low temperatures near the top of the cloud. As the ice particles grow large, they begin to fall and pull cold air down with them. This strong downdraft brings heavy rain or hail.

Step 3
During the final stage, the downdraft can spread out and block more warm air from moving upward into the cloud. The storm slows down and ends.

👁 **Visualize It!**

5 Describe What role does warm air play in the formation of a thunderstorm?

_____

_____

_____

Lightning is a Discharge of Electrical Energy

If you have ever shuffled your feet on a carpet, you may have felt a small shock when you touched a doorknob. If so, you have experienced how lightning forms. **Lightning** is an electric discharge that happens between a positively charged area and a negatively charged area. While you walk around, electrical charges can collect on your body. When you touch someone or something else, the charges jump to that person or object in a spark of electricity. In a similar way, electrical charges build up near the tops and bottoms of clouds as pellets of ice move up and down through the clouds. Suddenly, a flash of lightning will spark from one place to another.

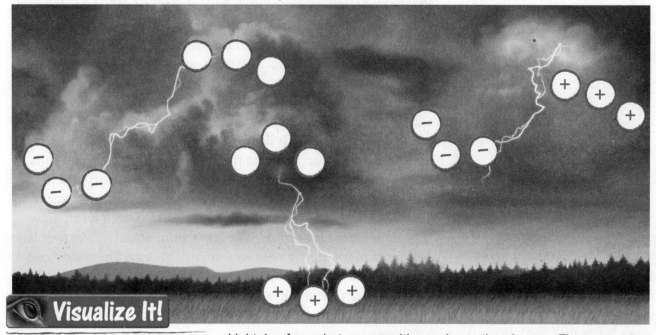

Visualize It!

6 Label Fill in the positive and negative charges in the appropriate spaces provided.

Lightning forms between positive and negative charges. The upper part of a cloud usually carries a positive electric charge. The lower part of the cloud carries mainly negative charges. Lightning is a big spark that jumps between parts of clouds, or between a cloud and Earth's surface.

Thunder Is a Result of Rapidly Expanding Air

Active Reading

7 Identify As you read, underline the explanation of what causes thunder during a storm.

When lightning strikes, the air along its path is heated to a high temperature. The superheated air quickly expands. The rapidly moving air causes the air to vibrate and release sound waves. The result is **thunder**, the sound created by the rapid expansion of air along a lightning strike.

You usually hear thunder a few seconds after you see a lightning strike, because light travels faster than sound. You can count the seconds between a lightning flash and the sound of thunder to figure out about how far away the lightning is. For every 3 seconds between lightning and its thunder, add about 1 km to the lightning strike's distance from you.

☑ Plan Ahead!

 **Active Reading**

8 Identify As you read, underline the definition of *hurricane*.

What do we know about hurricanes?

A **hurricane** is a tropical low-pressure system with winds blowing at speeds of 119 km/h (74 mi/h) or more—strong enough to uproot trees. Hurricanes are called typhoons when they form over the western Pacific Ocean and cyclones when they form over the Indian Ocean.

Hurricanes Need Water to Form and Grow

A hurricane begins as a group of thunderstorms moving over tropical ocean waters. Thunderstorms form in areas of low pressure. Near the equator, warm ocean water provides the energy that can turn a low-pressure center into a violent storm. As water evaporates from the ocean, energy is transferred from the ocean water into the air. This energy makes warm air rise faster. Tall clouds and strong winds develop. As winds blow across the water from different directions into the low-pressure center, the paths bend into a spiral. The winds blow faster and faster around the low-pressure center, which becomes the center of the hurricane.

As long as a hurricane stays above warm water, it can grow bigger and more powerful. As soon as a hurricane moves over land or over cooler water, it loses its source of energy. The winds lose strength and the storm dies out. If a hurricane moves over land, the rough surface of the land reduces the winds even more.

Hurricanes in the Northern Hemisphere usually move westward with the trade winds. Near land, however, they will often move north or even back out to sea.

Hurricane Ike moves into the Gulf of Mexico on September 10, 2008.

Atlantic Ocean

Path of Hurricane Ike

Gulf of Mexico

Caribbean Sea

Hurricanes Can Cause Extensive Damage

A hurricane can pound a coast with huge waves and sweep the land with strong winds and heavy rains. The storms cause damage and dangerous conditions in several ways. Hurricane winds can lift cars, uproot trees, and tear the roofs off buildings. Hurricanes may also produce tornadoes that can cause even more damage. Heavy rains from hurricanes may make rivers overflow their banks and flood nearby areas. When a hurricane moves into a coastal area, it also pushes a huge mass of ocean water known as a **storm surge**. In a storm surge, the sea level rises several meters, backing up rivers and flooding the shore. A storm surge can be the most destructive and deadliest part of a hurricane. Large waves add to the damage. A hurricane may affect an area for a few hours or a few days, but the damage may take weeks or even months to clean up.

Active Reading

9 Describe What are three of the dangers associated with hurricanes?

_____

_____

The storm surge and debris from Hurricane Ike cover a street on September 12, 2008, in Seabrook, Texas.

Think Outside the Book (Inquiry)

10 Apply With a classmate, discuss why hurricanes are more likely to make landfall in Florida than they are to hit California. You may need to refer to a map of ocean currents to find the answer.

© Houghton Mifflin Harcourt Publishing Company • Image Credits: AP Photo/Kim Christensen

☑ Secure Loose Objects!

What do we know about tornadoes?

A **tornado** is a destructive, rotating column of air that has very high wind speeds and that is sometimes visible as a funnel-shaped cloud. A tornado forms when a thunderstorm meets horizontal winds at a high altitude. These winds cause the warm air rising in the thunderstorm to spin. A storm cloud may form a thin funnel shape that has a very low pressure center. As the funnel reaches the ground, the higher-pressure air rushes into the low-pressure area. The result is high-speed winds, which cause the damage associated with tornadoes.

Clouds begin to rotate, signaling that a tornado may form.

The funnel cloud becomes visible as the tornado picks up dust from the ground or particles from the air.

The tornado moves along the ground before it dies out.

Think Outside the Book

11 **Illustrate** Read the description of the weather conditions that cause tornadoes and draw a sketch of what those conditions might look like.

© Houghton Mifflin Harcourt Publishing Company • Image Credits: (t) ©Jim Edds/Photo Researchers, Inc.; (c) ©Digital Vision/Getty Images; (b) ©Reed Timmer/SPL/Photo Researchers, Inc.

Most Tornadoes Happen in the Midwest

Tornadoes happen in many places, but they are most common in the United States in *Tornado Alley*. Tornado Alley reaches from Texas up through the midwestern United States, including Iowa, Kansas, Nebraska, and Ohio. Many tornadoes form in the spring and early summer, typically along a front between cool, dry air and warm, humid air.

Tornadoes Can Cause Extensive Damage

The danger of a tornado is mainly due to the high speed of its winds. Winds in a tornado's funnel may have speeds of more than 400 km/h. Most injuries and deaths caused by tornadoes happen when people are struck by objects blown by the winds or when they are trapped in buildings that collapse.

Active Reading

12 Identify As you read, underline what makes a tornado so destructive.

13 Summarize In the overlapping sections of the Venn diagram, list the characteristics that are shared by the different types of storms. In the outer sections, list the characteristics that are specific to each type of storm.

Thunderstorms

Hurricanes

Tornadoes

14 Conclude Write a summary that describes the information in the Venn diagram.

_____

_____

_____

☑ Be Prepared!

What can people do to prepare for severe weather?

Severe weather is weather that can cause property damage, injury, and sometimes death. Hail, lightning, high winds, tornadoes, hurricanes, and floods are all part of severe weather. Hailstorms can damage crops and cars and can break windows. Lightning starts many forest fires and kills or injures hundreds of people and animals each year. Winds and tornadoes can uproot trees and destroy homes. Flooding is also a leading cause of weather-related deaths. Most destruction from hurricanes results from flooding due to storm surges.

Think Outside the Book · Inquiry

15 Apply Research severe weather in your area and come up with a plan for safety.

Plan Ahead

Have a storm supply kit that contains a battery-operated radio, batteries, flashlights, candles, rain jackets, tarps, blankets, bottled water, canned food, and medicines. Listen to weather announcements. Plan and practice a safety route. A safety route is a planned path to a safe place.

Listen for Storm Updates

During severe weather, it is important to listen to local radio or TV stations. Severe weather updates will let you know the location of a storm. They will also let you know if the storm is getting worse. A *watch* is given when the conditions are ideal for severe weather. A *warning* is given when severe weather has been spotted or is expected within 24 h. During most kinds of severe weather, it is best to stay indoors and away from windows. However, in some situations, you may need to evacuate.

Follow Flood Safety Rules

Sometimes, a place can get so much rain that it floods, especially if it is a low-lying area. So, like storms, floods have watches and warnings. However, little advance notice can usually be given that a flood is coming. A flash flood is a flood that rises and falls very quickly. The best thing to do during a flood is to find a high place to stay until it is over. You should always stay out of floodwaters. Even shallow water can be dangerous because it can move fast.

What can people do to stay safe during thunderstorms?

Stay alert when thunderstorms are predicted or when dark, tall clouds are visible. If you are outside and hear thunder, seek shelter immediately and stay there for 30 min after the thunder ends. Heavy rains can cause sudden, or flash, flooding, and hailstones can damage property and harm living things.

Lightning is one of the most dangerous parts of a thunderstorm. Because lightning is attracted to tall objects, it is important to stay away from trees if you are outside. If you are in an open area, stay close to the ground so that you are not the tallest object in the area. If you can, get into a car. Stay away from ponds, lakes, or other bodies of water. If lightning hits water while you are swimming or wading in it, you could be hurt or killed. If you are indoors during a thunderstorm, avoid using electrical appliances, running water, and phone lines.

How can people stay safe during a tornado?

Tornadoes are too fast and unpredictable for you to attempt to outrun, even if you are in a car. If you see or hear a tornado, go to a place without windows, such as basement, a storm cellar, or a closet or hallway. Stay away from areas that are likely to have flying objects or other dangers. If you are outside, lie in a ditch or low-lying area. Protect your head and neck by covering them with your arms and hands.

How can people stay safe during a hurricane?

If your family lives where hurricanes may strike, have a plan to leave the area, and gather emergency supplies. If a hurricane is approaching your area, listen to weather reports for storm updates. Secure loose objects outside, and cover windows with storm shutters or boards. During a storm, stay indoors and away from windows. If ordered to evacuate the area, do so immediately. After a storm, be aware of downed power lines, hanging branches, and flooded areas.

16 Apply What would you do in each of these scenarios?

Scenario	What would you do?
You are swimming at an outdoor pool when you hear thunder in the distance.	
You and your family are watching TV when you hear a tornado warning that says a tornado has been spotted in the area.	
You are listening to the radio when the announcer says that a hurricane is headed your way and may make landfall in 3 days.	

☑ Use Sun Sense!

How can people protect their skin from the sun?

![Active Reading]

17 Identify As you read, underline when the sun's ray's are strongest during the day.

Human skin contains melanin, which is the body's natural protection against ultraviolet (UV) radiation from the sun. The skin produces more melanin when it is exposed to the sun, but UV rays will still cause sunburn when you spend too much time outside. It is particularly important to protect your skin when the sun's rays are strongest, usually between 10 A.M and 4 P.M.

Know the Sun's Hazards

It's easy to notice the effects of a sunburn. Sunburn usually appears within a few hours after sun exposure. It causes red, painful skin that feels hot to the touch. Prolonged exposure to the sun will lead to sunburn in even the darkest-skinned people. Sunburn can lead to skin cancer and premature aging of the skin. The best way to prevent sunburn is to protect your skin from the sun, even on cloudy days. UV rays pass right through clouds and can give you a false feeling of protection from the sun.

Wear Sunscreen and Protective Clothing

Even if you tan easily, you should still use sunscreen. For most people, a sun protection factor (SPF) of 30 or more will prevent burning for about 1.5 h. Babies and people who have pale skin should use an SPF of 45 or more. In addition, you can protect your skin and eyes in different ways. Seek the shade, and wear hats, sunglasses, and perhaps even UV light-protective clothing.

Have fun in the sun! Just be sure to protect your skin from harmful rays.

How can people protect themselves from summer heat?

Heat exhaustion is a condition in which the body has been exposed to high temperatures for an extended period of time. Symptoms include cold, moist skin, normal or near-normal body temperature, headache, nausea, and extreme fatigue. *Heat stroke* is a condition in which the body loses its ability to cool itself by sweating because the victim has become dehydrated.

Limit Outdoor Activities

When outdoor temperatures are high, be cautious about exercising outdoors for long periods of time. Pay attention to how your body is feeling, and go inside or to a shady spot if you are starting to feel light-headed or too warm.

Drink Water

Heat exhaustion and heat stroke can best be prevented by drinking 6 to 8 oz of water at least 10 times a day when you are active in warm weather. If you are feeling overheated, dizzy, nauseous, or are sweating heavily, drink something cool (not cold). Drink about half a glass of cool water every 15 min until you feel like your normal self.

Drinking water is one of the best things you can do to keep yourself healthy in hot weather.

Visualize It!

18 Describe List all the ways the people in the photo of the beach may have protected themselves from overexposure to the sun.

_____

_____

_____

_____

_____

_____

_____

Know the Signs of Heat Stroke

Active Reading **19 Identify** Underline signs of heat stroke in the paragraph below.

Heat stroke is life threatening, so it is important to know the signs and treatment for it. Symptoms of heat stroke include hot, dry skin; higher than normal body temperature; rapid pulse; rapid, shallow breathing; disorientation; and possible loss of consciousness.

What to Do In Case of Heat Stroke

☐ Seek emergency help immediately.

☐ If there are no emergency facilities nearby, move the person to a cool place.

☐ Cool the person's body by immersing it in a cool (not cold) bath or using wet towels.

☐ Do not give the person food or water if he or she is vomiting.

☐ Place ice packs under the person's armpits.

Visual Summary

To complete this summary, circle the correct word or phrase. Then use the key below to check your answers. You can use this page to review the main concepts of the lesson.

Severe Weather

Thunderstorms are intense weather systems that produce strong winds, heavy rain, lightning, and thunder.

20 One of the most dangerous parts of a thunderstorm is lightning / thunder.

A hurricane is a large, rotating tropical weather system with strong winds that can cause severe property damage.

21 An important step to plan for a hurricane is to buy raingear / stock a supply kit.

Tornadoes are rotating columns of air that touch the ground and can cause severe damage.

22 The damage from a tornado is mostly caused by associated thunderstorms / high-speed winds.

It is important to plan ahead and listen for weather updates in the event of severe weather.

23 One of the biggest dangers of storms that produce heavy rains or storm surges is flooding / low temperatures.

Prolonged exposure to the sun can cause sunburn, skin cancer, and heat-related health effects.

24 One of the best ways to avoid heat-related illnesses while in the sun is to stay active / drink water.

25 Synthesize What are three ways in which severe weather can be dangerous?

Lesson Review

Vocabulary

Draw a line that matches the term with the correct definition.

1 hurricane

2 tornado

3 severe weather

4 thunderstorm

5 storm surge

A a huge mass of ocean water that floods the shore

B a storm with lightning and thunder

C a violently rotating column of air stretching to the ground

D weather that can potentially destroy property or cause loss of life

E a tropical low-pressure system with winds of 119 km/h or more

Key Concepts

6 Thunder is caused by _____

7 An electrical discharge between parts of clouds or a cloud and the ground is called _____

8 The sun's ultraviolet rays can cause skin damage including sunburn and even skin _____

9 **Explain** How can a person prepare for hazardous weather well in advance?

_____

_____

_____

10 **Describe** What can people do to stay safe before and during a storm with high winds and heavy rains?

_____

_____

_____

_____

Critical Thinking

Use the map below to answer the following question.

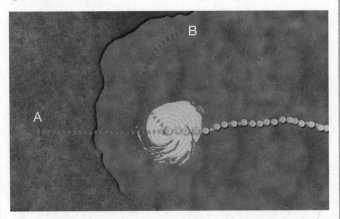

11 **Interpret** Would a hurricane be more likely to remain a hurricane if it reached point A or point B? Explain your answer.

_____

_____

_____

12 **Explain** Why do hurricanes form in tropical latitudes?

_____

_____

_____

13 **Describe** What two weather conditions are needed for tornadoes to form?

_____

_____

14 **Explain** Why is hail sometimes dangerous?

_____

_____

_____

15 **Summarize** What can you do to avoid overexposure to the sun's rays?

_____

_____

_____

My Notes

Weather Maps and Weather Prediction

ESSENTIAL QUESTION

What tools do we use to predict weather?

By the end of this lesson, you should understand how meteorologists forecast the weather using weather maps and other data.

Weather forecasters use radar and satellite images to warn people of the approach of severe weather.

🌐 Engage Your Brain

1 Describe Fill in the blank with the word or phrase that you think correctly completes the following sentences.

The job of a _____
is to analyze scientific data to predict future weather conditions.

The location, movement, and intensity of precipitation can be found by using

_____

The elements of weather that are measured and analyzed to make accurate forecasts include

_____

2 Assess What industry is represented in the photo below? What other industries rely on accurate weather forecasts?

_____

_____

✏️ Active Reading

3 Synthesize You can often define an unknown word if you know the meaning of its word parts. Use the word parts and sentence below to make an educated guess about the meaning of the word *meteorology*.

Word part	Meaning
meteoron	phenomenon in the sky
-ology	the study of, science of

Example sentence
Studying <u>meteorology</u> helps you to understand weather events.

meteorology:

_____

_____

Vocabulary Terms
• weather forecasting
• meteorology
• station model

4 Identify This list contains the vocabulary terms you'll learn in this lesson. As you read, circle the definition of each term.

Cloudy with a chance of ...

What is weather forecasting?

Looking at the weather outdoors in the morning helps you to decide what clothes to wear that day. Different observations give clues to the current weather. The leaves in the trees may be moving if it is windy. If the sky is gray and the streets are shiny, it may be raining.

Checking the weather forecast also helps determine how the weather might change. **Weather forecasting** is the analysis of scientific data to predict future weather conditions.

What elements of weather are forecast?

Weather forecasters study the elements of weather to make detailed predictions. The study of weather and Earth's atmosphere is called **meteorology** [mee•tee•uh•RAHL•uh•jee]. Scientists who study meteorology are called *meteorologists*.

Eight elements of weather are observed around the clock. These elements are air temperature, humidity, wind direction, wind speed, clouds, precipitation, atmospheric pressure, and visibility. Using these eight elements to make accurate weather forecasts helps people stay safe and comfortable. To make the best predictions, meteorologists need accurate data.

5 Infer Forest firefighters need accurate and detailed weather forecasts. What weather elements would these firefighters be most interested in? Explain.

_____

_____

_____

_____

_____

_____

 **Visualize It!**

6 Apply Identify three elements of weather that appear in this beach scene.

A _____

B _____

C _____

The Hurricane Hunters

Flying in stormy weather can be an uncomfortable and frightening experience. Yet, some pilots are trained to fly into the most intense storms. The Hurricane Hunters of the National Oceanic and Atmospheric Administration (NOAA) fly right into the eye of tropical storms and hurricanes to collect valuable data. Weather forecasters use the data to predict a storm's path and intensity.

Hurricane Hunter Planes

The weather-sensing equipment aboard NOAA's WP-3D Orion is quite advanced. The planes are equipped with radar in the nose, in the tail, and on the underside of the fuselage. Radiometers on the wings measure wind speed once every second. These and other data are sent immediately to the airplane's computer system.

UNITED STATES DEPT. OF COMM

Wind gust probe

Weather radar for 360-degree view

Sensors are released from the plane's belly.

Falling Dropsonde

A lightweight instrument package called a *dropsonde* [DRAHP•sahnd] is launched from the aircraft. As the dropsonde descends through the storm, it collects data twice every second. Data about temperature, humidity, wind speed, and air pressure are sent back to the plane.

Extend

Inquiry

7 Explain How do airplanes help weather forecasters make predictions about the movement and intensity of storms?

8 Research Find out about another technology that is used to gather weather data by sea or by air.

9 Assess Explain how this technology is used in an oral report, poster presentation, or slide show.

What's Going on *up There?*

How are weather data collected?

To predict the weather, meteorologists must look at data that come from different sources. Meteorologists use many kinds of advanced technologies to gather this data. These technologies are found at ground stations and in balloons, aircraft, and satellites.

By Ground Stations

Land-based ground stations, also called *automated surface stations*, collect weather data from the lower atmosphere 24 hours a day. A variety of weather-sensing instruments are found at these ground stations. These instruments measure pressure, temperature, humidity, precipitation, wind speed, visibility, and cloud cover. Many ground stations are located near airports and transmit computer-generated voice observations to aircraft regularly.

By Radar

Weather radar is useful for finding the location, movement, and intensity of storms. Radar works by bouncing radio waves off precipitation. The stronger the signal that is returned to the radar, the heavier the precipitation is. Also, the longer it takes for the signal to return to the radar, the farther away the precipitation is.

Doppler radar, a type of weather radar, can detect precipitation and air motion within a storm. This technology is important for detecting and tracking severe storms and tornadoes.

Satellites, balloons, and aircraft can provide wide views of Earth's weather systems.

Visualize It!

10 Apply Which town is experiencing the most severe weather?

_____

_____

11 Apply In which town is it raining lightly?

_____

_____

Colors represent the intensity of precipitation.

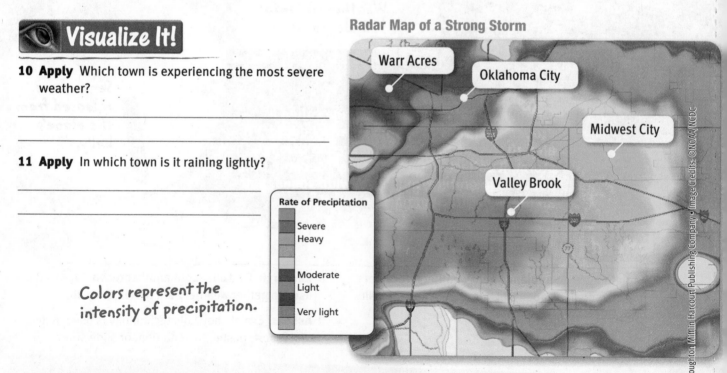

Radar Map of a Strong Storm

Warr Acres

Oklahoma City

Midwest City

Valley Brook

Rate of Precipitation

Severe
Heavy

Moderate
Light

Very light

By Balloons and Aircraft

Weather-sensing instruments carried by aircraft and balloons measure weather conditions in the middle to upper atmosphere. Aircraft can carry a variety of weather-sensing instruments and collect data in places far from ground stations, such as over oceans.

Weather balloons are released twice daily from stations around the world. These balloons collect weather information at different altitudes. Weather balloons carry a small instrument package called a radiosonde [RAY•dee•oh•sahnd]. Radiosondes measure atmospheric pressure, air temperature, and humidity up to about 32 km. They also measure wind speed and direction. Radiosondes send data by radio signal to ground stations.

Balloons such this one can gather weather data from high up in the atmosphere.

By Satellites

Orbiting weather satellites at high altitudes provide data on water vapor, cloud-top temperatures, and the movement of weather systems. Geostationary satellites and polar-orbiting satellites monitor Earth's weather. Geostationary weather satellites monitor Earth from a fixed position thousands of kilometers above Earth. Polar-orbiting satellites circle Earth and provide global information from hundreds of kilometers above Earth's surface. Cameras on satellites take images at regular intervals to track weather conditions on Earth. Digital images are sent back to ground stations. These images can be animated to show changes in weather over time.

Active Reading 12 **Compare** What is the difference between geostationary and polar-orbiting satellites?

_____

_____

Think Outside the Book Inquiry

13 **Describe** Research ways that weather predictions were made before the use of aircraft, balloons, and satellites.

What kinds of symbols and maps are used to analyze the weather?

In the United States, meteorologists with the National Weather Service (NWS) collect and analyze weather data. The NWS prepares weather maps and station models to make weather data easy to use and understand.

Station Models

A **station model** is a set of meteorological symbols that represent the weather at a particular observing station. Station models are often shown on weather maps. Placing many station models on a map makes it possible to see large weather patterns, such as fronts.

A station model is a small circle that is surrounded by a set of symbols and numbers that represent current weather data at a specific location. Key weather elements shown on a station model are temperature, wind speed and direction, cloud cover, air pressure, and dew point. Note that the pointer, or wind barb, for wind direction points *into* the wind.

Active Reading

14 Identify What are the key weather elements shown by a station model?

_____

_____

_____

_____

_____

Visualize It!

15 Observe Where are the temperature and dew point recorded on a station model?

_____

_____

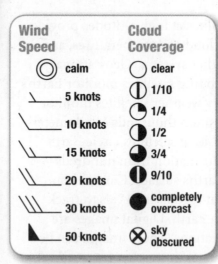

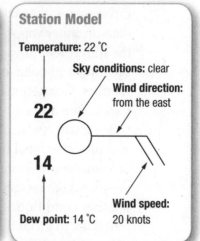

16 Apply Draw a station model below to represent the following conditions: air temperature 8 °C; dew point 6 °C; sky 1/2 overcast; wind 15 knots from the south.

Surface Weather Maps

Meteorologists commonly use surface weather maps to show forecasts on television. A surface weather map displays air pressure and the locations of fronts. Precipitation may also be shown.

Air pressure is shown by using isobars. Isobars are lines that connect points of equal air pressure and are marked in units called *millibars*. Isobars form closed loops. The center of these loops is marked with either a capital H (high) or L (low). A capital H represents a center of high pressure, and a capital L represents a center of low pressure.

Fronts are also shown on surface weather maps. Blue lines with blue triangles are cold fronts. Red lines with red half circles are warm fronts. Stationary fronts alternate between blue and red.

Visualize It!

17 Apply What type of front has recently passed through this area?

_____

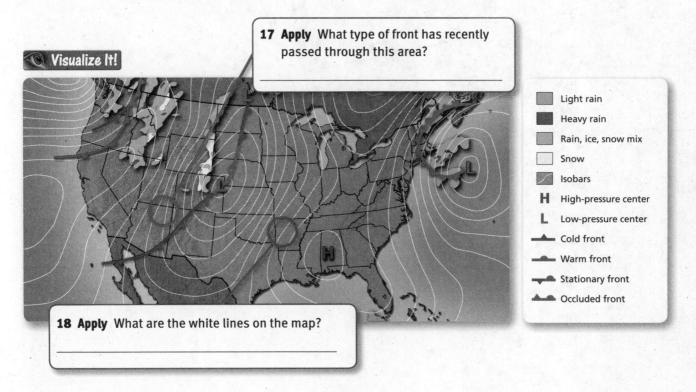

	Light rain
	Heavy rain
	Rain, ice, snow mix
	Snow
	Isobars
H	High-pressure center
L	Low-pressure center
	Cold front
	Warm front
	Stationary front
	Occluded front

18 Apply What are the white lines on the map?

_____

Upper-Air Charts

Another type of weather map used to analyze weather is the upper-air chart. Upper-air charts are based on data collected by instruments carried into the atmosphere by weather balloons.

Upper-air charts show wind and air pressure at middle and upper levels of Earth's atmosphere. Information from upper air charts indicates if and where weather systems will form, and if these systems will move, remain stationary, or fall apart. In addition, these charts are used to determine the position of jet streams. Airlines and airplane pilots use upper-air charts to determine flight paths and possible areas of turbulence.

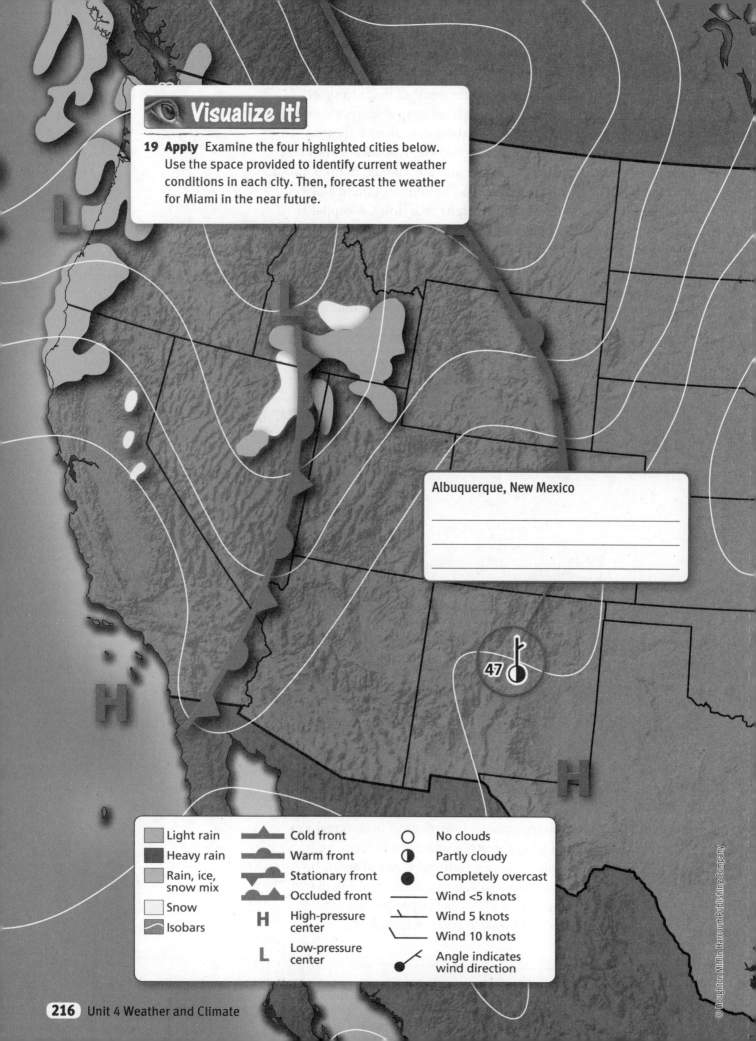

Visualize It!

19 Apply Examine the four highlighted cities below. Use the space provided to identify current weather conditions in each city. Then, forecast the weather for Miami in the near future.

Albuquerque, New Mexico

_____

_____

_____

47

Light rain		Cold front		No clouds
Heavy rain		Warm front		Partly cloudy
Rain, ice, snow mix		Stationary front		Completely overcast
Snow		Occluded front		Wind <5 knots
Isobars	**H**	High-pressure center		Wind 5 knots
	L	Low-pressure center		Wind 10 knots
				Angle indicates wind direction

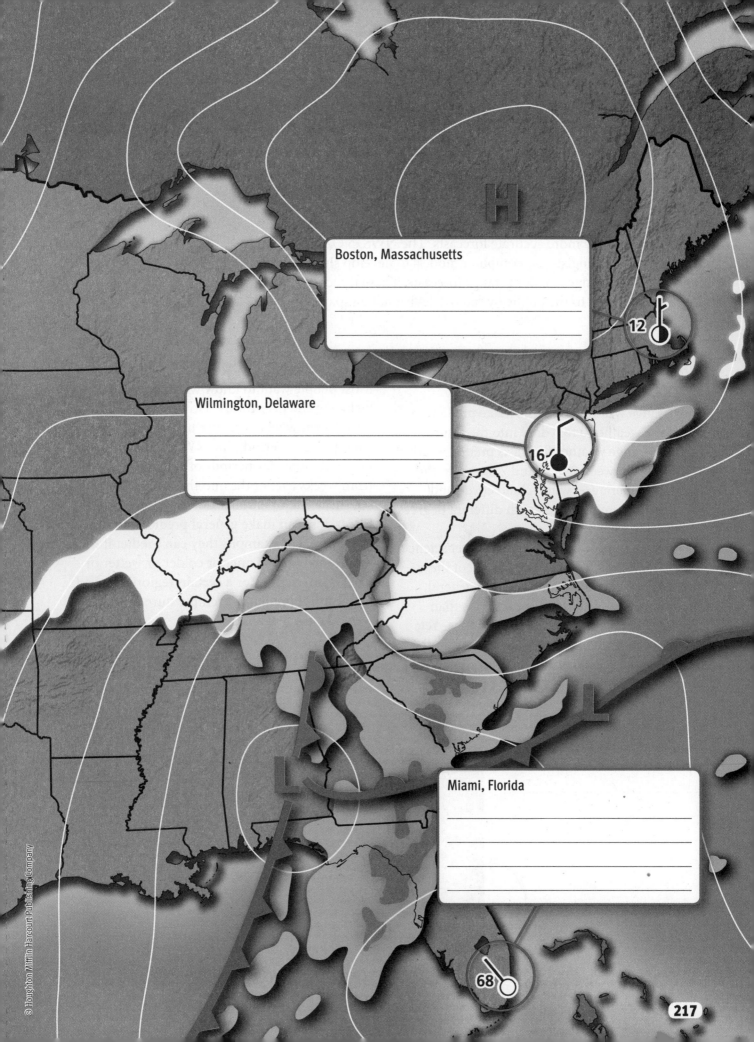

Boston, Massachusetts

_____
_____
_____

12

Wilmington, Delaware

_____
_____
_____

16

H

L

L

L

Miami, Florida

_____
_____
_____
_____

68

What are some types of weather forecasts?

As supercomputers have become faster in recent years, forecasts have also improved. Increasing amounts of weather data can be combined to create more accurate forecasts. The NWS, NOAA, and local meteorologists use computer models to develop short-range, medium-range, and long-range forecasts. These forecasts are made available to the public by radio, television, newspaper, and the Internet.

Short-Range and Medium-Range Weather Forecasts

Short-range weather forecasts make predictions about the weather 0 to 3 days into the future. Medium-range weather forecasts predict weather conditions between 3 days and 7 days into the future. Temperature, wind, cloud cover, and precipitation are predicted with different degrees of accuracy.

Weather forecasting is an imperfect science. Many variables affect weather, and all of these variables are changing constantly. In general, short-term forecasts are more accurate than forecasts made for longer periods of time. Yet, given the continuous changes that occur in the atmosphere, even short-range forecasts cannot always be accurate.

Long-Range Weather Forecasts

Most people want to know what the weather will be like in the near future. However, some people need to know what the weather will be like over a longer time period. The NWS issues long-range forecasts for periods of time that range from weeks to months into the future. Using sea surface temperatures and high-level winds, forecasters can make general predictions about the future. For example, they can predict if the weather will be warmer or colder or wetter or drier than average for a certain region. However, they cannot predict the temperature or if it will rain on a particular day.

20 Infer Why is it important for the farmer to know the long-range forecast?

_____

_____

_____

Some meteorologists prepare specialized forecasts for farmers.

Hazardous Weather Forecasts

An important job of meteorologists is to warn the public about severe weather. This information is shown as a weather "crawl" at the bottom of a television screen. The NWS issues three types of hazardous weather forecasts: weather advisories, weather watches, and weather warnings.

A weather advisory is issued when the expected weather conditions will not be a serious hazard but may cause inconvenience if caution is not used. When severe weather conditions are possible over a large geographic area, a weather watch is issued. People should prepare and have a plan of action in place in case a storm threatens. A weather warning is issued when weather conditions that pose a threat to life and property are happening or are about to happen. People who live in the path of the storm need to take immediate action.

Active Reading **21 Compare** What is the difference between a weather watch and a weather warning?

_____
_____
_____
_____
_____
_____
_____
_____

The National Weather Service issues weather advisories, weather watches, and weather warnings to inform the public about hazardous weather.

Visualize It!

22 Compose Write a caption for the photo based on a hazardous weather forecast.

_____

Visual Summary

To complete this summary, check the box that indicates true or false. Then use the key below to check your answers. You can use this page to review the main concepts of the lesson.

Weather Maps and Weather Prediction

Weather forecasting is the analysis of scientific data to predict likely future weather conditions.

	T	F
23	☐	☐

In order to forecast the weather, meteorologists gather weather data for five important weather elements.

Different kinds of weather data can be shown together on station models and weather maps.

18
12

	T	F
24	☐	☐

Two types of weather maps that meteorologists use to show the weather are surface weather maps and upper-air charts.

Weather data come from many sources on land and in the air.

	T	F
25	☐	☐

Weather balloons and aircraft allow for surface weather observations.

Meteorologists use computer models to make short-range, medium-range, and long-range weather forecasts.

	T	F
26	☐	☐

Three types of hazardous weather forecasts are weather advisories, weather watches, and weather warnings.

Answers: 23 F; 24 T; 25 F; 26 T

27 Synthesis Describe the technologies used to gather data, prepare a forecast, and broadcast a forecast for a town in the path of a hurricane.

Lesson Review

Vocabulary

Fill in the blank with the term that best completes the following sentences.

1 A _____ is a group of meteorological symbols that represents the weather at a particular observing station.

2 _____ is the analysis of scientific data to predict likely future weather conditions.

3 The scientific study of Earth's atmosphere and weather is called _____

Key Concepts

4 List What are the eight elements of weather that are observed for making weather forecasts?

_____

_____

_____

_____

5 Identify What kinds of data do surface weather maps provide?

_____

_____

_____

6 Summarize Describe each of the three types of hazardous weather forecasts.

_____

_____

_____

_____

_____

_____

_____

_____

_____

_____

Critical Thinking

Use the diagram to answer the following questions.

Mon	Tue	Wed	Thu	Fri
74°	70°	56°	56°	66°
62°	64°	48°	54°	56°

7 Analyze On what day will there likely be severe weather?

_____

8 Infer Between which two days will a cold front arrive? Explain.

_____

_____

_____

9 Diagram Draw a station model based on the Thursday forecast, if winds are 15 knots from the northwest.

10 Assess Why do you think weather observations are made frequently at airports around the world?

_____

_____

_____

_____

_____

_____

My Notes

J. Marshall Shepherd

METEOROLOGIST AND CLIMATOLOGIST

J. Marshall Shepherd

Dr. Marshall Shepherd, who works at the University of Georgia, has been interested in weather since he made his own weather-collecting instruments for a school science project. Although the instruments he uses today, like computers and satellites, are much larger and much more powerful than the ones he made in school, they give him some of the same information.

In his work, Dr. Shepherd tries to understand weather events, such as hurricanes and thunderstorms, and relate them to current weather and climate change. He once led a team that used space-based radar to measure rainfall over urban areas. The measurements confirmed that the areas downwind of major cities experience more rainfall in summer than other areas in the same region. He explained that the excess heat retained by buildings and roads changes the way the air circulates, and this causes rain clouds to form.

While the most familiar field of meteorology is weather forecasting, research meteorology is also used in air pollution control, weather control, agricultural planning, climate change studies, and even criminal and civil investigations.

Social Studies Connection

An almanac is a type of calendar that contains various types of information, including weather forecasts and astronomical data, for every day of the year. Many people used almanacs before meteorologists started to forecast the weather. Use an almanac from the library or the Internet to find out what the weather was on the day that you were born.

JOB BOARD

Atmospheric Scientist

What You'll Do: Collect and analyze data on Earth's air pressure, humidity, and winds to make short-range and long-range weather forecasts. Work around the clock during weather emergencies like hurricanes and tornadoes.

Where You Might Work: Weather data collecting stations, radio and television stations, or private consulting firms.

Education: A bachelor's degree in meteorology, or in a closely related field with courses in meteorology, is required. A master's degree is necessary for some jobs.

Airplane Pilot

What You'll Do: Fly airplanes containing passengers or cargo, or for crop dusting, search and rescue, or fire-fighting. Before flights, check the plane's control equipment and weather conditions. Plan a safe route. Pilots communicate with air traffic control during flight to ensure a safe flight and fill out paperwork after the flight.

Where You Might Work: Flying planes for airlines, the military, radio and tv stations, freight companies, flight schools, farms, national parks, or other businesses that use airplanes.

Education: Most pilots will complete a four-year college degree before entering a pilot program. Before pilots become certified and take to the skies, they need a pilot license and many hours of flight time and training.

Snow Plow Operator

What You'll Do: In areas that receive snowfall, prepare the roads by spreading a mixture of sand and salt on the roads when snow is forecast. After a snowfall, drive snow plows to clear snow from roads and walkways.

Where You Might Work: For public organizations or private companies in cities and towns that receive snowfall.

Education: In most states, there is no special license needed, other than a driver's license.

Climate

ESSENTIAL QUESTION

How is climate affected by energy from the sun and variations on Earth's surface?

By the end of this lesson, you should be able to describe the main factors that affect climate and explain how scientists classify climates.

Earth has a wide variety of climates, including polar climates like the one shown here. What kind of climate do you live in?

Lesson Labs

Quick Labs
- Determining Climate
- Factors That Affect Climate
- The Angles of the Sun's Rays

Field Lab
- How Land Features Affect Climate

Engage Your Brain

1 Predict Check T or F to show whether you think each statement is true or false.

T F

☐ ☐ Locations in Florida and Oregon receive the same amount of sunlight on any given day.

☐ ☐ Temperature is an important part of determining the climate of an area.

☐ ☐ The climate on even the tallest mountains near the equator is too warm for glaciers to form.

☐ ☐ Winds can move rain clouds from one location to another.

2 Infer Volcanic eruptions can send huge clouds of gas and dust into the air. These dust particles can block sunlight. How might the eruption of a large volcano affect weather for years to come?

_____

_____

_____

_____

_____

Active Reading

3 Synthesize You can often define an unknown word if you know the meaning of its word parts. Use the word parts and sentence below to make an educated guess about the meaning of the word *topography*.

Word part	Meaning
topos-	place
-graphy	writing

Example sentence
The <u>topography</u> of the area is varied, because there are hills, valleys, and flat plains all within a few square miles.

topography:

_____

_____

Vocabulary Terms
- weather
- climate
- latitude
- topography
- elevation
- surface currents

4 Apply As you learn the definition of each vocabulary term in this lesson, create your own definition or sketch to help you remember the meaning of the term.

How's the Climate?

What determines climate?

Weather conditions change from day to day. **Weather** is the condition of Earth's atmosphere at a particular time and place. **Climate**, on the other hand, describes the weather conditions in an area over a long period of time. For the most part, climate is determined by temperature and precipitation (pree•SIP•uh•tay•shuhn). But what factors affect the temperature and precipitation rates of an area? Those factors include latitude, wind patterns, elevation, locations of mountains and large bodies of water, and nearness to ocean currents.

Temperature

Temperature patterns are an important feature of climate. Although the average temperature of an area over a period of time is useful information, using only average temperatures to describe climate can be misleading. Areas that have similar average temperatures may have very different temperature ranges.

A temperature range includes all of the temperatures in an area, from the coldest temperature extreme to the warmest temperature extreme. Organisms that thrive in a region are those that can survive the temperature extremes in that region. Temperature ranges provide more information about an area and are unique to the area. Therefore, temperature ranges are a better indicator of climate than are temperature averages.

Active Reading

5 Identify As you read, underline two elements of weather that are important in determining climate.

Visualize It!

6 Infer How might the two different climates shown below affect the daily lives of the people who live there?

_____

_____

_____

_____

Desert region

Polar region

Precipitation

Precipitation, such as rain, snow, or hail, is also an important part of climate. As with temperature, the average yearly precipitation alone is not the best way to describe a climate. Two places that have the same average yearly precipitation may receive that precipitation in different patterns during the year. For example, one location may receive small amounts of precipitation throughout the year. This pattern would support plant life all year long. Another location may receive all of its precipitation in a few months of the year. These months may be the only time in which plants can grow. So, the pattern of precipitation in a region can determine the types of plants that grow there and the length of the growing season. Therefore, the pattern of precipitation is a better indicator of the local climate than the average precipitation alone.

Think Outside the Book Inquiry

8 Apply With a classmate, discuss what condition, other than precipitation, is likely related to better plant growth in the temperate area shown directly below than in the desert on the bottom right.

Visualize It!

7 Interpret Match the climates represented in the bar graph below to the photos by writing *A*, *B*, or *C* in the blank circles.

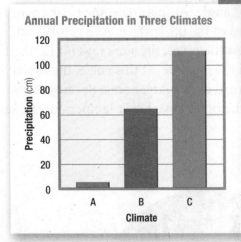

Annual Precipitation in Three Climates

○ There are enough resources in the area for plants to thickly cover the ground.

○ Some plants that grow in deserts have long roots to reach the water deep underground.

○ Conditions in a tropical forest allow lots of plants to grow quickly and closely together.

Here Comes the Sun!

How is the sun's energy related to Earth's climate?

The climate of an area is directly related to the amount of energy from the sun, or *solar energy*, that the area receives. This amount depends on the latitude (LAHT•ih•tood) of the area. **Latitude** is the angular distance in degrees north and south from the equator. Different latitudes receive different amounts of solar energy. The available solar energy powers the water cycle and winds, which affect the temperature, precipitation, and other factors that determine the local climate.

Latitude Affects the Amount of Solar Energy an Area Receives and that Area's Climate

Latitude helps determine the temperature of an area, because latitude affects the amount of solar energy an area receives. The figure below shows how the amount of solar energy reaching Earth's surface varies with latitude. Notice that the sun's rays travel in lines parallel to one another. Near the equator, the sun's rays hit Earth directly, at almost a 90° angle. At this angle, the solar energy is concentrated in a small area of Earth's surface. As a result, that area has high temperatures. At the poles, the sun's rays hit Earth at a lesser angle than they do at the equator. At this angle, the same amount of solar energy is spread over a larger area. Because the energy is less concentrated, the poles have lower temperatures than areas near the equator do.

Active Reading

9 Identify As you read, underline how solar energy affects the climate of an area.

Visualize It!

10 Analyze What is the difference between the sun's rays that strike at the equator and the sun's rays that strike at the poles?

_____

_____

_____

_____

The amount of solar energy an area receives depends on latitude.

Drawing is not to scale.

The Sun Powers the Water Cycle

It is easy to see how the water cycle affects weather and climate. For example, when it rains or snows, you see precipitation. In the water cycle, energy from the sun warms the surface of the ocean or other body of water. Some of the liquid water evaporates, becoming invisible water vapor, a gas. When cooled, some of the vapor condenses, turning into droplets of liquid water and forming clouds. Some water droplets collide, becoming larger. Once large enough, they fall to Earth's surface as precipitation.

11 Apply Using the figure below, explain how the water cycle affects the climate of an area.

_____

_____

_____

_____

_____

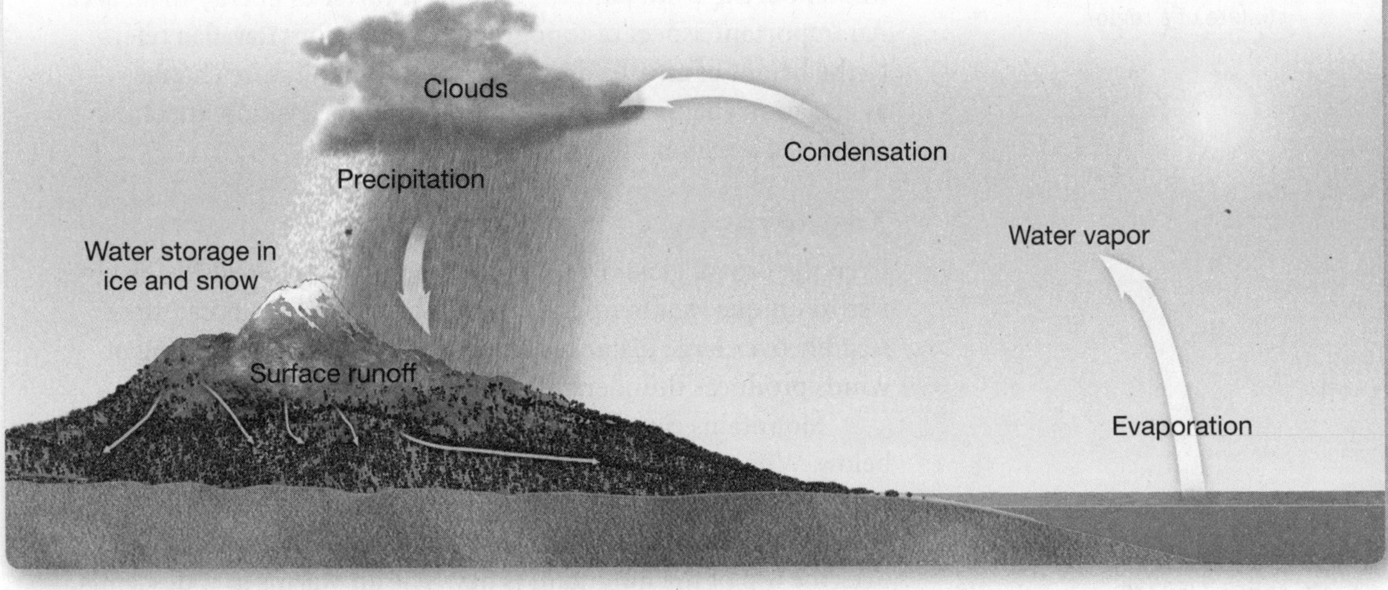

Clouds

Condensation

Precipitation

Water vapor

Water storage in ice and snow

Surface runoff

Evaporation

The Sun Powers Wind

The sun warms Earth's surface unevenly, creating areas of different air pressure. As air moves from areas of higher pressure to areas of lower pressure, it is felt as wind, as shown below. Global and local wind patterns transfer energy around Earth's surface, affecting global and local temperatures. Winds also carry water vapor from place to place. If the air cools enough, the water vapor will condense and fall as precipitation. The speed, direction, temperature, and moisture content of winds affect the climate and weather of the areas they move through.

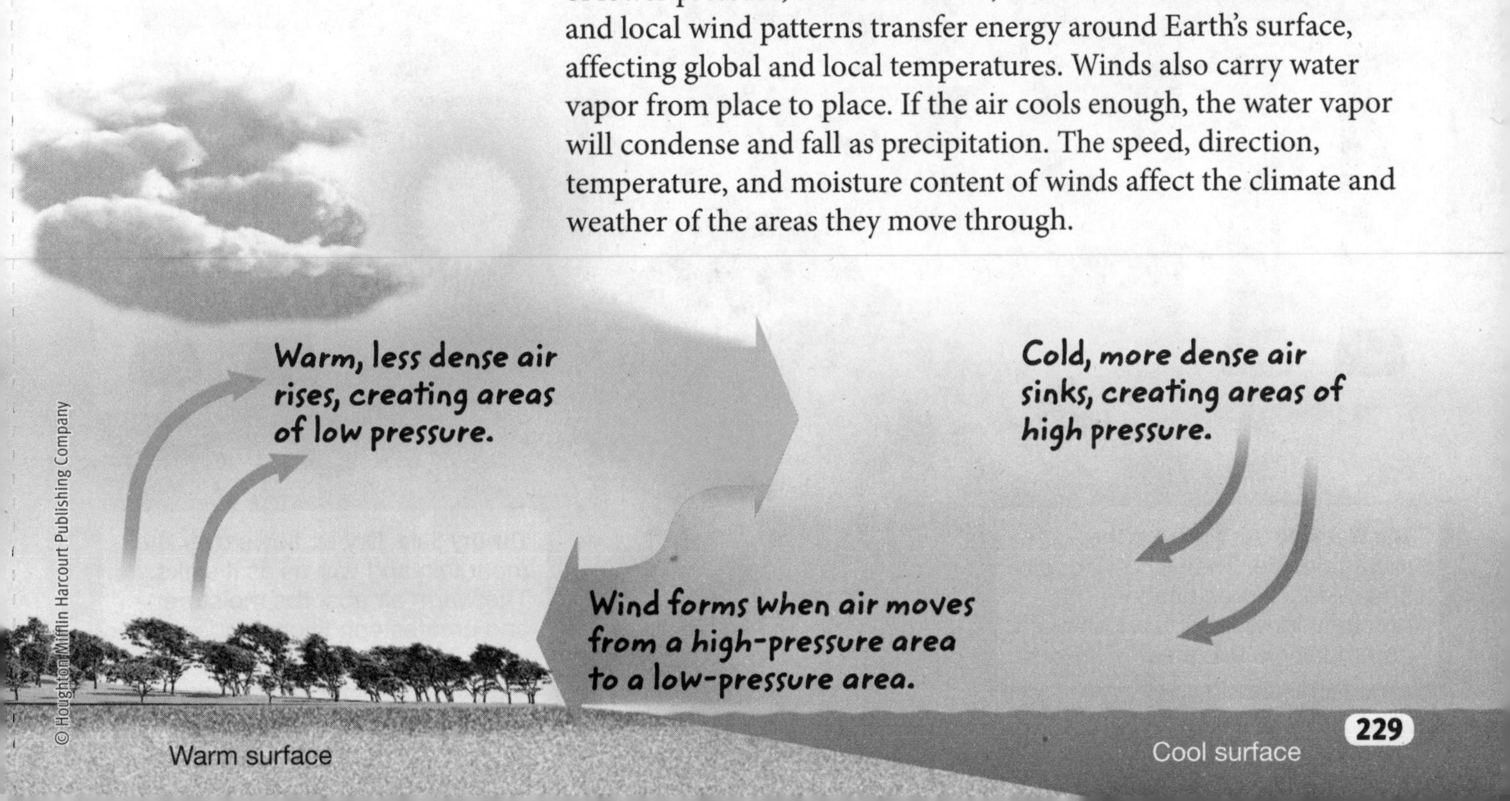

Warm, less dense air rises, creating areas of low pressure.

Cold, more dense air sinks, creating areas of high pressure.

Wind forms when air moves from a high-pressure area to a low-pressure area.

Warm surface

Cool surface

Latitude Isn't Everything

How do Earth's features affect climate?

On land, winds have to flow around or over features on Earth's surface, such as mountains. The surface features of an area combine to form its **topography** (tuh•POG•ruh•fee). Topography influences the wind patterns and the transfer of energy in an area. An important aspect of topography is elevation. **Elevation** refers to the height of an area above sea level. Temperature changes as elevation changes. Thus, topography and elevation affect the climate of a region.

Topography Can Affect Winds

Even the broad, generally flat topography of the Great Plains gives rise to unique weather patterns. On the plains, winds can flow steadily over large distances before they merge. This mixing of winds produces thunderstorms and even tornadoes.

Mountains can also affect the climate of an area, as shown below. When moist air hits a mountain, it is forced to rise up the side of the mountain. The rising air cools and often releases rain, which supports plants on the mountainside. The air that moves over the top of the mountain is dry. The air warms as it descends, creating a dry climate, which supports desert formation. Such areas are said to be in a *rain shadow*, because the air has already released all of its water by the time that it reaches this side of the mountain.

12 Identify As you read, underline how topography affects the climate of a region.

13 Apply Circle the rain gauge in each set that corresponds to how much rain each side of the mountain is likely to receive.

The Rain Shadow Effect

The Wet Side Air rises up the mountainside. The rising air cools and releases precipitation. The precipitation supports a lush plant community in this area.

The Dry Side Dry air flows over the mountain and warms as it sinks. The warm air absorbs moisture and creates conditions under which deserts may develop.

Elevation Influences Temperature

Elevation has a very strong effect on the temperature of an area. If you rode a cable car up a mountain, the temperature would decrease by about 6.5 °C (11.7 °F) for every kilometer you rose in elevation. Why does it get colder as you move higher up? Because the lower atmosphere is mainly warmed by Earth's surface that is directly below it. The warmed air lifts to higher elevations, where it expands and cools. Even close to the equator, temperatures at high elevations can be very cold. For example, Mount Kilimanjaro in Tanzania is close to the equator, but it is still cold enough at the peak to support a permanent glacier. The example below shows how one mountain can have several types of climates.

Visualize It!

14 Apply Circle the thermometer that shows the most likely temperature for each photo at different elevations.

Effects of Elevation

Haleakala, Maui

Elevation: 3,048 m (10,000 ft)

Elevation: 0 m (sea level)

15 Infer Generally, why are there no trees above a certain elevation on very tall mountains?

_____

_____

Waterfront Property

How do large bodies of water affect climate?

Large bodies of water, such as the ocean, can influence an area's climate. Water absorbs and releases energy as heat more slowly than land does. So, water helps moderate the temperature of nearby land. Sudden or extreme temperature changes rarely take place on land near large bodies of water. The state of Michigan, which is nearly surrounded by the Great Lakes, has more moderate temperatures than places far from large bodies of water at the same latitude. California's coastal climate is also influenced by a large body of water—the ocean. Places that are inland, but that are at the same latitude as a given place on California's coast, experience wider ranges of temperature.

Crescent City, California
Temperature Range:
4 °C to 19 °C
Latitude 41.8°N

Council Bluffs, Iowa
Temperature Range:
-11 °C to 30.5 °C
Latitude 41.3°N

Cleveland, Ohio
Temperature Range:
-4 °C to 28 °C
Latitude 41.4°N

GULF STREAM

ANTILLES CURRENT

CARIBBEAN CURRENT

Visualize It!

16 Apply Explain the difference in temperature ranges between Crescent City, Council Bluffs, and Cleveland.

_____

_____

_____

_____

_____

_____

How do ocean currents affect climate?

An *ocean current* is the movement of water in a certain direction. There are many different currents in the oceans. Ocean currents move water and distribute energy and nutrients around the globe. The currents on the surface of the ocean are called **surface currents.** Surface currents are driven by winds and carry warm water away from the equator and carry cool water away from the poles.

Cold currents cool the air in coastal areas, while warm currents warm the air in coastal areas. Thus, currents moderate global temperatures. For example, the Gulf Stream is a surface current that moves warm water from the Gulf of Mexico northeastward, toward Great Britain and Europe. The British climate is mild because of the warm Gulf Stream waters. Polar bears do not wander the streets of Great Britain, as they might in Natashquan, Canada, which is at a similar latitude.

NORWAY CURRENT

Natashquan, Canada
Temperature Range:
-18 °C to 14 °C
Latitude: 50.2°N

London, England
Temperature Range:
2 °C to 22 °C
Latitude 51.5°N

LABRADOR CURRENT

NORTH ATLANTIC CURRENT

GULF STREAM

ATLANTIC OCEAN

17 Summarize How do currents distribute heat around the globe?

_____

_____

_____

Visualize It!

18 Infer How do you think that the Canary current affects the temperature in the Canary Islands?

_____

_____

_____

CANARY CURRENT

Canary Islands, Spain
Temperature Range:
12 °C to 26 °C
Latitude 28°N

NORTH EQUATORIAL CURRENT

Zoning Out

What are the three major climate zones?

Earth has three major types of climate zones: tropical, temperate, and polar. These zones are shown below. Each zone has a distinct temperature range that relates to its latitude. Each of these zones has several types of climates. These different climates result from differences in topography, winds, ocean currents, and geography.

Active Reading

19 Identify Underline the factor that determines the temperature ranges in each zone.

Temperate

Temperate climates have an average temperature below 18 °C (64 °F) in the coldest month and an average temperature above 10 °C (50 °F) in the warmest month. There are five temperate zone subclimates: marine west coast climates, steppe climates, humid continental climate, humid subtropical climate, and Mediterranean climate. The temperate zone is characterized by lower temperatures than the tropical zone. It is located between the tropical zone and the polar zone.

Visualize It!

20 Label What climate zone is this?

_____

Polar

The polar zone, at latitudes of 66.5° and higher, is the coldest climate zone. Temperatures rarely rise above 10 °C (50 °F) in the warmest month. The climates of the polar regions are referred to as the *polar climates*. There are three types of polar zone subclimates: subarctic climates, tundra climates, and polar ice cap climates.

ARCTIC OCEAN

NORTH AMERICA

ATLANTIC OCEAN

23.5°N

0°–Equator

PACIFIC OCEAN

SOUTH AMERICA

23.5°S

66.5°S

SOUTH

21 Summarize Fill in the table for either the factor that affects climate or the effect on climate the given factor has.

Factor	Effect on climate
Latitude	
	Cooler temperatures as you travel up a tall mountain
Winds	
	Moderates weather so that highs and lows are less extreme
Surface ocean currents	
	Impacts wind patterns and the transfer of energy in an area

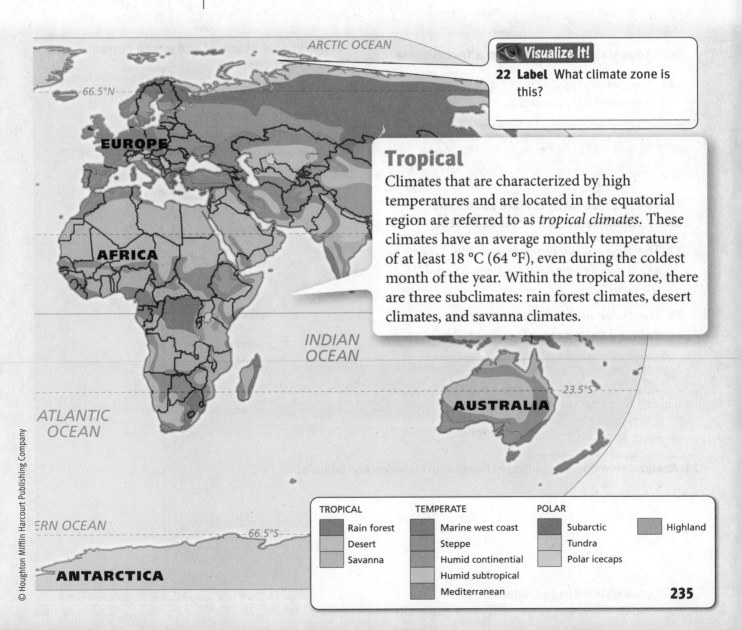

ARCTIC OCEAN

66.5°N

EUROPE

AFRICA

INDIAN OCEAN

23.5°S

AUSTRALIA

ATLANTIC OCEAN

66.5°S

ERN OCEAN

ANTARCTICA

Visualize It!

22 Label What climate zone is this?

Tropical

Climates that are characterized by high temperatures and are located in the equatorial region are referred to as *tropical climates*. These climates have an average monthly temperature of at least 18 °C (64 °F), even during the coldest month of the year. Within the tropical zone, there are three subclimates: rain forest climates, desert climates, and savanna climates.

TROPICAL	TEMPERATE	POLAR	
Rain forest	Marine west coast	Subarctic	Highland
Desert	Steppe	Tundra	
Savanna	Humid continental	Polar icecaps	
	Humid subtropical		
	Mediterranean		

Visual Summary

To complete this summary, circle the correct word or phrase. Then, use the key below to check your answers. You can use this page to review the main concepts of the lesson.

Climate

Temperature and precipitation are used to describe climate.

23 Climate is the characteristic weather conditions in a place over a short/long period.

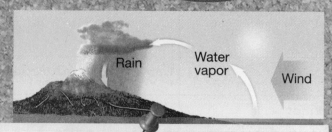

Rain
Water vapor
Wind

Winds transfer energy and moisture to new places.

24 Winds can affect the amount of precipitation in/elevation of an area.

Both topography and elevation affect climate.

25 Temperatures decrease as elevation increases/decreases.

Large bodies of water and ocean currents both affect climate.

26 Large bodies of water affect the climate of nearby land when cool waters absorb energy as heat from the warm air/cold land.

There are three main climate zones and many subclimates within those zones.

27 The three main types of climate zones are polar, temperate, and equatorial/tropical.

28 The three main climate zones are determined by elevation/latitude.

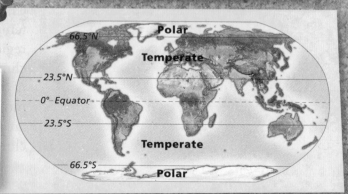

66.5°N — Polar
Temperate
23.5°N
0° Equator
23.5°S
Temperate
66.5°S — Polar

29 **Analyze** How does temperature change with elevation and latitude?

Lesson Review

Vocabulary

In your own words, define the following terms.

1 topography

_____

_____

2 climate

_____

_____

Key Concepts

Fill in the table below.

Factor	Effect on Climate
3 Identify Latitude	
4 Identify Elevation	
5 Identify Large bodies of water	
6 Identify Wind	

7 Explain What provides Great Britain with a moderate climate? How?

_____

_____

_____

8 Identify What are two characteristics used to describe the climate of an area?

_____

_____

Critical Thinking

Use the image below to answer the following question.

9 Explain Location A receives nearly 200 cm of rain each year, while Location B receives only 30 cm. Explain why Location A gets so much more rain. Use the words *rain shadow* and *precipitation* in your answer.

_____

_____

_____

_____

_____

_____

_____

10 Analyze What climate zone are you in if the temperatures are always very warm? Where is this zone located on Earth?

_____

11 Analyze How does the sun's energy affect the climate of an area?

_____

_____

_____

_____

_____

My Notes

Climate Change

ESSENTIAL QUESTION

What are the causes and effects of climate change?

By the end of this lesson, you should be able to describe climate change and the causes and effects of climate change.

Temperatures are rising in the Arctic. Warmer temperatures cause the ice sheets to freeze later and melt sooner. With less time on the ice to hunt for seals, polar bears are struggling to survive.

Engage Your Brain

1 Predict Check T or F to show whether you think each statement is true or false.

T F

☐ ☐ There have been periods on Earth when the climate was colder than the climate is today.

☐ ☐ The ocean does not play a role in climate.

☐ ☐ Earth's climate is currently warming.

☐ ☐ Humans are contributing to changes in climate.

2 Describe Write your own caption relating this photo to climate change.

_____

_____

_____

Active Reading

3 Apply Many scientific terms, such as *greenhouse effect*, also have everyday meanings. Use context clues to write your own definition for the words *greenhouse* and *effect*.

Example sentence
The <u>greenhouse</u> is filled with tropical plants that are found in Central America.

greenhouse:

_____

_____

_____

Example sentence
What are some of the <u>effects</u> of staying up too late?

effect:

_____

_____

_____

Vocabulary Terms

• ice age
• greenhouse effect
• global warming

4 Identify As you read, create a reference card for each vocabulary term. On one side of the card, write the term and its meaning. On the other side, draw an image that illustrates or makes a connection to the term. These cards can be used as bookmarks in the text so that you can refer to them while studying.

The Temps are a–Changin'

What are some natural causes of climate change?

The weather conditions in an area over a long period of time are called *climate*. Natural factors have changed Earth's climate many times during our planet's history. Natural changes in climate can be long-term or short-term.

Movement of Tectonic Plates

Tectonic plate motion has contributed to long-term climate change over billions of years. And Earth's plates are still moving!

The present continents once fit together as a single landmass called *Pangaea* (pan•JEE•uh). Pangaea began to break up about 200 million years ago. By 20 million years ago, the continents had moved close to their current positions. Some continents grew warmer as they moved closer to the equator. Other continents, such as Antarctica, moved to colder, higher latitudes.

The eruption of Mt. Pinatubo sent ash and gases as high as 34 km into the atmosphere.

 **Visualize It!**

5 Infer Today, Antarctica is the coldest desert on Earth. But fossils of trees and dinosaurs have been found on this harsh continent. Explain how life could thrive on ancient Antarctica.

_____

_____

_____

_____

EURASIA

NORTH AMERICA

Tethys Sea

SOUTH AMERICA

AFRICA

INDIA

AUSTRALIA

ANTARCTICA

Antarctica was part of the supercontinent Pangaea about 250 million years ago. Antarctica is located at the South Pole today.

EURASIA

NORTH AMERICA

AFRICA

PACIFIC OCEAN

SOUTH AMERICA

ATLANTIC OCEAN

INDIAN OCEAN

AUSTRALIA

ANTARCTICA

If you look closely at the current shapes of the continents, you can see how they once fit together to form Pangaea.

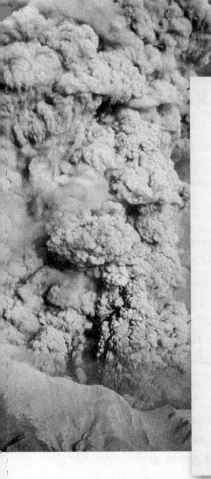

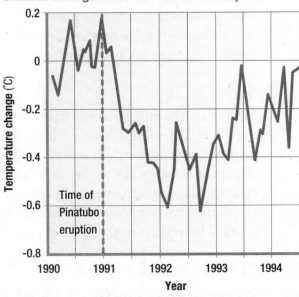

Climate Change After Mt. Pinatubo Eruption

Temperature change (°C) vs. Year (1990–1994)

Time of Pinatubo eruption

Source: Goddard Institute for Space Studies, NASA, 1997

This graph shows the *change* in average global temperature, not the actual temperature.

Particles in the Atmosphere

Short-term changes in climate can be due to natural events that send *particulates* into the atmosphere. Particulates are tiny, solid particles that are suspended in air or water. They absorb some of the sun's energy and reflect some of the sun's energy back into space. This process temporarily lowers temperatures on Earth.

Where do particulates come from? Asteroid impacts throw large amounts of dust into the atmosphere. Dust from the asteroid that struck near Mexico around 65 million years ago would have blocked the sun's rays. This reduction in sunlight may have limited photosynthesis in plants. The loss of plant life may have caused the food chain to collapse and led to dinosaur extinction.

Volcanic eruptions also release enormous clouds of ash and gases into the atmosphere. Particulates from large eruptions can circle Earth. The average global surface temperature fell by about 0.5 °C for several years after the 1991 eruption of Mt. Pinatubo in the Philippines. Twenty million tons of sulfur dioxide and 5 km³ of ash were blasted into the atmosphere. The sulfur-rich gases combined with water to form an Earth-cooling haze.

 **Active Reading** **7 Describe** Give one example of a long-term and one example of a short-term change in climate caused by natural factors.

_____

_____

Visualize It!

6 Analyze What happened to global temperatures after the eruption of Mt. Pinatubo? How long did this effect last?

_____

_____

_____

What are some causes of repeating patterns of climate change?

From day to day, or even year to year, the weather can change quite a lot. Some of these changes are relatively unpredictable, but others are due to predictable patterns or cycles. These patterns are the result of changes in the way energy is distributed around Earth.

Sun Cycles

Most of Earth's energy comes from the sun. And the output from the sun is very slightly higher during times of higher sunspot activity. Sunspots are dark areas on the sun that appear and disappear. Sunspot activity tends to increase and decrease in a cycle that lasts approximately 11 years. The effect of this sunspot cycle on global temperatures is not dramatic. But studies show a possible link between the sunspot cycle and global rain patterns.

El Niño and La Niña

Changes in ocean temperature also affect climate. During El Niño years, ocean temperatures are higher than usual in the tropical Pacific Ocean. The warmer water causes changes in global weather patterns. Some areas are cooler and wetter than normal. Other areas are warmer and dryer than normal.

The opposite effect occurs during La Niña years. Ocean temperatures are cooler than normal in the equatorial eastern Pacific Ocean. El Niño and La Niña conditions usually alternate, and both can lead to conditions such as droughts and flooding.

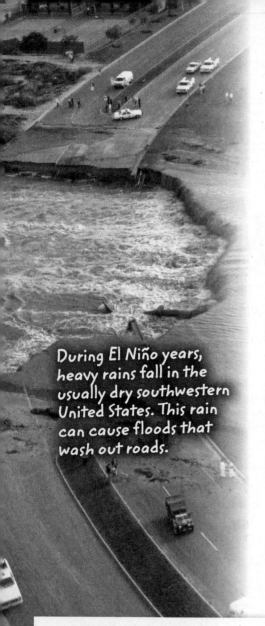

During El Niño years, heavy rains fall in the usually dry southwestern United States. This rain can cause floods that wash out roads.

Do the Math

8 Calculate About what percentage of years are El Niño years, with warmer than average ocean temperatures? About what percentage are La Niña years? About what percentage are neither El Niño or La Niña years?

_____

_____

Cycles of El Niño and La Niña

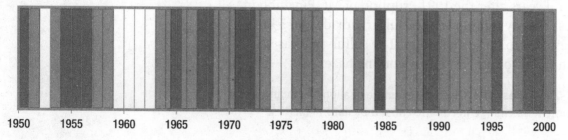

| 1950 | 1955 | 1960 | 1965 | 1970 | 1975 | 1980 | 1985 | 1990 | 1995 | 2000 |

■ La Niña years
■ El Niño years

Source: International Research Institute for Climate and Society, Columbia University, 2007

During the last 2 million years, continental ice sheets have expanded far beyond the polar regions. There have been multiple advances of ice sheets (glacial periods) and retreats of ice sheets (interglacial periods). The timeline shows recent glacial and interglacial periods.

Cycles of the Recent Ice Age

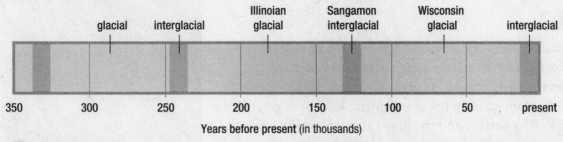

glacial | interglacial | Illinoian glacial | Sangamon interglacial | Wisconsin glacial | interglacial

350   300   250   200   150   100   50   present

Years before present (in thousands)

☐ Glacial period
☐ Interglacial period

Source: NOAA Paleoclimatology, 2007

Much of North America was covered with thick ice sheets during the last glacial period. This glacial period ended 10,000 to 14,000 years ago.

NORTH AMERICA

PACIFIC OCEAN

ATLANTIC OCEAN

☐ Land covered by ice
— Ice Age shoreline
— Present-day shoreline
— Present-day border

Ice Ages

The geological record shows that at different times Earth's climate has been both cooler *and* warmer than it is today. Earth's history contains multiple extremely cold periods when thick sheets of ice covered much of the continents. These periods are called *ice ages*. An **ice age** is a long period of cooling during which ice sheets spread beyond the polar regions. The exact cause of ice ages is not fully understood. Some hypotheses propose that ice ages include changes in Earth's orbit, shifts in the balance of incoming and outgoing solar radiation, and changes in heat exchange rates between the equator and the poles.

Geologic evidence indicates that ice ages occur over widely spaced intervals of time—approximately every 200 million years. Each ice age lasts for millions of years. The most recent ice age began about 2 million years ago, with its peak about 20,000 years ago. Large ice sheets still cover Greenland and Antarctica.

9 Infer Locate your home state on the map. Then, describe the climate your state likely experienced during the last glacial period.

_____

_____

_____

Active Reading **10 List** What are some possible causes of ice ages?

_____

Is It Getting HOTTER?

How do humans affect climate change?

Although natural events cause climate change, human activities may also affect Earth's climate. Human activities can cause the planet to warm when greenhouse gases are released into the atmosphere. Certain gases in the atmosphere, known as *greenhouse gases*, warm Earth's surface and the lower atmosphere by a process called the *greenhouse effect*. The **greenhouse effect** is the process by which gases in the atmosphere absorb and radiate energy as heat back to Earth. Greenhouse gases include carbon dioxide (CO_2), water vapor, methane, and nitrous oxide. Without greenhouse gases, energy would escape into space, and Earth would be colder. Two ways that humans release greenhouse gases into the atmosphere are by burning fossil fuels and by deforestation.

Active Reading **11 List** What are four greenhouse gases?

Smokestacks from a coal-burning power plant release water vapor and carbon dioxide into the atmosphere. Water vapor and carbon dioxide are greenhouse gases.

By Burning Fossil Fuels

There is now evidence to support the idea that humans are causing a rise in global CO_2 levels. Burning fossil fuels, such as gasoline and coal, adds greenhouse gases to the atmosphere. Since the 1950s, scientists have measured increasing levels of CO_2 and other greenhouse gases in the atmosphere. During this same period, the average global surface temperature has also been rising.

Correlation is when two sets of data show patterns that can be related. Both CO_2 level and average global surface temperature have been increasing over the same period of time, as shown by the graphs on the following page. So, there is a correlation between CO_2 levels in Earth's atmosphere and rising temperature. However, even though the two trends can be correlated, this does not show causation, or that one causes the other. In order to show causation, an explanation for how one change causes another has to be accepted. The explanation lies in the greenhouse effect. CO_2 is a greenhouse gas. An increase in greenhouse gases will warm Earth's surface and lower atmosphere. As greenhouse gas levels in the atmosphere have been rising, Earth's surface temperatures have been increasing, and so have temperatures in Earth's lower atmosphere. This shows that it is likely that rising CO_2 levels are causing global warming.

By Deforestation

Some processes, such as burning fossil fuels, add CO_2 and other carbon-based gases to the atmosphere. Processes that emit carbon into the atmosphere are called *carbon sources*. Processes such as the growth of plants and trees remove carbon from the atmosphere. Processes that remove carbon from the atmosphere are called *carbon sinks*. Deforestation is the mass removal of trees for farming, timber, and land development. The loss of trees represents the loss of an important carbon sink. Deforestation often includes the burning of trees, which is another source of carbon dioxide. So deforestation affects the amount of carbon in the atmosphere by converting a carbon sink into a carbon source.

Scientists think that the deforestation of rain forests plays a large role in greenhouse gas emissions. Tropical deforestation is thought to release 1.5 billion tons of carbon each year.

Active Reading **12 Describe** How does deforestation affect the amount of carbon dioxide that is in the atmosphere?

_____

_____

Deforestation is one of the leading sources of greenhouse gases.

Visualize It!

13 Apply Based on the trend shown in the graph, how do you expect CO_2 levels to change over the next 20 years?

_____

_____

14 Explain Describe the changes in average global temperature during the years represented by the CO_2 graph.

_____

_____

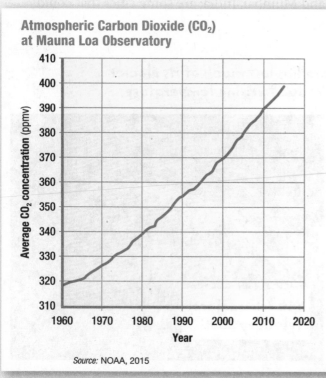

Atmospheric Carbon Dioxide (CO_2) at Mauna Loa Observatory

Source: NOAA, 2015

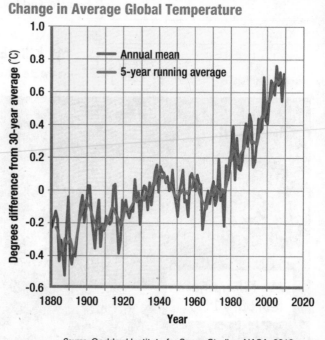

Change in Average Global Temperature

- Annual mean
- 5-year running average

Source: Goddard Institute for Space Studies, NASA, 2010

What are some predicted effects of climate change?

Data show that the world's climate has been warming in recent years. **Global warming** is a gradual increase in average global temperature. Global warming will affect global weather patterns, global sea level, and life on Earth.

Effects on the Atmosphere

Studies show that the average global surface temperature has increased by about 0.3 °C to 0.8 °C over the last 100 years. Even small changes in temperature can greatly affect weather and precipitation. Scientists predict that warming will generate more severe weather. Predictions suggest that storms will be more powerful and occur more frequently. It has also been predicted that as much as half of Earth's surface may be affected by drought.

Effects on the Hydrosphere and Cryosphere

Much of the ice on Earth occurs in glaciers in mountains, arctic sea ice, and ice sheets that cover Greenland and Antarctica. As temperatures increase, some of this ice will melt. A 2010 report observed record-setting hot temperatures, which resulted in record ice melt of the Greenland ice sheet.

When ice on land melts, global sea level rises because water flows into the ocean. Global sea level rose by 10 to 20 cm during the 1900s. Scientists project that sea level may rise 29–82 cm by 2100. Higher sea level is expected to increase flooding in coastal areas, some of which are highly populated. New York City; Shanghai, China; and Mumbai, India; are some cities that could be affected.

15 Infer How do melting ice caps and glaciers affect sea level?

_____

_____

_____

Mt. Kilimanjaro has lost much of its glacier in recent years due to rising temperatures.

Mt. Kilimanjaro
February 1993

Mt. Kilimanjaro
February 2000

A warmer climate may force some species northward, including sugar maples.

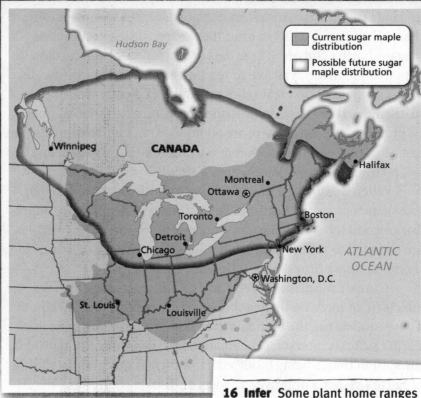

Current sugar maple distribution

Possible future sugar maple distribution

Hudson Bay

CANADA

Winnipeg

Montreal
Ottawa ⊛

Toronto

Detroit

Chicago

Halifax

Boston

New York

Washington, D.C. ⊛

ATLANTIC OCEAN

St. Louis

Louisville

Effects on the Biosphere

Active Reading **17 Summarize** Underline some of the effects of predicted climate change on the biosphere.

Scientists predict that global warming will change ecosystems. These changes may threaten the survival of many plant and animal species. Some species may move to cooler areas or even go extinct. Some butterflies, foxes, and alpine plants have already moved north to cooler climates. In Antarctica, emperor penguin populations could be reduced by as much as 95 percent by the end of this century if sea ice loss continues at its current rate. On the other hand, some species may benefit from expanded habitats in a warmer world.

Changes in temperature and precipitation will affect crops and livestock. If Earth warms more than a few degrees Celsius, many of the world's farms could suffer. Higher temperatures, reduced rainfall, and severe flooding can reduce crop production. Changes in weather will especially affect developing countries with large rural areas, such as countries in South Asia.

Warmer temperatures could increase the number of heat-related deaths and deaths from certain diseases, such as malaria. However, deaths associated with extreme cold could decrease.

16 Infer Some plant home ranges are shifting northward due to regional warming. What might happen to plant populations that are unable to spread northward?

_____
_____
_____
_____

How are climate predictions made?

Instruments have been placed in the atmosphere, in the oceans, on land, and in space to collect climate data. NASA now has more than a dozen spacecraft in orbit that are providing continuous data on Earth's climate. These data are added to historical climate data that are made available to researchers at centers worldwide. The data are used to create climate models. *Climate models* use mathematical formulas to describe how different variables affect Earth's climate. Today, there are about a dozen climate models that can be used to simulate different parts of the Earth system and the interactions that take place between them.

When designing a model to predict future climate change, scientists first model Earth's current climate system. If the model does a good job describing current conditions, then the variables are changed to reflect future conditions. Scientists usually run the model multiple times using different variables.

Climate models are the means by which scientists predict the effects of an increase in greenhouse gases on future global climate. These models use the best data available about the ways in which Earth's systems interact. No climate model can perfectly reproduce the system that is being modeled. However, as our understanding of Earth's systems improves, models of climate change are becoming more accurate.

Visualize It!

18 Predict As Earth is warming, the oceans are rising. This is due to both melting ice and the expansion of water as it warms. Predict what the change in sea level will be by the year 2025 if the current trend continues. You may draw on the graph to extend the current trend.

_____

_____

_____

Sea level has been rising steadily since 1993. By the year 2014, global average sea level had risen 67 mm above the 1993 average, represented by 0 on the graph.

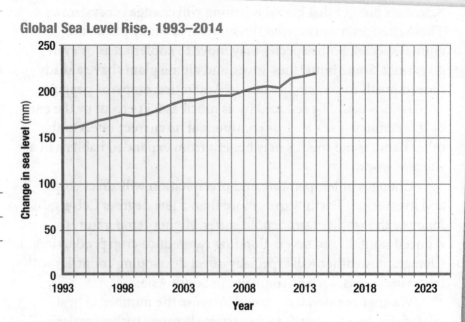

Global Sea Level Rise, 1993–2014

Source: Bulletin of the American Meteorological Society, 2015

Think Clean and Green

How can people reduce their impact on climate change?

People can take action to reduce climate change and its effects. Countries are working together to reduce their impact on Earth's climate. Communities and individuals are also doing their part to reduce greenhouse gas emissions.

Reduce Greenhouse Gas Emissions

The Kyoto Protocol, an international environmental agreement to reduce greenhouse gas emissions, was adopted in 1997. The Kyoto Protocol is the only existing international treaty in which nations have agreed to reduce CO_2 emissions. As of 2010, 191 countries had signed the protocol. At present, the Kyoto Protocol faces many complex challenges. One of the greatest challenges is that developing nations, which will be the largest future sources of CO_2 emissions, did not sign the protocol.

Individuals can reduce their impact on climate by conserving energy, increasing energy efficiency, and reducing the use of fossil fuels. Greenhouse gas emissions can be reduced by driving less and by switching to nonpolluting energy sources. Simple energy conservation solutions include turning off lights and replacing light bulbs. Recycling and reusing products also reduce energy use.

For most materials, recycling uses less energy than making products from scratch. That means less greenhouse gases are emitted.

Do the Math You Try It

19 Calculate How much energy is saved by using recycled aluminum to make new aluminum cans instead of making aluminum cans from raw materials?

_____

_____

20 Calculate By what percentage does recycling aluminum reduce energy use?

_____

_____

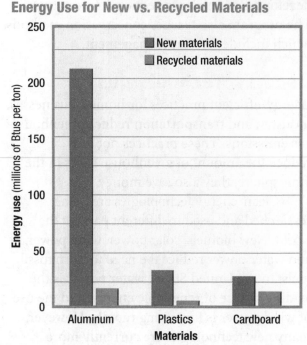

Energy Use for New vs. Recycled Materials

Source: US EPA Solid Waste Management and Greenhouse Gases, 2002

- Reduce use of automobile.
- Use new, cleaner technologies.
- Plant a tree.

Reduce the Rate of Deforestation

Deforestation contributes up to 20 percent of greenhouse gases globally. Planting trees and supporting reforestation programs are ways that carbon sources can be balanced by carbon sinks. Another solution is to educate people about the importance of the carbon that is stored in forests for stabilizing climate. In 2008, the United Nations began a program called REDD, or *Reducing Emissions from Deforestation and Forest Degradation*. REDD offers incentives to developing countries to reduce deforestation. The program also teaches conservation methods, which include forestry management.

Use New Technologies

Energy-efficient practices for homes, businesses, industry, and transportation reduce greenhouse gas emissions. These practices not only reduce the amount of greenhouse gases in the atmosphere, they also save money.

Clean-energy technologies are being researched and used in different parts of the world. New biofuels, solar power, wind power, and water power reduce the need to burn fossil fuels. In the United States, water power is the leading source of renewable energy, and the use of wind power is increasing rapidly. However, many new technologies are currently more expensive than fossil fuels.

21 Summarize Use the table to summarize ways in which sources of greenhouse gases in the atmosphere can be reduced.

Sources of greenhouse gases	Ways to reduce greenhouse gases
cars	Walk or use bikes more often.

What are some economic and political issues related to climate change?

Active Reading **22 Identify** Underline some of the economic and political issues that are related to climate change.

Climate change affects the entire Earth, no matter where greenhouse gases are produced. This makes climate change a global issue. The scientific concerns that climate change poses are not the only issues that have to be taken into account. There are economic and political issues involving climate change that are equally important.

Climate change is an economic issue. The cost of climate change includes the costs of crop failure, storm damage, and human disease. However, developing countries may not be able to afford technologies needed to reduce human impact on climate.

Climate change is also a political issue. Political action can lead to regulations that reduce greenhouse gas emissions. However, these laws may be challenged by groups who disagree with the need for change or disagree about what needs to change. No matter what choices are made to handle the challenges of climate change, it will take groups of people working together to make a difference.

Think Outside the Book **Inquiry**

23 Apply Research a recent extreme weather event from anywhere in the world. How might this event be related to climate change? Present your findings to the class as a news report or poster.

Climate change may make unusual weather the new norm. Rome, Italy, was brought to a standstill by unusually cold and snowy weather in 2010.

In Australia, years of unusually dry and hot weather led to devastating forest fires in 2009. Australia also suffered damaging floods in 2010.

24 Predict What are the possible economic and social consequences of unusually warm weather in a cold climate or unusually cool weather in a warm climate?

_____

_____

_____

Visual Summary

To complete this summary, fill in the blanks with the missing word or phrase. Then, use the key below to check your answers. You can use this page to review the main concepts of the lesson.

Natural factors have changed Earth's climate many times during Earth's history.

25 _____ have moved across Earth's surface over time and once formed a supercontinent called Pangaea.

Global warming affects many of Earth's systems.

27 If average global surface temperature continues to rise, then severe storms may become more _____

Climate Change

Greenhouse gases have a warming effect on the surface of Earth.

26 Scientists think that there is a connection between rising levels of _____ and rising _____

There are steps that people can take to reduce their impact on climate change.

28 People can reduce their impact on climate change by reducing greenhouse emissions and deforestation, and by _____

Sample answers: 25 Tectonic plates; 26 CO₂ (carbon dioxide); global temperatures; 27 frequent; 28 using new technologies

29 Synthesize How can burning fossil fuels cause global warming?

Lesson Review

Vocabulary

Fill in the blank with the term that best completes the following sentences.

1 _____ is a gradual increase in average global surface temperature.

2 A long period of climate cooling during which ice sheets spread beyond the polar regions is called a(n) _____

3 The warming of Earth's surface and lower atmosphere that occurs when greenhouse gases absorb and reradiate energy is called the

_____

Key Concepts

4 Identify What are some natural events that have caused changes in Earth's climate?

_____

_____

_____

_____

5 Identify What are some predicted effects of climate change linked to global warming?

_____

_____

_____

_____

_____

6 Summarize List ways in which humans can reduce the rate of climate change.

_____

_____

_____

_____

_____

Critical Thinking

Use the graph to answer the following questions.

Change in Average Global Temperature

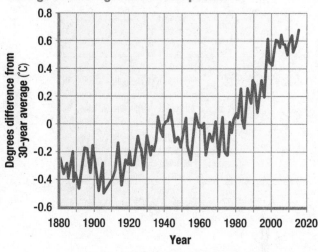

Source: Goddard Institute for Space Studies, NASA, 2015

7 Analyze Describe the trend shown in this graph. Why is it helpful to have many decades of data to make a graph such as this?

_____

_____

_____

_____

8 Infer What might cause average global surface temperature to rise and fall from year to year?

_____

_____

_____

_____

9 Infer Why might some countries be more reluctant than others to take steps to reduce levels of greenhouse gases?

_____

_____

_____

_____

_____

_____

My Notes

Unit 4 Big Idea

Air pressure, temperature, air movement, and humidity in the atmosphere affect both weather and climate.

Lesson 1

ESSENTIAL QUESTION

What is weather and how can we describe types of weather conditions?

Describe elements of weather and explain how they are measured.

Lesson 2

ESSENTIAL QUESTION

How do clouds form, and how are clouds classified?

Describe the formation and classification of clouds.

Lesson 3

ESSENTIAL QUESTION

How do the water cycle and other global patterns affect local weather?

Explain how global patterns in Earth's system influence weather.

Lesson 4

ESSENTIAL QUESTION

How can humans protect themselves from hazardous weather?

Describe the major types of hazardous weather and the ways human beings can protect themselves from hazardous weather and from sun exposure.

Lesson 5

ESSENTIAL QUESTION

What tools do we use to predict weather?

Understand how meteorologists forecast the weather using weather maps and other data.

Lesson 6

ESSENTIAL QUESTION

How is climate affected by energy from the sun and variations on Earth's surface?

Describe the main factors that affect climate and explain how scientists classify climates.

Lesson 7

ESSENTIAL QUESTION

What are the causes and effects of climate change?

Describe climate change and the causes and effects of climate change.

Connect ESSENTIAL QUESTIONS
Lessons 3 and 5

1 Synthesize Explain how a change in air pressure can signal a change in weather.

_____

_____

Think Outside the Book

2 Synthesize Choose one of these activities to help synthesize what you have learned in this unit.

☐ Using what you learned in lessons 1, 2, 3, and 4, present a poster about water vapor and the formation of severe weather.

☐ Using what you learned in lessons 5, 6, and 7, explain in a short essay how weather predictions might change if additional greenhouse gases in Earth's atmosphere caused Earth to warm by several degrees C.

Name _____

Vocabulary

Fill in each blank with the term that best completes the following sentences.

1 _____ is the ratio of the amount of water vapor in the air to the amount of water vapor needed to reach saturation at a given temperature.

2 White, thin clouds with a feathery appearance are called _____.

3 A(n) _____ is a violently rotating column of air stretching from a cloud to the ground.

4 _____ is the characteristic weather conditions in an area over a long period of time.

5 A long period of climate cooling during which ice sheets spread beyond the polar regions is called a(n) _____.

Key Concepts

Read each question below, and circle the best answer.

6 The graph shows the temperatures recorded at school one day.

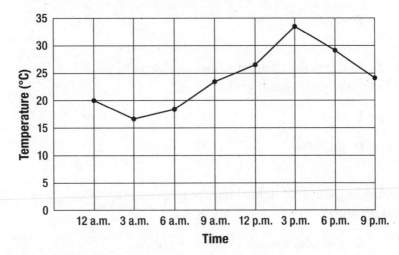

What can these temperature data tell us?

A The highest temperature of the day occurred at 6 p.m.

B The amount of water vapor in the air changed that day.

C The amount of energy as heat in the air changed during that day.

D The climate changed between 3 a.m. and 3 p.m.

7 Which of these types of weather data is measured using a barometer?

   A air pressure   **C** relative humidity

   B precipitation   **D** wind speed

8 The picture below shows the four parts of the water cycle labeled A, B, C, and D.

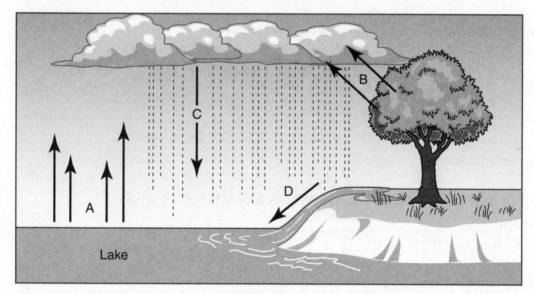

If rain (C) is falling as part of a thunderstorm, which type of clouds are shown?

   A altostratus clouds   **C** cumulonimbus clouds

   B cirrus clouds   **D** stratus clouds

9 If it rained all day but stopped and then cooled down considerably at night, what weather phenomenon would you likely see that night?

   A fog   **C** sleet

   B hail   **D** thunder

10 What results when air surrounding a bolt of lightning experiences a rapid increase in temperature and pressure?

   A A tornado forms.   **C** Thunder sounds.

   B Hail forms.   **D** Rain condenses.

11 Refer to the regions A, B, C, and D shown on the U.S. map below.

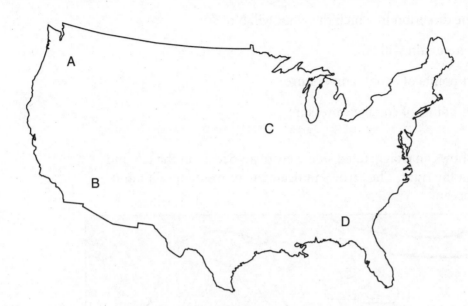

In which of these directions is the jet stream most likely to flow?

A from D to C

C from C to A

B from A to C

D from C to B

12 Which of the following should you do to escape a flood?

A Seek a high, safe point above the floodwaters and wait for assistance.

B Walk carefully into the floodwaters to get to safety.

C Swim through the floodwaters until you find a safer place.

D Use a lifejacket or flotation device to help you wade through the floodwaters.

13 What are the two main factors that determine climate?

A temperature and wind

B temperature and precipitation

C air pressure and humidity

D wind and precipitation

14 What do the curved concentric lines on weather forecast maps show?

   A The lines show the direction in which the wind will blow.

   B The lines show where rain will fall.

   C The lines connect points of equal temperature.

   D The lines connect points of equal air pressure.

15 The picture below shows an exaggerated side view of an ocean on the left and a mountain range on the right. The arrows indicate the movement of air and moisture from the ocean.

Which region is most likely to have a dry, desert-like climate?

   A region R   **C** region T

   B region S   **D** region W

16 Which of these is not a currently predicted effect of global climate change?

   A rising sea levels

   B increased precipitation everywhere on the globe

   C reduction in Arctic sea ice

   D more severe storms

17 The graph below shows the amount of carbon dioxide measured in the atmosphere between about 1960 and 2005.

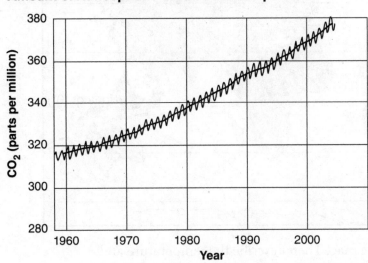

Amount of Atmospheric Carbon Dioxide per Year

What conclusion can you make from the data displayed in the graph?

A The amount of carbon dioxide in the atmosphere more than doubled between 1960 and 2000.

B An increasing number of cars on the road between 1960 and 2000 caused an increase in carbon dioxide levels in the atmosphere.

C There was an overall increase in the level of carbon dioxide in the atmosphere between 1960 and 2000.

D Average global temperatures increased between 1960 and 2000 as a result of the increase in carbon dioxide in the atmosphere.

Critical Thinking

Answer the following questions in the space provided.

18 Explain generally what makes a cloud form.

_____

_____

Describe one specific situation in which a cloud can form.

_____

_____

19 Explain two ways in which forecasters collect weather data.

_____

_____

20 The map below shows the three different climate zones on Earth.

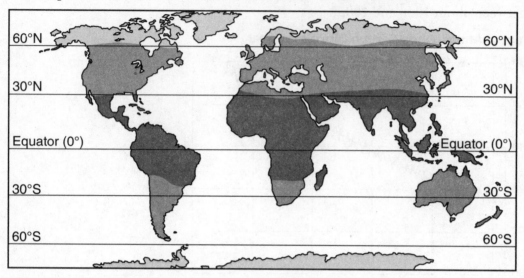

Label each climate zone on the map. Then describe the temperature and precipitation typical of each zone.

_____

_____

_____

Explain how latitude affects the climate of each zone.

_____

_____

_____

Connect ESSENTIAL QUESTIONS
Lessons 1, 2, 3, 4, and 6

Answer the following question in the space provided.

21 Even if you do not live on a coast, the movement of water in the oceans and water vapor in the atmosphere over the oceans does affect your weather. Using what you learned in lessons 1, 2, 3, 4, and 6, describe how the water cycle and the global movement of water through ocean currents and winds affect the climate of your local region.

_____

_____

_____

_____

_____

_____

21st Century Skills
⟨Technology⟩
and Coding

This breathtaking image of Earth was taken from the International Space Station, an international laboratory orbiting Earth. The operation of the International Space Station is controlled by 52 computers and millions of lines of computer code. Its many high-tech features include solar panels that power the laboratory and a human-like robotic astronaut.

This is Robonaut 2, a robot designed to do routine maintenance at the International Space Station.

Data Driven

What is computer science?

If you like computer technology and learning about how computers work, computer science might be for you. *Computer science* is the study of computer technology and how data is processed, stored, and accessed by computers. Computer science is an important part of many other areas, including science, math, engineering, robotics, medicine, game design, and 3D animation.

Computer technology is often described in terms of *hardware*, which are the physical components, and *software*, which are the programs or instructions that a computer runs. Computer scientists must understand how hardware and software work together. Computer scientists may develop new kinds of useful computer software. Or they may work with engineers to improve existing computer hardware.

The first electronic computer, the computer ENIAC (Electronic Numerical Integrator And Computer), was developed at the University of Pennsylvania in 1946.

The integrated circuit (IC), first developed in the 1950s, was instrumental in the development of small computer components.

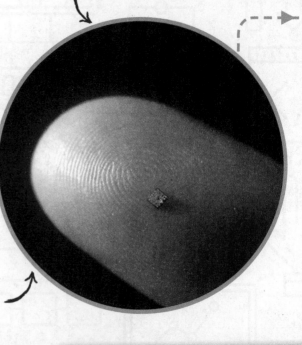

The development of the IC made it possible to reduce the overall size of computers and their components and to increase their processing speed.

How has computer technology changed over time?

Modern digital computer technology is less than 100 years old. Yet in that short amount of time, it has advanced rapidly. The earliest digital computers could perform only a limited number of tasks and were the size of an entire room. Over the decades, engineers continued to develop smaller, faster, and more powerful computers. Today's computers can process hundreds of millions of instructions per second!

Computer scientists and engineers think about what people want or need from computer technology. The most advanced hardware is not useful if people do not know how to use it. So computer scientists and engineers work to create software that is reliable, useful, and easy to use. Today's tablet computers, cell phones, and video game consoles can be used without any special training.

Advances in digital computer technology have help make computers cheaper and easier to operate, which has allowed many more people to work and play with them.

1 Compare Are modern computers simpler or more complex than early computers? Explain.

_____

_____

_____

Computer Logic

What do computer scientists do?

Many people enjoy developing computer technology for fun. Learning how to create mobile phone games or Internet-enabled gadgets can be rewarding hobbies. For some people, that hobby may one day become a career in computer science. Working in computer science is a bit like solving a puzzle. Applying knowledge of how computers work to solve real-world problems requires collaboration, creativity, and logical step-by-step thinking.

This is a kayak folded up.

They collaborate across many disciplines

Computers are valuable tools in math and science because they can perform complex calculations very quickly. Computers are useful to many other fields, too. For example, animators use computer technology to create realistic lighting effects in 3D animated films. Mechanics use computers to diagnose problems in car systems. For every field that relies on special software or computer technology, there is an opportunity for computer scientists and engineers to collaborate and develop solutions for those computing needs. Computer scientists must be able to define and understand the problems presented to them and to communicate and work with experts in other fields to develop the solutions.

Computational origami is a computer program used to model the ways in which different materials, including paper, can be folded. It combines computer science and the art of paper folding to create new technologies, such as this kayak.

Tracking software helps biologists study animal behavior.

satellite →

satellite data receiving center

satellite data processing center

transmitter

They help solve real-world problems

Some computer scientists carry out theoretical research. Others apply computer science concepts to develop software. Theoretical computer science and practical software development help solve real-world problems. For example, biologists need ways to safely and accurately track endangered animals. Computer science theories on artificial intelligence and pattern recognition have been applied to advanced animal-tracking technologies, such as satellite transmitters and aerial cameras. New kinds of image processing software now allow biologists to analyze the collected data in different ways.

They use logical, step-by-step thinking

Computers perform tasks given to them, and they do this very well. But in order to get the results they expect, computer scientists and programmers must write very accurate instructions. Computer science and programming requires logical thinking, deductive reasoning, and a good understanding of cause-and-effect relationships. When designing software, computer scientists must consider every possible user action and how the computer should respond to each action.

2 Explain How is computer science helping this scientist do her research?

_____

_____

_____

_____

Transmitters can be attached to animals to help track their movements.

Up to <Code>

How is computer software created?

Imagine that you are using a computer at the library to learn more about the history of electronic music. You use the library's database application to start searching for Internet resources. You also do a search to look for audio recordings. Finally, you open a word processor to take notes on the computer. Perhaps without realizing it, you've used many different pieces of software. Have you ever wondered how computer software is created?

Computer software is designed to address a need

Computer software can help us to learn more about our world. It can be useful to business. Or it can simply entertain us. Whatever its purpose, computer software should fulfill some human want or need. The first steps in creating software are precisely defining the need or want being addressed and planning how the software will work.

Computer software source code is written in a programming language

The instructions that tell a computer how to run video games, word processors, and other kinds of software are not written in a human language. They are written in a special programming language, or *code*. Javascript, C++, and Python are examples of programming languages. Programming languages—like human languages—must follow certain rules in order to be understood by the computer. A series of instructions written in a programming language is called *source code*.

Identifying what need a computer program addresses is one of the first development steps.

Source code is revised

Sometimes, programmers make mistakes in their code. Many programming environments have a feature that alerts the programmer to certain errors, such as spelling mistakes in commands, missing portions of code, or logical errors in the sequence of instructions. However, many mistakes go undetected, too. Some errors may cause the program to function incorrectly or not at all. When this happens, the programmer must identify the error, correct it, and test the software again.

3 Identify This source code contains an error. Infer where the error is located. What does this code "tell" the computer to do? Write your answers below.

_____

_____

_____

_____

Computer software is user tested, and revised

Once the software is created, it must be tested thoroughly to make sure it does not fail or behave in unexpected ways. It must also be tested to ensure that it meets users' needs. The creators of a piece of software might observe how people use it. Or they might ask users to provide feedback on certain features and test the software again.

```
13
14   # Scores are not tied, so check
15   # which player wins the round
16 ▾ if player1_score > player2_score:
17       print ("Player 1 wins!")
18 ▾ else:
19       prnt ("Player 2 wins!")
20

! Syntax error, line 19
```

Test running a program is important for finding and fixing errors in the code.

Play it Safe

How should I work with computers?

It is easy to lose track of time when you're sitting in front of a computer or game console. It's also easy to forget that things you say or do online can be seen and shared by many different people. Here are some tips for using computers safely and responsibly.

✓ **Maintain good posture**

Time can pass by quickly when you are working on a computer or another device. Balance computer time with other activities, including plenty of physical activity. When you are sitting at a computer, sit upright with your shoulders relaxed. Your eyes should be level with the top of the monitor and your feet should be flat on the ground.

✓ **Observe electrical safety**

Building your own electronics projects can be fun, but it's important to have an understanding of circuits and electrical safety first. Otherwise, you could damage your components or hurt yourself. The potential for an electrical shock is real when you open up a computer, work with frayed cords or, use ungrounded plugs or attempt to replace parts without understanding how to do so safely. Ask an adult for help before starting any projects. Also, avoid using a connected computer during thunderstorms.

head and neck in a straight, neutral position

shoulders are relaxed

wrists are straight

feet are flat on the ground

Good posture will help you avoid the aches and injuries related to sitting in front of a computer for a long time.

✓ Handle and maintain computers properly

Be cautious when handling and transporting electronic devices. Dropping them or spilling liquids on them could cause serious damage. Keep computers away from dirt, dust, liquids, and moisture. Never use wet cleaning products unless they are specifically designed for use on electronics. Microfiber cloths can be used to clear smudges from device screens. Spilled liquids can cause circuits to short out and hardware to corrode. If a liquid spills on a device, unplug it and switch it off immediately, remove the battery and wipe up as much of the liquid inside the device as possible. Don't switch the device back on until it is completely dry.

✓ Do not post private information online

Talk to your family about rules for Internet use. Do not use the Internet to share private information such as photographs, your phone number, or your address. Do not respond to requests for personal details from people you do not know.

✓ Treat yourself and others with respect

It is important to treat others with respect when on the Internet. Don't send or post messages online that you wouldn't say to someone in person. Unfortunately, not everyone acts respectfully while online. Some people may say hurtful things to you or send you unwanted messages. Do not reply to unwanted messages. Alert a trusted adult to any forms of contact, such as messages or photos, that make you feel uncomfortable.

4 Apply Fill in the chart below with a suitable response to each scenario.

SCENARIO	YOUR RESPONSE
You receive a text message from an online store asking for your home address.	
You've been lying down in front of a laptop, and you notice that your neck is feeling a little sore.	
You need to take a laptop computer with you on your walk to school.	
You want to try assembling a robotics kit with a friend.	
Someone posts unfriendly comments directed at you.	

Career in Computing:
Game Programmer

What do video game programmers do?

Creating your own universe with its own set of rules is fun. Just ask a programmer who works on video games!

What skills are needed in game programming?

A programmer should know how to write code, but there are other important skills a programmer needs as well. An understanding of physics and math is important for calculating how objects move and interact in a game. Game programmers usually work on a team with other people, such as artists, designers, writers, and musicians. They must be able to communicate effectively, and ideally, the programmer should understand the other team members' roles.

How can I get started with game development?

You don't need a big budget or years of experience to try it out. There are books, videos, and websites that can help you get started. When you're first experimenting with game development, start small. Try making a very simple game like Tic-Tac-Toe. Once you've mastered that, you can try something more complex.

5 Brainstorm Why would working on a team be important to the game development process?

_____

_____

_____

Look It Up!

References

Mineral Properties

Here are five steps to take in mineral identification:

1 Determine the color of the mineral. Is it light-colored, dark-colored, or a specific color?

2 Determine the luster of the mineral. Is it metallic or non-metallic?

3 Determine the color of any powder left by its streak.

4 Determine the hardness of your mineral. Is it soft, hard, or very hard? Using a glass plate, see if the mineral scratches it.

5 Determine whether your sample has cleavage or any special properties.

TERMS TO KNOW	DEFINITION
adamantine	a non-metallic luster like that of a diamond
cleavage	how a mineral breaks when subject to stress on a particular plane
luster	the state or quality of shining by reflecting light
streak	the color of a mineral when it is powdered
submetallic	between metallic and nonmetallic in luster
vitreous	glass-like type of luster

Silicate Minerals					
Mineral	Color	Luster	Streak	Hardness	Cleavage and Special Properties
Beryl	deep green, pink, white, bluish green, or yellow	vitreous	white	7.5–8	1 cleavage direction; some varieties fluoresce in ultraviolet light
Chlorite	green	vitreous to pearly	pale green	2–2.5	1 cleavage direction
Garnet	green, red, brown, black	vitreous	white	6.5–7.5	no cleavage
Hornblende	dark green, brown, or black	vitreous	none	5–6	2 cleavage directions
Muscovite	colorless, silvery white, or brown	vitreous or pearly	white	2–2.5	1 cleavage direction
Olivine	olive green, yellow	vitreous	white or none	6.5–7	no cleavage
Orthoclase	colorless, white, pink, or other colors	vitreous	white or none	6	2 cleavage directions
Plagioclase	colorless, white, yellow, pink, green	vitreous	white	6	2 cleavage directions
Quartz	colorless or white; any color when not pure	vitreous or waxy	white or none	7	no cleavage

Nonsilicate Minerals

Mineral	Color	Luster	Streak	Hardness	Cleavage and Special Properties
Native Elements					
Copper	copper-red	metallic	copper-red	2.5–3	no cleavage
Diamond	pale yellow or colorless	adamantine	none	10	4 cleavage directions
Graphite	black to gray	submetallic	black	1–2	1 cleavage direction
Carbonates					
Aragonite	colorless, white, or pale yellow	vitreous	white	3.5–4	2 cleavage directions; reacts with hydrochloric acid
Calcite	colorless or white to tan	vitreous	white	3	3 cleavage directions; reacts with weak acid; double refraction
Halides					
Fluorite	light green, yellow, purple, bluish green, or other colors	vitreous	none	4	4 cleavage directions; some varieties fluoresce
Halite	white	vitreous	white	2.0–2.5	3 cleavage directions
Oxides					
Hematite	reddish brown to black	metallic to earthy	dark red to red-brown	5.6–6.5	no cleavage; magnetic when heated
Magnetite	iron-black	metallic	black	5.5–6.5	no cleavage; magnetic
Sulfates					
Anhydrite	colorless, bluish, or violet	vitreous to pearly	white	3–3.5	3 cleavage directions
Gypsum	white, pink, gray, or colorless	vitreous, pearly, or silky	white	2.0	3 cleavage directions
Sulfides					
Galena	lead-gray	metallic	lead-gray to black	2.5–2.8	3 cleavage directions
Pyrite	brassy yellow	metallic	greenish, brownish, or black	6–6.5	no cleavage

References

Geologic Time Scale

Geologists developed the geologic time scale to represent the 4.6 billion years of Earth's history that have passed since Earth formed. This scale divides Earth's history into blocks of time. The boundaries between these time intervals (shown in millions of years ago or mya in the table below), represent major changes in Earth's history. Some boundaries are defined by mass extinctions, major changes in Earth's surface, and/or major changes in Earth's climate.

The four major divisions that encompass the history of life on Earth are Precambrian time, the Paleozoic era, the Mesozoic era, and the Cenozoic era. The largest divisions are eons. **Precambrian time** is made up of the first three eons, over 4 billion years of Earth's history.

The **Paleozoic era** lasted from 542 mya to 251 mya. All major plant groups, except flowering plants, appeared during this era. By the end of the era, reptiles, winged insects, and fishes had also appeared. The largest known mass extinction occurred at the end of this era.

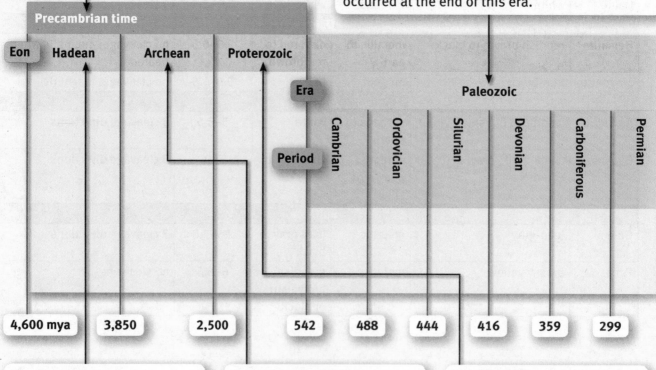

Eon	Hadean	Archean	Proterozoic						
Precambrian time									
Era					Paleozoic				
Period				Cambrian	Ordovician	Silurian	Devonian	Carboniferous	Permian

4,600 mya   3,850   2,500   542   488   444   416   359   299

The **Hadean eon** lasted from about 4.6 billion years ago (bya) to 3.85 bya. It is described based on evidence from meteorites and rocks from the moon.

The **Archean eon** lasted from 3.85 bya to 2.5 bya. The earliest rocks from Earth that have been found and dated formed at the start of this eon.

The **Proterozoic eon** lasted from 2.5 bya to 542 mya. The first organisms, which were single-celled organisms, appeared during this eon. These organisms produced so much oxygen that they changed Earth's oceans and Earth's atmosphere.

Divisions of Time

The divisions of time shown here represent major changes in Earth's surface and when life developed and changed significantly on Earth. As new evidence is found, the boundaries of these divisions may shift. The Phanerozoic eon is divided into three eras. The beginning of each of these eras represents a change in the types of organisms that dominated Earth. And, each era is commonly characterized by the types of organisms that dominated the era. These eras are divided into periods, and periods are divided into epochs.

The **Mesozoic era** lasted from 251 mya to 65.5 mya. During this era, many kinds of dinosaurs dominated land, and giant lizards swam in the ocean. The first birds, mammals, and flowering plants also appeared during this time. About two-thirds of all land species went extinct at the end of this era.

The **Phanerozoic eon** began 542 mya. We live in this eon.

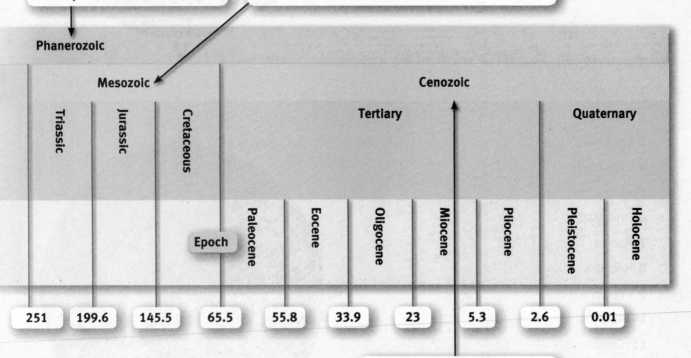

The **Cenozoic era** began 65.5 mya and continues today. Mammals dominate this era. During the Mesozoic era, mammals were small in size but grew much larger during the Cenozoic era. Primates, including humans, appeared during this era.

Phanerozoic

Mesozoic

Cenozoic

Tertiary

Quaternary

Triassic | Jurassic | Cretaceous

Paleocene | Eocene | Oligocene | Miocene | Pliocene | Pleistocene | Holocene

Epoch

| 251 | 199.6 | 145.5 | 65.5 | 55.8 | 33.9 | 23 | 5.3 | 2.6 | 0.01 |

Star Charts for the Northern Hemisphere

A star chart is a map of the stars in the night sky. It shows the names and positions of constellations and major stars. Star charts can be used to identify constellations and even to orient yourself using Polaris, the North Star.

Because Earth moves through space, different constellations are visible at different times of the year. The star charts on these pages show the constellations visible during each season in the Northern Hemisphere.

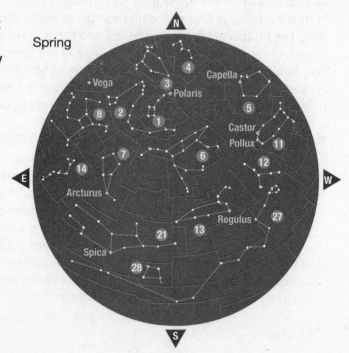

Spring

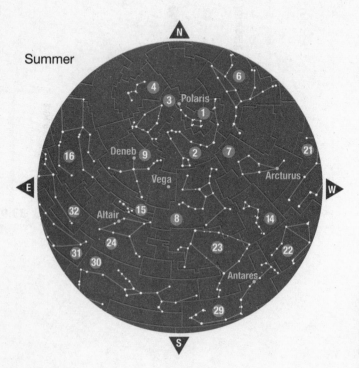

Summer

Constellations

1 Ursa Minor

2 Draco

3 Cepheus

4 Cassiopeia

5 Auriga

6 Ursa Major

7 Boötes

8 Hercules

9 Cygnus

10 Perseus

11 Gemini

12 Cancer

13 Leo

14 Serpens

15 Sagitta

16 Pegasus

17 Pisces

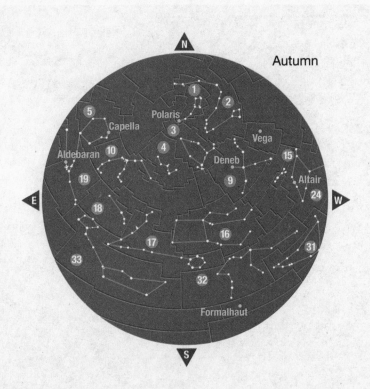

Autumn

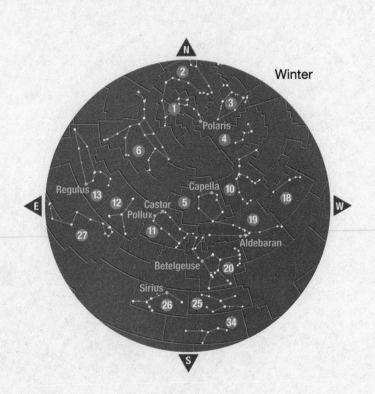

Winter

Constellations

18 Aries

19 Taurus

20 Orion

21 Virgo

22 Libra

23 Ophiuchus

24 Aquila

25 Lepus

26 Canis Major

27 Hydra

28 Corvus

29 Scorpius

30 Sagittarius

31 Capricornus

32 Aquarius

33 Cetus

34 Columba

World Map

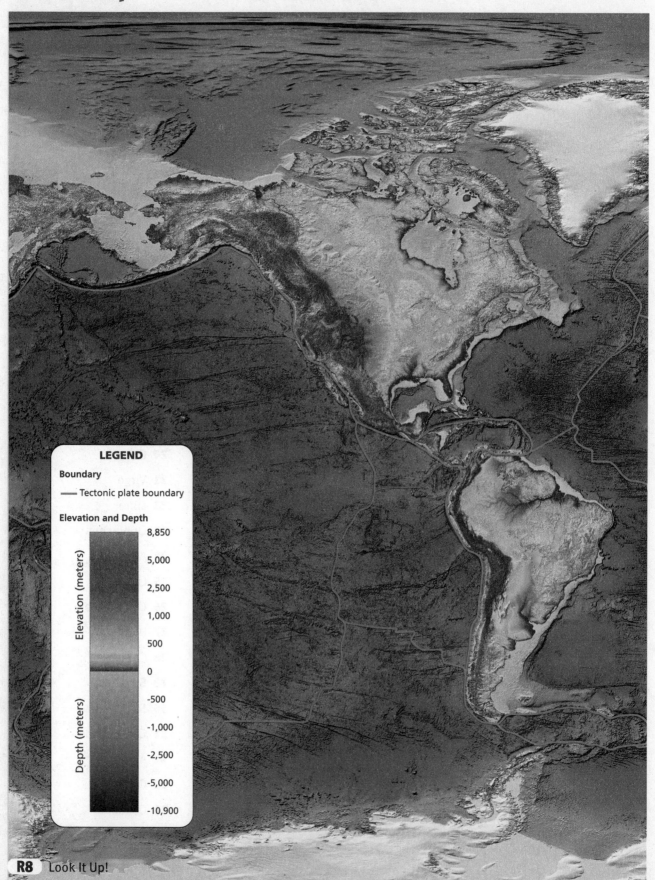

LEGEND

Boundary

—— Tectonic plate boundary

Elevation and Depth

Elevation (meters)

8,850
5,000
2,500
1,000
500
0

Depth (meters)

-500
-1,000
-2,500
-5,000
-10,900

References

Classification of Living Things

Domains and Kingdoms

All organisms belong to one of three domains: Domain Archaea, Domain Bacteria, or Domain Eukarya. Some of the groups within these domains are shown below. (Remember that genus names are italicized.)

Domain Archaea

The organisms in this domain are single-celled prokaryotes, many of which live in extreme environments.

Archaea		
Group	**Example**	**Characteristics**
Methanogens	*Methanococcus*	produce methane gas; can't live in oxygen
Thermophiles	*Sulpholobus*	require sulphur; can't live in oxygen
Halophiles	*Halococcus*	live in very salty environments; most can live in oxygen

Domain Bacteria

Organisms in this domain are single-celled prokaryotes and are found in almost every environment on Earth.

Bacteria		
Group	**Example**	**Characteristics**
Bacilli	*Escherichia*	rod shaped; some bacilli fix nitrogen; some cause disease
Cocci	*Streptococcus*	spherical shaped; some cause disease; can form spores
Spirilla	*Treponema*	spiral shaped; cause diseases such as syphilis and Lyme disease

Domain Eukarya

Organisms in this domain are single-celled or multicellular eukaryotes.

Kingdom Protista Many protists resemble fungi, plants, or animals, but are smaller and simpler in structure. Most are single celled.

Protists		
Group	**Example**	**Characteristics**
Sarcodines	*Amoeba*	radiolarians; single-celled consumers
Ciliates	*Paramecium*	single-celled consumers
Flagellates	*Trypanosoma*	single-celled parasites
Sporozoans	*Plasmodium*	single-celled parasites
Euglenas	*Euglena*	single celled; photosynthesize
Diatoms	*Pinnularia*	most are single celled; photosynthesize
Dinoflagellates	*Gymnodinium*	single celled; some photosynthesize
Algae	*Volvox*	single celled or multicellular; photosynthesize
Slime molds	*Physarum*	single celled or multicellular; consumers or decomposers
Water molds	powdery mildew	single celled or multicellular; parasites or decomposers

Kingdom Fungi Most fungi are multicellular. Their cells have thick cell walls. Fungi absorb food from their environment.

Fungi		
Group	**Examples**	**Characteristics**
Threadlike fungi	bread mold	spherical; decomposers
Sac fungi	yeast; morels	saclike; parasites and decomposers
Club fungi	mushrooms; rusts; smuts	club shaped; parasites and decomposers
Lichens	British soldier	a partnership between a fungus and an alga

Kingdom Plantae Plants are multicellular and have cell walls made of cellulose. Plants make their own food through photosynthesis. Plants are classified into divisions instead of phyla.

Plants		
Group	**Examples**	**Characteristics**
Bryophytes	mosses; liverworts	no vascular tissue; reproduce by spores
Club mosses	*Lycopodium;* ground pine	grow in wooded areas; reproduce by spores
Horsetails	rushes	grow in wetland areas; reproduce by spores
Ferns	spleenworts; sensitive fern	large leaves called fronds; reproduce by spores
Conifers	pines; spruces; firs	needlelike leaves; reproduce by seeds made in cones
Cycads	*Zamia*	slow growing; reproduce by seeds made in large cones
Gnetophytes	*Welwitschia*	only three living families; reproduce by seeds
Ginkgoes	*Ginkgo*	only one living species; reproduce by seeds
Angiosperms	all flowering plants	reproduce by seeds made in flowers; fruit

Kingdom Animalia Animals are multicellular. Their cells do not have cell walls. Most animals have specialized tissues and complex organ systems. Animals get food by eating other organisms.

Animals		
Group	**Examples**	**Characteristics**
Sponges	glass sponges	no symmetry or specialized tissues; aquatic
Cnidarians	jellyfish; coral	radial symmetry; aquatic
Flatworms	planaria; tapeworms; flukes	bilateral symmetry; organ systems
Roundworms	*Trichina;* hookworms	bilateral symmetry; organ systems
Annelids	earthworms; leeches	bilateral symmetry; organ systems
Mollusks	snails; octopuses	bilateral symmetry; organ systems
Echinoderms	sea stars; sand dollars	radial symmetry; organ systems
Arthropods	insects; spiders; lobsters	bilateral symmetry; organ systems
Chordates	fish; amphibians; reptiles; birds; mammals	bilateral symmetry; complex organ systems

References

Periodic Table of the Elements

| 13 |
| **Al** |
| Aluminum |
| 26.98 |

- Atomic number
- Chemical symbol
- Element name
- Average atomic mass

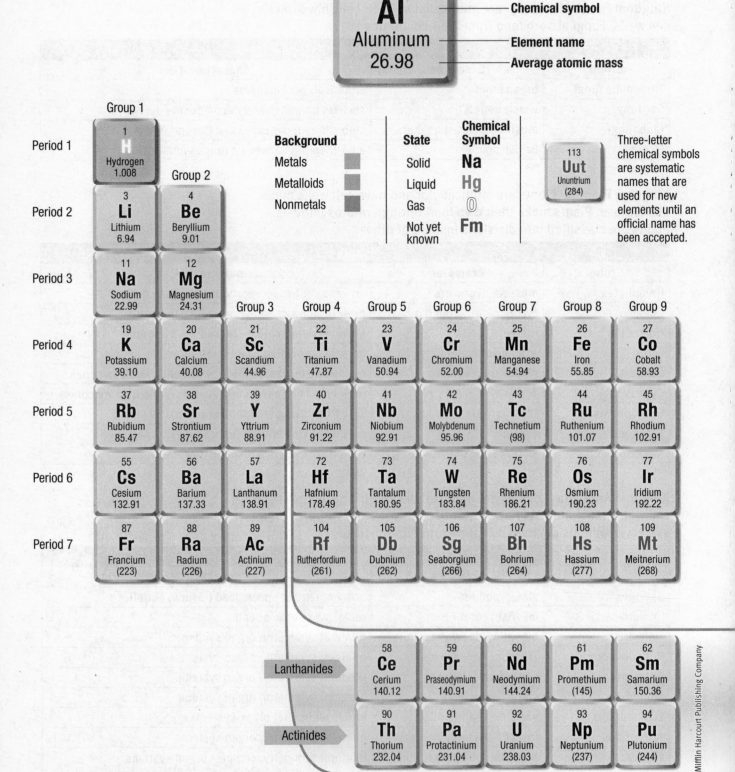

Background
- Metals
- Metalloids
- Nonmetals

State / **Chemical Symbol**
- Solid — **Na**
- Liquid — **Hg**
- Gas — ⓪
- Not yet known — **Fm**

| 113 |
| **Uut** |
| Ununtrium |
| (284) |

Three-letter chemical symbols are systematic names that are used for new elements until an official name has been accepted.

Group 1

Period 1
| 1 |
| **H** |
| Hydrogen |
| 1.008 |

Group 2

Period 2
3	4
Li	**Be**
Lithium	Beryllium
6.94	9.01

Period 3
11	12
Na	**Mg**
Sodium	Magnesium
22.99	24.31

		Group 3	Group 4	Group 5	Group 6	Group 7	Group 8	Group 9
Period 4	19 **K** Potassium 39.10	20 **Ca** Calcium 40.08	21 **Sc** Scandium 44.96	22 **Ti** Titanium 47.87	23 **V** Vanadium 50.94	24 **Cr** Chromium 52.00	25 **Mn** Manganese 54.94	26 **Fe** Iron 55.85	27 **Co** Cobalt 58.93
Period 5	37 **Rb** Rubidium 85.47	38 **Sr** Strontium 87.62	39 **Y** Yttrium 88.91	40 **Zr** Zirconium 91.22	41 **Nb** Niobium 92.91	42 **Mo** Molybdenum 95.96	43 **Tc** Technetium (98)	44 **Ru** Ruthenium 101.07	45 **Rh** Rhodium 102.91
Period 6	55 **Cs** Cesium 132.91	56 **Ba** Barium 137.33	57 **La** Lanthanum 138.91	72 **Hf** Hafnium 178.49	73 **Ta** Tantalum 180.95	74 **W** Tungsten 183.84	75 **Re** Rhenium 186.21	76 **Os** Osmium 190.23	77 **Ir** Iridium 192.22
Period 7	87 **Fr** Francium (223)	88 **Ra** Radium (226)	89 **Ac** Actinium (227)	104 **Rf** Rutherfordium (261)	105 **Db** Dubnium (262)	106 **Sg** Seaborgium (266)	107 **Bh** Bohrium (264)	108 **Hs** Hassium (277)	109 **Mt** Meitnerium (268)

Lanthanides
58	59	60	61	62
Ce	**Pr**	**Nd**	**Pm**	**Sm**
Cerium	Praseodymium	Neodymium	Promethium	Samarium
140.12	140.91	144.24	(145)	150.36

Actinides
90	91	92	93	94
Th	**Pa**	**U**	**Np**	**Pu**
Thorium	Protactinium	Uranium	Neptunium	Plutonium
232.04	231.04	238.03	(237)	(244)

The International Union of Pure and Applied Chemistry (IUPAC) has determined that, because of isotopic variance, the average atomic mass is best represented by a range of values for each of the following elements: hydrogen, lithium, boron, carbon, nitrogen, oxygen, silicon, sulfur, chlorine, and thallium. However, the values in this table are appropriate for everyday calculations.

Elements with atomic numbers of 95 and above are not known to occur naturally, even in trace amounts. They have only been synthesized in the lab. The physical and chemical properties of elements with atomic numbers 100 and above cannot be predicted with certainty. The states for elements with atomic numbers 100 and above are therefore shown as not yet known.

Group 18

2
He
Helium
4.003

Group 13	Group 14	Group 15	Group 16	Group 17
5	6	7	8	9	10
B	**C**	**N**	**O**	**F**	**Ne**
Boron	Carbon	Nitrogen	Oxygen	Fluorine	Neon
10.81	12.01	14.01	16.00	19.00	20.18
13	14	15	16	17	18
Al	**Si**	**P**	**S**	**Cl**	**Ar**
Aluminum	Silicon	Phosphorus	Sulfur	Chlorine	Argon
26.98	28.09	30.97	32.06	35.45	39.95

Group 10	Group 11	Group 12					
28	29	30	31	32	33	34	35	36
Ni	**Cu**	**Zn**	**Ga**	**Ge**	**As**	**Se**	**Br**	**Kr**
Nickel	Copper	Zinc	Gallium	Germanium	Arsenic	Selenium	Bromine	Krypton
58.69	63.55	65.38	69.72	72.63	74.92	78.96	79.90	83.80
46	47	48	49	50	51	52	53	54
Pd	**Ag**	**Cd**	**In**	**Sn**	**Sb**	**Te**	**I**	**Xe**
Palladium	Silver	Cadmium	Indium	Tin	Antimony	Tellurium	Iodine	Xenon
106.42	107.87	112.41	114.82	118.71	121.76	127.60	126.90	131.29
78	79	80	81	82	83	84	85	86
Pt	**Au**	**Hg**	**Tl**	**Pb**	**Bi**	**Po**	**At**	**Rn**
Platinum	Gold	Mercury	Thallium	Lead	Bismuth	Polonium	Astatine	Radon
195.08	196.97	200.59	204.38	207.2	208.98	(209)	(210)	(222)
110	111	112	113	114	115	116	117	118
Ds	**Rg**	**Cn**	**Uut**	**Fl**	**Uup**	**Lv**	**Uus**	**Uuo**
Darmstadtium	Roentgenium	Copernicium	Ununtrium	Flerovium	Ununpentium	Livermorium	Ununseptium	Ununoctium
(271)	(272)	(285)	(284)	(289)	(288)	(293)	(294)	(294)

63	64	65	66	67	68	69	70	71
Eu	**Gd**	**Tb**	**Dy**	**Ho**	**Er**	**Tm**	**Yb**	**Lu**
Europium	Gadolinium	Terbium	Dysprosium	Holmium	Erbium	Thulium	Ytterbium	Lutetium
151.96	157.25	158.93	162.50	164.93	167.26	168.93	173.05	174.97
95	96	97	98	99	100	101	102	103
Am	**Cm**	**Bk**	**Cf**	**Es**	**Fm**	**Md**	**No**	**Lr**
Americium	Curium	Berkelium	Californium	Einsteinium	Fermium	Mendelevium	Nobelium	Lawrencium
(243)	(247)	(247)	(251)	(252)	(257)	(258)	(259)	(262)

© Houghton Mifflin Harcourt Publishing Company

References

Physical Science Refresher

Atoms and Elements

Every object in the universe is made of matter. **Matter** is anything that takes up space and has mass. All matter is made of atoms. An **atom** is the smallest particle into which an element can be divided and still be the same element. An **element**, in turn, is a substance that cannot be broken down into simpler substances by chemical means. Each element consists of only one kind of atom. An element may be made of many atoms, but they are all the same kind of atom.

Atomic Structure

Atoms are made of smaller particles called **electrons, protons,** and **neutrons.** Electrons have a negative electric charge, protons have a positive charge, and neutrons have no electric charge. Together, protons and neutrons form the **nucleus,** or small dense center, of an atom. Because protons are positively charged and neutrons are neutral, the nucleus has a positive charge. Electrons move within an area around the nucleus called the **electron cloud.** Electrons move so quickly that scientists cannot determine their exact speeds and positions at the same time.

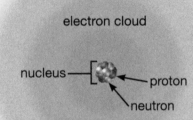

electron cloud

nucleus — proton

neutron

Atomic Number

To help distinguish one element from another, scientists use the atomic numbers of atoms. The **atomic number** is the number of protons in the nucleus of an atom. The atoms of a certain element always have the same number of protons.

When atoms have an equal number of protons and electrons, they are uncharged, or electrically neutral. The atomic number equals the number of electrons in an uncharged atom. The number of neutrons, however, can vary for a given element. Atoms of the same element that have different numbers of neutrons are called **isotopes**.

Periodic Table of the Elements

In the periodic table, each element in the table is in a separate box. And the elements are arranged from left to right in order of increasing atomic number. That is, an uncharged atom of each element has one more electron and one more proton than an uncharged atom of the element to its left. Each horizontal row of the table is called a **period.** Changes in chemical properties of elements across a period correspond to changes in the electron arrangements of their atoms.

Each vertical column of the table is known as a **group.** A group lists elements with similar physical and chemical properties. For this reason, a group is also sometimes called a family. The elements in a group have similar properties because their atoms have the same number of electrons in their outer energy level. For example, the elements helium, neon, argon, krypton, xenon, and radon all have similar properties and are known as the noble gases.

Molecules and Compounds

When two or more elements join chemically, they form a **compound**. A compound is a new substance with properties different from those of the elements that compose it. For example, water, H_2O, is a compound formed when hydrogen (H) and oxygen (O) combine. The smallest complete unit of a compound that has the properties of that compound is called a **molecule**. A chemical formula indicates the elements in a compound. It also indicates the relative number of atoms of each element in the compound. The chemical formula for water is H_2O. So, each water molecule consists of two atoms of hydrogen and one atom of oxygen. The subscript number after the symbol for an element shows how many atoms of that element are in a single molecule of the compound.

Chemical Equations

A chemical reaction occurs when a chemical change takes place. A chemical equation describes a chemical reaction using chemical formulas. The equation indicates the substances that react and the substances that are produced. For example, when carbon and oxygen combine, they can form carbon dioxide, shown in the equation below: $C + O_2 \longrightarrow CO_2$

Acids, Bases, and pH

An **ion** is an atom or group of chemically bonded atoms that has an electric charge because it has lost or gained one or more electrons. When an acid, such as hydrochloric acid, HCl, is mixed with water, it separates into ions. An **acid** is a compound that produces hydrogen ions, H^+, in water. The hydrogen ions then combine with a water molecule to form a hydronium ion, H_3O^+. A **base**, on the other hand, is a substance that produces hydroxide ions, OH^-, in water.

To determine whether a solution is acidic or basic, scientists use pH. The **pH** of a solution is a measure of the hydronium ion concentration in a solution. The pH scale ranges from 0 to 14. Acids have a pH that is less than 7. The lower the number, the more acidic the solution. The middle point, pH = 7, is neutral, neither acidic nor basic. Bases have a pH that is greater than 7. The higher the number is, the more basic the solution.

The pH of Some Common Materials

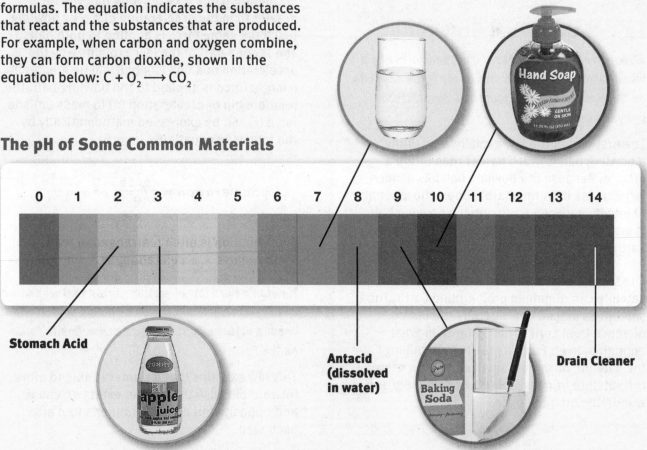

Stomach Acid

Antacid (dissolved in water)

Baking Soda

Hand Soap

Drain Cleaner

apple juice

References

Physical Laws and Useful Equations

Law of Conservation of Mass

Mass cannot be created or destroyed during ordinary chemical or physical changes.

The total mass in a closed system is always the same no matter how many physical changes or chemical reactions occur.

Law of Conservation of Energy

Energy can be neither created nor destroyed.

The total amount of energy in a closed system is always the same. Energy can be changed from one form to another, but all of the different forms of energy in a system always add up to the same total amount of energy, no matter how many energy conversions occur. `

Law of Universal Gravitation

All objects in the universe attract each other by a force called gravity. The size of the force depends on the masses of the objects and the distance between the objects.

The first part of the law explains why lifting a bowling ball is much harder than lifting a marble. Because the bowling ball has a much larger mass than the marble does, the amount of gravity between Earth and the bowling ball is greater than the amount of gravity between Earth and the marble.

The second part of the law explains why a satellite can remain in orbit around Earth. The satellite is placed at a carefully calculated distance from Earth. This distance is great enough to keep Earth's gravity from pulling the satellite down, yet small enough to keep the satellite from escaping Earth's gravity and wandering off into space.

Newton's Laws of Motion

Newton's first law of motion states that an object at rest remains at rest, and an object in motion remains in motion at constant speed and in a straight line unless acted on by an unbalanced force.

The first part of the law explains why a football will remain on a tee until it is kicked off or until a gust of wind blows it off. The second part of the law explains why a bike rider will continue moving forward after the bike comes to an abrupt stop. Gravity and the friction of the sidewalk will eventually stop the rider.

Newton's second law of motion states that the acceleration of an object depends on the mass of the object and the amount of force applied.

The first part of the law explains why the acceleration of a 4 kg bowling ball will be greater than the acceleration of a 6 kg bowling ball if the same force is applied to both balls. The second part of the law explains why the acceleration of a bowling ball will be greater if a larger force is applied to the bowling ball. The relationship of acceleration (a) to mass (m) and force (F) can be expressed mathematically by the following equation:

$$acceleration = \frac{force}{mass}, \text{ or } a = \frac{F}{m}$$

This equation is often rearranged to read *force = mass × acceleration, or F = m × a*

Newton's third law of motion states that whenever one object exerts a force on a second object, the second object exerts an equal and opposite force on the first.

This law explains that a runner is able to move forward because the ground exerts an equal and opposite force on the runner's foot after each step.

Average speed

$$average\ speed = \frac{total\ distance}{total\ time}$$

Example:
A bicycle messenger traveled a distance of 136 km in 8 h. What was the messenger's average speed?

$$\frac{136\ km}{8\ h} = 17\ km/h$$

The messenger's average speed was **17 km/h**.

Average acceleration

$$average\ acceleration = \frac{final\ velocity - starting\ velocity}{time\ it\ takes\ to\ change\ velocity}$$

Example:
Calculate the average acceleration of an Olympic 100 m dash sprinter who reached a velocity of 20 m/s south at the finish line. The race was in a straight line and lasted 10 s.

$$\frac{20\ m/s - 0\ m/s}{10\ s} = 2\ m/s/s$$

The sprinter's average acceleration was **2 m/s/s south**.

Net force
Forces in the Same Direction

When forces are in the same direction, add the forces together to determine the net force.

Example:
Calculate the net force on a stalled car that is being pushed by two people. One person is pushing with a force of 13 N northwest, and the other person is pushing with a force of 8 N in the same direction.

$$13\ N + 8\ N = 21\ N$$

The net force is **21 N northwest**.

Forces in Opposite Directions

When forces are in opposite directions, subtract the smaller force from the larger force to determine the net force. The net force will be in the direction of the larger force.

Example:
Calculate the net force on a rope that is being pulled on each end. One person is pulling on one end of the rope with a force of 12 N south. Another person is pulling on the opposite end of the rope with a force of 7 N north.

$$12\ N - 7\ N = 5\ N$$

The net force is **5 N south**.

Pressure

Pressure is the force exerted over a given area. The SI unit for pressure is the pascal. Its symbol is Pa.

$$pressure = \frac{force}{area}$$

Example:
Calculate the pressure of the air in a soccer ball if the air exerts a force of 10 N over an area of 0.5 m².

$$pressure = \frac{10N}{0.5\ m^2} = \frac{20N}{m^2} = 20\ Pa$$

The pressure of the air inside the soccer ball is **20 Pa**.

Reading and Study Skills

A How-To Manual for Active Reading

This book belongs to you, and you are invited to write in it. In fact, the book won't be complete until you do. Sometimes you'll answer a question or follow directions to mark up the text. Other times you'll write down your own thoughts. And when you're done reading and writing in the book, the book will be ready to help you review what you learned and prepare for tests.

Active Reading Annotations

Before you read, you'll often come upon an Active Reading prompt that asks you to underline certain words or number the steps in a process. Here's an example.

Active Reading

12 Identify In this paragraph, number the sequence of sentences that describe replication.

Marking the text this way is called **annotating,** and your marks are called **annotations.** Annotating the text can help you identify important concepts while you read.

There are other ways that you can annotate the text. You can draw an asterisk (*) by vocabulary terms, mark unfamiliar or confusing terms and information with a question mark (?), and mark main ideas with a <u>double underline</u>. And you can even invent your own marks to annotate the text!

Other Annotating Opportunities

Keep your pencil, pen, or highlighter nearby as you read, so you can make a note or highlight an important point at any time. Here are a few ideas to get you started.

- Notice the headings in red and blue. The blue headings are questions that point to the main idea of what you're reading. The red headings are answers to the questions in the blue ones. Together these headings outline the content of the lesson. After reading a lesson, you could write your own answers to the questions.

- Notice the bold-faced words that are highlighted in yellow. They are highlighted so that you can easily find them again on the page where they are defined. As you read or as you review, challenge yourself to write your own sentence using the bold-faced term.

- Make a note in the margin at any time. You might
  - Ask a "What if" question
  - Comment on what you read
  - Make a connection to something you read elsewhere
  - Make a logical conclusion from the text

Use your own language and abbreviations. Invent a code, such as using circles and boxes around words to remind you of their importance or relation to each other. Your annotations will help you remember your questions for class discussions, and when you go back to the lesson later, you may be able to fill in what you didn't understand the first time you read it. Like a scientist in the field or in a lab, you will be recording your questions and observations for analysis later.

Active Reading Questions

After you read, you'll often come upon Active Reading questions that ask you to think about what you've just read. You'll write your answer underneath the question. Here's an example.

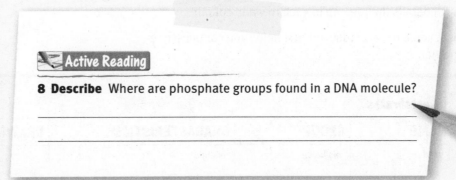

Active Reading

8 Describe Where are phosphate groups found in a DNA molecule?

_____

_____

This type of question helps you sum up what you've just read and pull out the most important ideas from the passage. In this case the question asks you to **describe** the structure of a DNA molecule that you have just read about. Other times you may be asked to do such things as **apply** a concept, **compare** two concepts, **summarize** a process, or **identify a cause-and-effect** relationship. You'll be strengthening those critical thinking skills that you'll use often in learning about science.

Reading and Study Skills

Using Graphic Organizers to Take Notes

Graphic organizers help you remember information as you read it for the first time and as you study it later. There are dozens of graphic organizers to choose from, so the first trick is to choose the one that's best suited to your purpose. Following are some graphic organizers to use for different purposes.

To remember lots of information	To relate a central idea to subordinate details	To describe a process	To make a comparison
• Arrange data in a Content Frame • Use Combination Notes to describe a concept in words and pictures	• Show relationships with a Mind Map or a Main Idea Web • Sum up relationships among many things with a Concept Map	• Use a Process Diagram to explain a procedure • Show a chain of events and results in a Cause-and-Effect Chart	• Compare two or more closely related things in a Venn Diagram

Content Frame

1 Make a four-column chart.

2 Fill the first column with categories (e.g., snail, ant, earthworm) and the first row with descriptive information (e.g., group, characteristic, appearance).

3 Fill the chart with details that belong in each row and column.

4 When you finish, you'll have a study aid that helps you compare one category to another.

Invertebrates

NAME	GROUP	CHARACTERISTICS	DRAWING
snail	mollusks	mangle	
ant	arthropods	six legs, exoskeleton	
earthworm	segmented worms	segmented body, circulatory and digestive systems	
heartworm	roundworms	digestive system	
sea star	echinoderms	spiny skin, tube feet	
jellyfish	cnidarians	stinging cells	

Combination Notes

1 Make a two-column chart.

2 Write descriptive words and definitions in the first column.

3 Draw a simple sketch that helps you remember the meaning of the term in the second column.

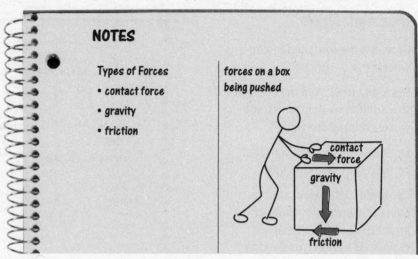

Mind Map

1 Draw an oval, and inside it write a topic to analyze.

2 Draw two or more arms extending from the oval. Each arm represents a main idea about the topic.

3 Draw lines from the arms on which to write details about each of the main ideas.

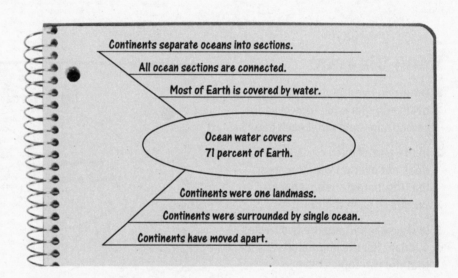

Main Idea Web

1 Make a box and write a concept you want to remember inside it.

2 Draw boxes around the central box, and label each one with a category of information about the concept (e.g., definition, formula, descriptive details).

3 Fill in the boxes with relevant details as you read.

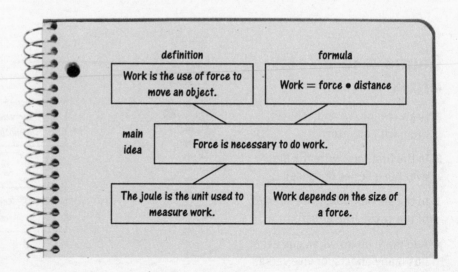

Reading and Study Skills

Concept Map

1 Draw a large oval, and inside it write a major concept.

2 Draw an arrow from the concept to a smaller oval, in which you write a related concept.

3 On the arrow, write a verb that connects the two concepts.

4 Continue in this way, adding ovals and arrows in a branching structure, until you have explained as much as you can about the main concept.

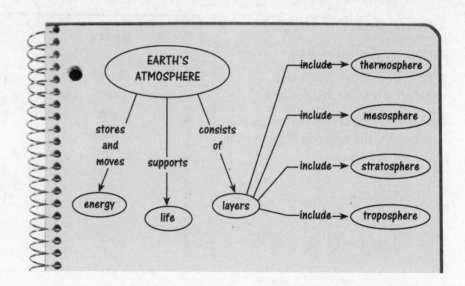

Venn Diagram

1 Draw two overlapping circles or ovals—one for each topic you are comparing—and label each one.

2 In the part of each circle that does not overlap with the other, list the characteristics that are unique to each topic.

3 In the space where the two circles overlap, list the characteristics that the two topics have in common.

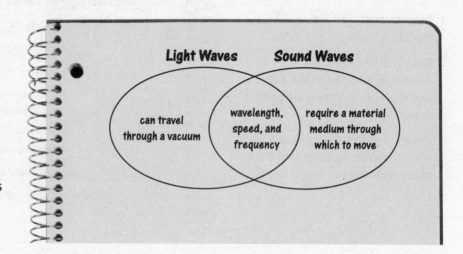

Cause-and-Effect Chart

1 Draw two boxes and connect them with an arrow.

2 In the first box, write the first event in a series (a cause).

3 In the second box, write a result of the cause (the effect).

4 Add more boxes when one event has many effects, or vice versa.

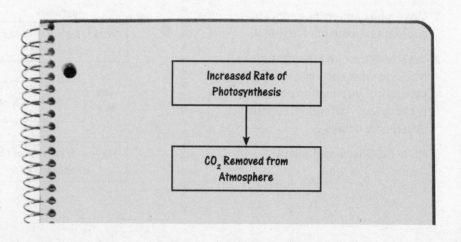

Process Diagram

A process can be a never-ending cycle. As you can see in this technology design process, engineers may backtrack and repeat steps, they may skip steps entirely, or they may repeat the entire process before a useable design is achieved.

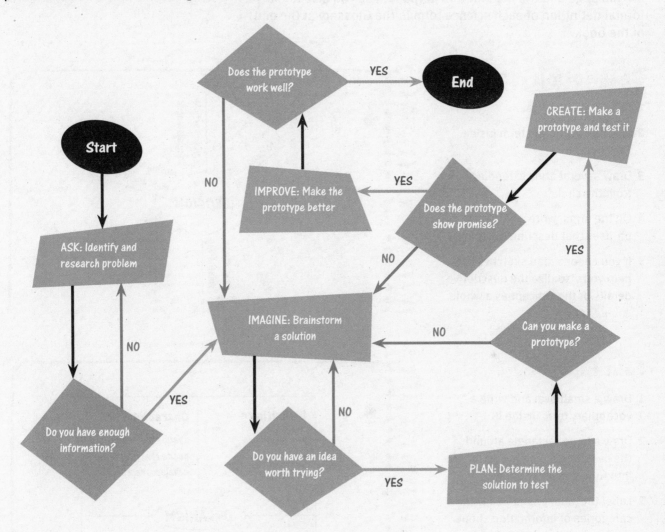

Reading and Study Skills

Using Vocabulary Strategies

Important science terms are highlighted where they are first defined in this book. One way to remember these terms is to take notes and make sketches when you come to them. Use the strategies on this page and the next for this purpose. You will also find a formal definition of each science term in the Glossary at the end of the book.

Description Wheel

1 Draw a small circle.

2 Write a vocabulary term inside the circle.

3 Draw several arms extending from the circle.

4 On the arms, write words and phrases that describe the term.

5 If you choose, add sketches that help you visualize the descriptive details or the concept as a whole.

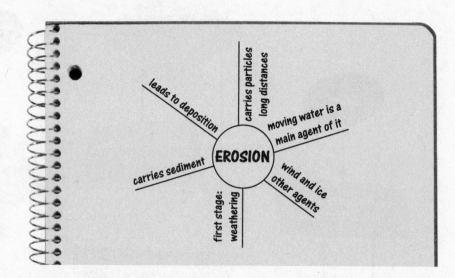

Four Square

1 Draw a small oval and write a vocabulary term inside it.

2 Draw a large rectangle around the oval, and divide the rectangle into four smaller squares.

3 Label the smaller squares with categories of information about the term, such as: definition, characteristics, examples, non-examples, appearance, and root words.

4 Fill the squares with descriptive words and drawings that will help you remember the overall meaning of the term and its essential details.

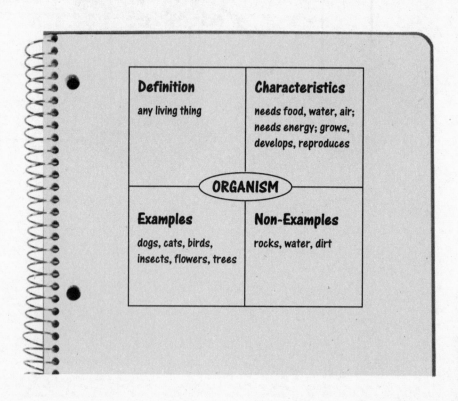

Frame Game

1 Draw a small rectangle, and write a vocabulary term inside it.

2 Draw a larger rectangle around the smaller one. Connect the corners of the larger rectangle to the corners of the smaller one, creating four spaces that frame the word.

3 In each of the four parts of the frame, draw or write details that help define the term. Consider including a definition, essential characteristics, an equation, examples, and a sentence using the term.

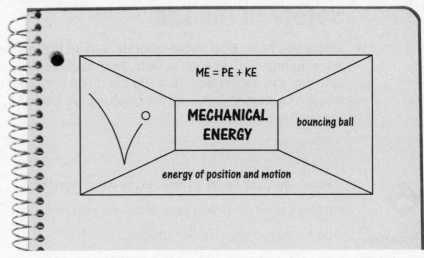

Magnet Word

1 Draw horseshoe magnet, and write a vocabulary term inside it.

2 Add lines that extend from the sides of the magnet.

3 Brainstorm words and phrases that come to mind when you think about the term.

4 On the lines, write the words and phrases that describe something essential about the term.

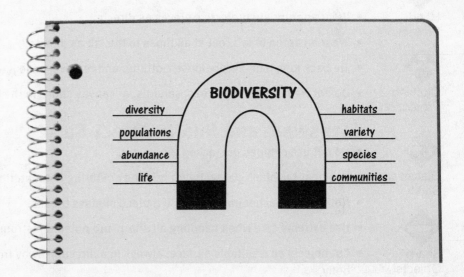

Word Triangle

1 Draw a triangle, and add lines to divide it into three parts.

2 Write a term and its definition in the bottom section of the triangle.

3 In the middle section, write a sentence in which the term is used correctly.

4 In the top section, draw a small picture to illustrate the term.

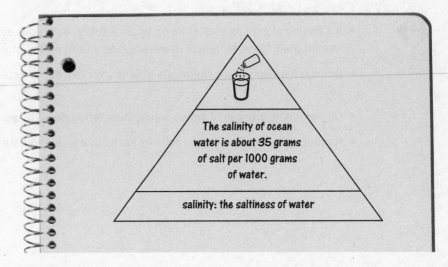

Science Skills

Safety in the Lab

Before you begin work in the laboratory, read these safety rules twice. Before starting a lab activity, read all directions and make sure that you understand them. Do not begin until your teacher has told you to start. If you or another student are injured in any way, tell your teacher immediately.

Dress Code

Eye
Protection

Hand
Protection

Clothing
Protection

- Wear safety goggles at all times in the lab as directed.
- If chemicals get into your eyes, flush your eyes immediately.
- Do not wear contact lenses in the lab.
- Do not look directly at the sun or any intense light source or laser.
- Do not cut an object while holding the object in your hand.
- Wear appropriate protective gloves as directed.
- Wear an apron or lab coat at all times in the lab as directed.
- Tie back long hair, secure loose clothing, and remove loose jewelry.
- Do not wear open-toed shoes, sandals, or canvas shoes in the lab.

Glassware and Sharp Object Safety

Glassware
Safety

Sharp
Objects
Safety

- Do not use chipped or cracked glassware.
- Use heat-resistant glassware for heating or storing hot materials.
- Notify your teacher immediately if a piece of glass breaks.
- Use extreme care when handling all sharp and pointed instruments.
- Cut objects on a suitable surface, always in a direction away from your body.

Chemical Safety

Chemical
Safety

- If a chemical gets on your skin, on your clothing, or in your eyes, rinse it immediately (shower, faucet or eyewash fountain) and alert your teacher.
- Do not clean up spilled chemicals unless your teacher directs you to do so.
- Do not inhale any gas or vapor unless directed to do so by your teacher.
- Handle materials that emit vapors or gases in a well-ventilated area.

Electrical Safety

Electrical Safety

- Do not use equipment with frayed electrical cords or loose plugs.
- Do not use electrical equipment near water or when clothing or hands are wet.
- Hold the plug housing when you plug in or unplug equipment.

Heating and Fire Safety

Heating Safety

- Be aware of any source of flames, sparks, or heat (such as flames, heating coils, or hot plates) before working with any flammable substances.
- Know the location of lab fire extinguishers and fire-safety blankets.
- Know your school's fire-evacuation routes.
- If your clothing catches on fire, walk to the lab shower to put out the fire.
- Never leave a hot plate unattended while it is turned on or while it is cooling.
- Use tongs or appropriate insulated holders when handling heated objects.
- Allow all equipment to cool before storing it.

Wafting

Plant and Animal Safety

Plant Safety

Animal Safety

- Do not eat any part of a plant.
- Do not pick any wild plants unless your teacher instructs you to do so.
- Handle animals only as your teacher directs.
- Treat animals carefully and respectfully.
- Wash your hands thoroughly after handling any plant or animal.

Cleanup

Proper Waste Disposal

Hygienic Care

- Clean all work surfaces and protective equipment as directed by your teacher.
- Dispose of hazardous materials or sharp objects only as directed by your teacher.
- Keep your hands away from your face while you are working on any activity.
- Wash your hands thoroughly before you leave the lab or after any activity.

Science Skills

Designing, Conducting, and Reporting an Experiment

An experiment is an organized procedure to study something under specific conditions. Use the following steps of the scientific method when designing or conducting a controlled experiment.

1 Identify a Research Problem

Every day, you make observations by using your senses to gather information. Careful observations lead to good questions, and good questions can lead you to an experiment. Imagine, for example, that you pass a pond every day on your way to school, and you notice green scum beginning to form on top of it. You wonder what it is and why it seems to be growing. You list your questions, and then you do a little research to find out what is already known. A good place to start a research project is at the library. A library catalog lists all of the resources available to you at that library and often those found elsewhere. Begin your search by using:

- keywords or main topics.

- similar words, or synonyms, of your keyword.

The types of resources that will be helpful to you will depend on the kind of information you are interested in. And, some resources are more reliable for a given topic than others. Some different kinds of useful resources are:

- magazines and journals (or periodicals)—articles on a topic.

- encyclopedias—a good overview of a topic.

- books on specific subjects—details about a topic.

- newspapers—useful for current events.

The Internet can also be a great place to find information. Some of your library's reference materials may even be online. When using the Internet, however, it is especially important to make sure you are using appropriate and reliable sources. Websites of universities and government agencies are usually more accurate and reliable than websites created by individuals or businesses. Decide which sources are relevant and reliable for your topic. If in doubt, check with your teacher.

Take notes as you read through the information in these resources. You will probably come up with many questions and ideas for which you can do more research as needed. Once you feel you have enough information, think about the questions you have on the topic. Then, write down the problem that you want to investigate. Your notes might look like these.

© Houghton Mifflin Harcourt Publishing Company

Research Questions	Research Problem	Library and Internet Resources
• How do algae grow? • How do people measure algae? • What kind of fertilizer would affect the growth of algae? • Can fertilizer and algae be used safely in a lab? How?	How does fertilizer affect the algae in a pond?	Pond fertilization: initiating an algal bloom – from University of California Davis website. Blue-Green algae in Wisconsin waters-from the Department of Natural Resources of Wisconsin website.

As you gather information from reliable sources, record details about each source, including author name(s), title, date of publication, and/or web address. Make sure to also note the specific information that you use from each source. Staying organized in this way will be important when you write your report and create a bibliography or works cited list. Recording this information and staying organized will help you credit the appropriate author(s) for the information that you have gathered.

Representing someone else's ideas or work as your own, (without giving the original author credit), is known as plagiarism. Plagiarism can be intentional or unintentional. The best way to make sure that you do not commit plagiarism is to always do your own work and to always give credit to others when you use their words or ideas.

Current scientific research is built on scientific research and discoveries that have happened in the past. This means that scientists are constantly learning from each other and combining ideas to learn more about the natural world through investigation. But, a good scientist always credits the ideas and research that they have gathered from other people to those people. There are more details about crediting sources and creating a bibliography under step 9.

2 Make a Prediction

A prediction is a statement of what you expect will happen in your experiment. Before making a prediction, you need to decide in a general way what you will do in your procedure. You may state your prediction in an if-then format.

Prediction

If the amount of fertilizer in the pond water is increased, then the amount of algae will also increase.

Science Skills

3 Form a Hypothesis

Many experiments are designed to test a hypothesis. A hypothesis is a tentative explanation for an expected result. You have predicted that additional fertilizer will cause additional algae growth in pond water; your hypothesis should state the connection between fertilizer and algal growth.

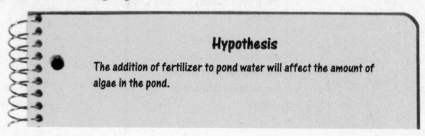

Hypothesis

The addition of fertilizer to pond water will affect the amount of algae in the pond.

4 Identify Variables to Test the Hypothesis

The next step is to design an experiment to test the hypothesis. The experimental results may or may not support the hypothesis. Either way, the information that results from the experiment may be useful for future investigations.

Experimental Group and Control Group

An experiment to determine how two factors are related has a control group and an experimental group. The two groups are the same, except that the investigator changes a single factor in the experimental group and does not change it in the control group.

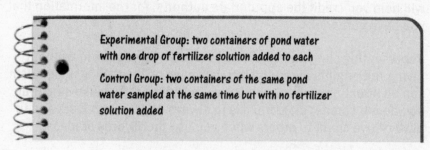

Experimental Group: two containers of pond water with one drop of fertilizer solution added to each

Control Group: two containers of the same pond water sampled at the same time but with no fertilizer solution added

Variables and Constants

In a controlled experiment, a variable is any factor that can change. Constants are all of the variables that are kept the same in both the experimental group and the control group.

The independent variable is the factor that is manipulated or changed in order to test the effect of the change on another variable. The dependent variable is the factor the investigator measures to gather data about the effect.

Independent Variable	Dependent Variable	Constants
Amount of fertilizer in pond water	Growth of algae in the pond water	• Where and when the pond water is obtained • The type of container used • Light and temperature conditions where the water is stored

5 Write a Procedure

Write each step of your procedure. Start each step with a verb, or action word, and keep the steps short. Your procedure should be clear enough for someone else to use as instructions for repeating your experiment.

Procedure

1. Use the masking tape and the marker to label the containers with your initials, the date, and the identifiers "Jar 1 with Fertilizer," "Jar 2 with Fertilizer," "Jar 1 without Fertilizer," and "Jar 2 without Fertilizer."

2. Put on your gloves. Use the large container to obtain a sample of pond water.

3. Divide the water sample equally among the four smaller containers.

4. Use the eyedropper to add one drop of fertilizer solution to the two containers labeled, "Jar 1 with Fertilizer," and "Jar 2 with Fertilizer".

5. Cover the containers with clear plastic wrap. Use the scissors to punch ten holes in each of the covers.

6. Place all four containers on a window ledge. Make sure that they all receive the same amount of light.

7. Observe the containers every day for one week.

8. Use the ruler to measure the diameter of the largest clump of algae in each container, and record your measurements daily.

Science Skills

6 Experiment and Collect Data

Once you have all of your materials and your procedure has been approved, you can begin to experiment and collect data. Record both quantitative data (measurements) and qualitative data (observations), as shown below.

Algal Growth and Fertilizer

Date and Time	Experimental Group		Control Group		Observations
	Jar 1 with Fertilizer (diameter of algal clump in mm)	Jar 2 with Fertilizer (diameter of algal clump in mm)	Jar 1 without Fertilizer (diameter of algal clump in mm)	Jar 2 without Fertilizer (diameter of algal clump in mm)	
5/3 4:00 p.m.	0	0	0	0	condensation in all containers
5/4 4:00 p.m.	0	3	0	0	tiny green blobs in Jar 2 with fertilizer
5/5 4:15 p.m.	4	5	0	3	green blobs in Jars 1 and 2 with fertilizer and Jar 2 without fertilizer
5/6 4:00 p.m.	5	6	0	4	water light green in Jar 2 with fertilizer
5/7 4:00 p.m.	8	10	0	6	water light green in Jars 1 and 2 with fertilizer and Jar 2 without fertilizer
5/8 3:30 p.m.	10	18	0	6	cover off of Jar 2 with fertilizer
5/9 3:30 p.m.	14	23	0	8	drew sketches of each container

Drawings of Samples Viewed Under Microscope on 5/9 at 100x

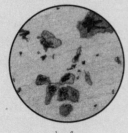

Jar 1 with Fertilizer

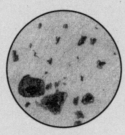

Jar 2 with Fertilizer

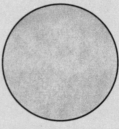

Jar 1 without Fertilizer

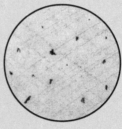

Jar 2 without Fertilizer

7 Analyze Data

After you complete your experiment, you must analyze all of the data you have gathered. Tables, statistics, and graphs are often used in this step to organize and analyze both the qualitative and quantitative data. Sometimes, your qualitative data are best used to help explain the relationships you see in your quantitative data.

Computer graphing software is useful for creating a graph from data that you have collected. Most graphing software can make line graphs, pie charts, or bar graphs from data that has been organized in a spreadsheet. Graphs are useful for understanding relationships in the data and for communicating the results of your experiment.

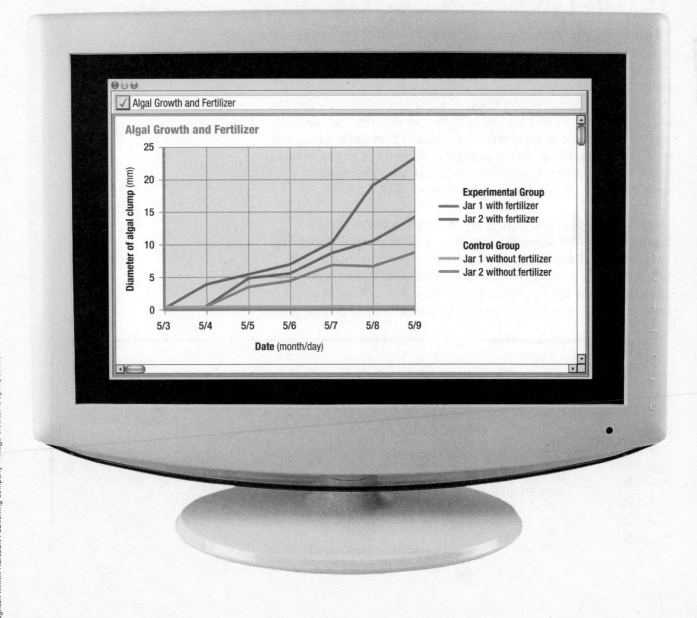

8 Make Conclusions

To draw conclusions from your experiment, first, write your results. Then, compare your results with your hypothesis. Do your results support your hypothesis? What have you learned?

Conclusion

More algae grew in the pond water to which fertilizer had been added than in the pond water to which fertilizer had not been added. My hypothesis was supported. I conclude that it is possible that the growth of algae in ponds can be influenced by the input of fertilizer.

9 Create a Bibliography or Works Cited List

To complete your report, you must also show all of the newspapers, magazines, journals, books, and online sources that you used at every stage of your investigation. Whenever you find useful information about your topic, you should write down the source of that information. Writing down as much information as you can about the subject can help you or someone else find the source again. You should at least record the author's name, the title, the date and where the source was published, and the pages in which the information was found. Then, organize your sources into a list, which you can title Bibliography or Works Cited.

Usually, at least three sources are included in these lists. Sources are listed alphabetically, by the authors' last names. The exact format of a bibliography can vary, depending on the style preferences of your teacher, school, or publisher. Also, books are cited differently than journals or websites. Below is an example of how different kinds of sources may be formatted in a bibliography.

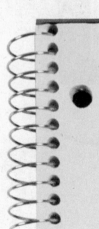

BOOK: Hauschultz, Sara. Freshwater Algae. Brainard, Minnesota: Northwoods Publishing, 2011.

ENCYCLOPEDIA: Lasure, Sedona. "Algae is not all just pond scum." Encyclopedia of Algae. 2009.

JOURNAL: Johnson, Keagan. "Algae as we know it." Sci Journal, vol 64. (September 2010): 201-211.

WEBSITE: Dout, Bill. "Keeping algae scum out of birdbaths." Help Keep Earth Clean. News. January 26, 2011. <www.SaveEarth.org>.

Using a Microscope

Scientists use microscopes to see very small objects that cannot easily be seen with the eye alone. A microscope magnifies the image of an object so that small details may be observed. A microscope that you may use can magnify an object 400 times—the object will appear 400 times larger than its actual size.

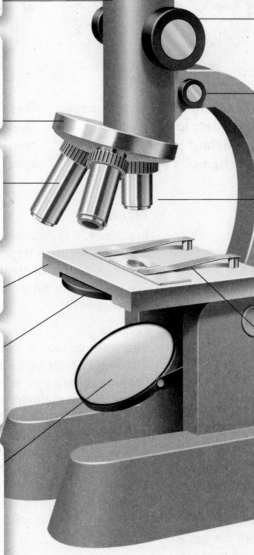

Eyepiece Objects are viewed through the eyepiece. The eyepiece contains a lens that commonly magnifies an image ten times.

Coarse Adjustment This knob is used to focus the image of an object when it is viewed through the low-power lens.

Fine Adjustment This knob is used to focus the image of an object when it is viewed through the high-power lens.

Low-Power Objective Lens This is the smallest lens on the nosepiece. It magnifies images about 10 times.

Arm The arm supports the body above the stage. Always carry a microscope by the arm and base.

Stage Clip The stage clip holds a slide in place on the stage.

Base The base supports the microscope.

Body The body separates the lens in the eyepiece from the objective lenses below.

Nosepiece The nosepiece holds the objective lenses above the stage and rotates so that all lenses may be used.

High-Power Objective Lens This is the largest lens on the nosepiece. It magnifies an image approximately 40 times.

Stage The stage supports the object being viewed.

Diaphragm The diaphragm is used to adjust the amount of light passing through the slide and into an objective lens.

Mirror or Light Source Some microscopes use light that is reflected through the stage by a mirror. Other microscopes have their own light sources.

Science Skills

Measuring Accurately

Precision and Accuracy

When you do a scientific investigation, it is important that your methods, observations, and data be both precise and accurate.

Low precision: The darts did not land in a consistent place on the dartboard.

Precision, but not accuracy: The darts landed in a consistent place, but did not hit the bull's eye.

Prescision and accuracy: The darts landed consistently on the bull's eye.

Precision

In science, *precision* is the exactness and consistency of measurements. For example, measurements made with a ruler that has both centimeter and millimeter markings would be more precise than measurements made with a ruler that has only centimeter markings. Another indicator of precision is the care taken to make sure that methods and observations are as exact and consistent as possible. Every time a particular experiment is done, the same procedure should be used. Precision is necessary because experiments are repeated several times and if the procedure changes, the results might change.

Example

Suppose you are measuring temperatures over a two-week period. Your precision will be greater if you measure each temperature at the same place, at the same time of day, and with the same thermometer than if you change any of these factors from one day to the next.

Accuracy

In science, it is possible to be precise but not accurate. *Accuracy* depends on the difference between a measurement and an actual value. The smaller the difference, the more accurate the measurement.

Example

Suppose you look at a stream and estimate that it is about 1 meter wide at a particular place. You decide to check your estimate by measuring the stream with a meter stick, and you determine that the stream is 1.32 meters wide. However, because it is difficult to measure the width of a stream with a meter stick, it turns out that your measurement was not very accurate. The stream is actually 1.14 meters wide. Therefore, even though your estimate of about 1 meter was less precise than your measurement, your estimate was actually more accurate.

Graduated Cylinders

How to Measure the Volume of a Liquid with a Graduated Cylinder

- Be sure that the graduated cylinder is on a flat surface so that your measurement will be accurate.

- When reading the scale on a graduated cylinder, be sure to have your eyes at the level of the surface of the liquid.

- The surface of the liquid will be curved in the graduated cylinder. Read the volume of the liquid at the bottom of the curve, or meniscus (muh-NIHS-kuhs).

- You can use a graduated cylinder to find the volume of a solid object by measuring the increase in a liquid's level after you add the object to the cylinder.

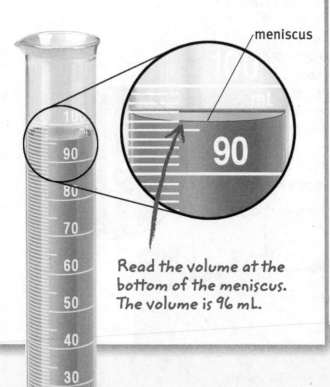

meniscus

Read the volume at the bottom of the meniscus. The volume is 96 mL.

Metric Rulers

How to Measure the Length of a Leaf with a Metric Ruler

1 Lay a ruler flat on top of the leaf so that the 1-centimeter mark lines up with one end. Make sure the ruler and the leaf do not move between the time you line them up and the time you take the measurement.

2 Look straight down on the ruler so that you can see exactly how the marks line up with the other end of the leaf.

3 Estimate the length by which the leaf extends beyond a marking. For example, the leaf below extends about halfway between the 4.2-centimeter and 4.3-centimeter marks, so the apparent measurement is about 4.25 centimeters.

4 Remember to subtract 1 centimeter from your apparent measurement, since you started at the 1-centimeter mark on the ruler and not at the end. The leaf is about 3.25 centimeters long (4.25 cm − 1 cm = 3.25 cm).

Science Skills

Triple Beam Balance

This balance has a pan and three beams with sliding masses, called riders. At one end of the beams is a pointer that indicates whether the mass on the pan is equal to the masses shown on the beams.

How to Measure the Mass of an Object

1 Make sure the balance is zeroed before measuring the mass of an object. The balance is zeroed if the pointer is at zero when nothing is on the pan and the riders are at their zero points. Use the adjustment knob at the base of the balance to zero it.

2 Place the object to be measured on the pan.

3 Move the riders one notch at a time away from the pan. Begin with the largest rider. If moving the largest rider one notch brings the pointer below zero, begin measuring the mass of the object with the next smaller rider.

4 Change the positions of the riders until they balance the mass on the pan and the pointer is at zero. Then add the readings from the three beams to determine the mass of the object.

300 g	position of largest rider
90 g	position of middle rider
+ 3 g	position of smallest rider
393 g	mass of beaker and water

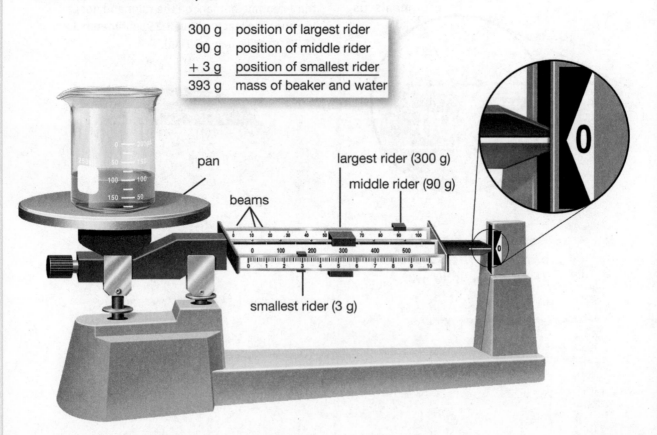

pan

beams

largest rider (300 g)

middle rider (90 g)

smallest rider (3 g)

Using the Metric System and SI Units

Scientists use International System (SI) units for measurements of distance, volume, mass, and temperature. The International System is based on powers of ten and the metric system of measurement.

Basic SI Units		
Quantity	Name	Symbol
length	meter	m
volume	liter	L
mass	gram	g
temperature	kelvin	K

SI Prefixes		
Prefix	Symbol	Power of 10
kilo-	k	1000
hecto-	h	100
deca-	da	10
deci-	d	0.1 or $\frac{1}{10}$
centi-	c	0.01 or $\frac{1}{100}$
milli-	m	0.001 or $\frac{1}{1000}$

Changing Metric Units

You can change from one unit to another in the metric system by multiplying or dividing by a power of 10.

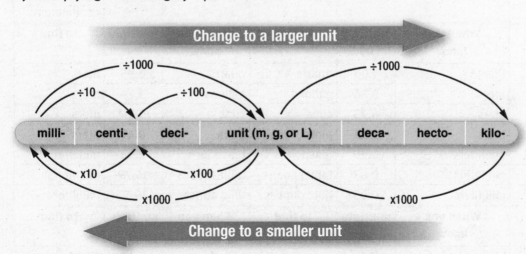

Example

Change 0.64 liters to milliliters.
1 Decide whether to multiply or divide.
2 Select the power of 10.

Change to a smaller unit by multiplying

mL ◄─── x 1000 ─── L

0.64 x 1000 = 640.

ANSWER 0.64 L = 640 mL

Example

Change 23.6 grams to kilograms.
1 Decide whether to multiply or divide.
2 Select the power of 10.

Change to a larger unit by dividing

g ─── ÷ 1000 ──► kg

26.3 ÷ 1000 = 0.0263

ANSWER 23.6 g = 0.0236 kg

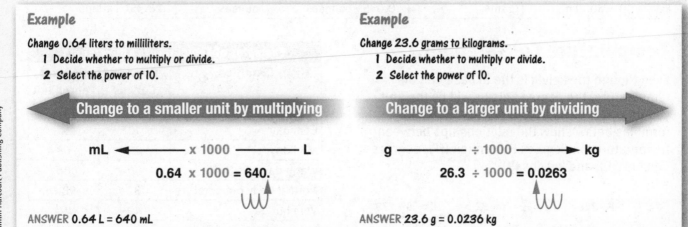

Science Skills

Converting Between SI and U.S. Customary Units

Use the chart below when you need to convert between SI units and U.S. customary units.

SI Unit	From SI to U.S. Customary			From U.S. Customary to SI		
Length	**When you know**	**multiply by**	**to find**	**When you know**	**multiply by**	**to find**
kilometer (km) = 1000 m	kilometers	0.62	miles	miles	1.61	kilometers
meter (m) = 100 cm	meters	3.28	feet	feet	0.3048	meters
centimeter (cm) = 10 mm	centimeters	0.39	inches	inches	2.54	centimeters
millimeter (mm) = 0.1 cm	millimeters	0.04	inches	inches	25.4	millimeters
Area	**When you know**	**multiply by**	**to find**	**When you know**	**multiply by**	**to find**
square kilometer (km²)	square kilometers	0.39	square miles	square miles	2.59	square kilometers
square meter (m²)	square meters	1.2	square yards	square yards	0.84	square meters
square centimeter (cm²)	square centimeters	0.155	square inches	square inches	6.45	square centimeters
Volume	**When you know**	**multiply by**	**to find**	**When you know**	**multiply by**	**to find**
liter (L) = 1000 mL	liters	1.06	quarts	quarts	0.95	liters
	liters	0.26	gallons	gallons	3.79	liters
	liters	4.23	cups	cups	0.24	liters
	liters	2.12	pints	pints	0.47	liters
milliliter (mL) = 0.001 L	milliliters	0.20	teaspoons	teaspoons	4.93	milliliters
	milliliters	0.07	tablespoons	tablespoons	14.79	milliliters
	milliliters	0.03	fluid ounces	fluid ounces	29.57	milliliters
Mass	**When you know**	**multiply by**	**to find**	**When you know**	**multiply by**	**to find**
kilogram (kg) = 1000 g	kilograms	2.2	pounds	pounds	0.45	kilograms
gram (g) = 1000 mg	grams	0.035	ounces	ounces	28.35	grams

Temperature Conversions

Even though the kelvin is the SI base unit of temperature, the degree Celsius will be the unit you use most often in your science studies. The formulas below show the relationships between temperatures in degrees Fahrenheit (°F), degrees Celsius (°C), and kelvins (K).

$$°C = \frac{5}{9} \ (°F - 32) \qquad °F = \frac{9}{5} \ °C + 32 \qquad K = °C + 273$$

Examples of Temperature Conversions		
Condition	**Degrees Celsius**	**Degrees Fahrenheit**
Freezing point of water	32	0
Cool day	10	50
Mild day	20	68
Warm day	30	86
Normal body temperature	37	98.6
Very hot day	40	104
Boiling point of water	100	212

Math Refresher

Performing Calculations

Science requires an understanding of many math concepts. The following pages will help you review some important math skills.

Mean

The mean is the sum of all values in a data set divided by the total number of values in the data set. The mean is also called the *average*.

Example

Find the mean of the following set of numbers: 5, 4, 7, and 8.

Step 1 Find the sum.

$5 + 4 + 7 + 8 = 24$

Step 2 Divide the sum by the number of numbers in your set. Because there are four numbers in this example, divide the sum by 4.

$24 \div 4 = 6$

Answer The average, or mean, is 6.

Median

The median of a data set is the middle value when the values are written in numerical order. If a data set has an even number of values, the median is the mean of the two middle values.

Example

To find the median of a set of measurements, arrange the values in order from least to greatest. The median is the middle value.

13 mm   14 mm   16 mm   21 mm   23 mm

Answer The median is 16 mm.

Mode

The mode of a data set is the value that occurs most often.

Example

To find the mode of a set of measurements, arrange the values in order from least to greatest and determine the value that occurs most often.

13 mm, 14 mm, 14 mm, 16 mm,
21 mm, 23 mm, 25 mm

Answer The mode is 14 mm.

A data set can have more than one mode or no mode. For example, the following data set has modes of 2 mm and 4 mm:

2 mm   2 mm   3 mm   4 mm   4 mm

The data set below has no mode, because no value occurs more often than any other.

2 mm   3 mm   4 mm   5 mm

Math Refresher

Ratios

A **ratio** is a comparison between numbers, and it is usually written as a fraction.

Example

Find the ratio of thermometers to students if you have 36 thermometers and 48 students in your class.

Step 1 Write the ratio.

$$\frac{36 \text{ thermometers}}{48 \text{ students}}$$

Step 2 Simplify the fraction to its simplest form.

$$\frac{36}{48} = \frac{36 \div 12}{48 \div 12} = \frac{3}{4}$$

The ratio of thermometers to students is 3 to 4 or 3:4.

Proportions

A **proportion** is an equation that states that two ratios are equal.

$$\frac{3}{1} = \frac{12}{4}$$

To solve a proportion, you can use cross-multiplication. If you know three of the quantities in a proportion, you can use cross-multiplication to find the fourth.

Example

Imagine that you are making a scale model of the solar system for your science project. The diameter of Jupiter is 11.2 times the diameter of the Earth. If you are using a plastic-foam ball that has a diameter of 2 cm to represent the Earth, what must the diameter of the ball representing Jupiter be?

$$\frac{11.2}{1} = \frac{x}{2 \text{ cm}}$$

Step 1 Cross-multiply.

$$\frac{11.2}{1} = \frac{x}{2}$$

$$11.2 \times 2 = x \times 1$$

Step 2 Multiply.

$$22.4 = x \times 1$$

$$x = 22.4 \text{ cm}$$

You will need to use a ball that has a diameter of 22.4 cm to represent Jupiter.

Rates

A **rate** is a ratio of two values expressed in different units. A unit rate is a rate with a denominator of 1 unit.

Example

A plant grew 6 centimeters in 2 days. The plant's rate of growth was $\frac{6 \text{ cm}}{2 \text{ days}}$.

To describe the plant's growth in centimeters per day, write a unit rate.

Divide numerator and denominator by 2:

$$\frac{6 \text{ cm}}{2 \text{ days}} = \frac{6 \text{ cm} \div 2}{2 \text{ days} \div 2}$$

Simplify:

$$= \frac{3 \text{ cm}}{1 \text{ day}}$$

Answer The plant's rate of growth is 3 centimeters per day.

Percent

A **percent** is a ratio of a given number to 100. For example, $85\% = 85/100$. You can use percent to find part of a whole.

Example
What is 85% of 40?

Step 1   Rewrite the percent as a decimal by moving the decimal point two places to the left.

$$0.85$$

Step 2   Multiply the decimal by the number that you are calculating the percentage of.

$$0.85 \times 40 = 34$$

85% of 40 is 34.

Decimals

To **add** or **subtract decimals**, line up the digits vertically so that the decimal points line up. Then, add or subtract the columns from right to left. Carry or borrow numbers as necessary.

Example
Add the following numbers: 3.1415 and 2.96.

Step 1   Line up the digits vertically so that the decimal points line up.

$$\begin{array}{r} 3.1415 \\ + 2.96 \\ \hline \end{array}$$

Step 2   Add the columns from right to left, and carry when necessary.

$$\begin{array}{r} 3.1415 \\ + 2.96 \\ \hline 6.1015 \end{array}$$

The sum is 6.1015.

Fractions

A **fraction** is a ratio of two nonzero whole numbers.

Example
Your class has 24 plants. Your teacher instructs you to put 5 plants in a shady spot. What fraction of the plants in your class will you put in a shady spot?

Step 1   In the denominator, write the total number of parts in the whole.

$$\frac{?}{24}$$

Step 2   In the numerator, write the number of parts of the whole that are being considered.

$$\frac{5}{24}$$

So, $\frac{5}{24}$ of the plants will be in the shade.

Math Refresher

Simplifying Fractions

It is usually best to express a fraction in its simplest form. Expressing a fraction in its simplest form is called **simplifying a fraction**.

Example

Simplify the fraction $\frac{30}{45}$ to its simplest form.

Step 1   Find the largest whole number that will divide evenly into both the numerator and denominator. This number is called the greatest common factor (GCF).

Factors of the numerator 30:
1, 2, 3, 5, 6, 10, 15, 30

Factors of the denominator 45:
1, 3, 5, 9, 15, 45

Step 2   Divide both the numerator and the denominator by the GCF, which in this case is 15.

$$\frac{30}{45} = \frac{30 \div 15}{45 \div 15} = \frac{2}{3}$$

Thus, $\frac{30}{45}$ written in its simplest form is $\frac{2}{3}$.

Adding and Subtracting Fractions

To **add** or **subtract fractions** that have the same denominator, simply add or subtract the numerators.

Examples

$\frac{3}{5} + \frac{1}{5} = ?$ and $\frac{3}{4} - \frac{1}{4} = ?$

Step 1   Add or subtract the numerators.
$$\frac{3}{5} + \frac{1}{5} = \frac{4}{} \text{ and } \frac{3}{4} - \frac{1}{4} = \frac{2}{}$$

Step 2   Write in the common denominator, which remains the same.
$$\frac{3}{5} + \frac{1}{5} = \frac{4}{5} \text{ and } \frac{3}{4} - \frac{1}{4} = \frac{2}{4}$$

Step 3   If necessary, write the fraction in its simplest form.
$$\frac{4}{5} \text{ cannot be simplified, and } \frac{2}{4} = \frac{1}{2}.$$

To **add** or **subtract** fractions that have **different denominators**, first find the least common denominator (LCD).

Examples

$\frac{1}{2} + \frac{1}{6} = ?$ and $\frac{3}{4} - \frac{2}{3} = ?$

Step 1   Write the equivalent fractions that have a common denominator.
$$\frac{3}{6} + \frac{1}{6} = ? \text{ and } \frac{9}{12} - \frac{8}{12} = ?$$

Step 2   Add or subtract the fractions.
$$\frac{3}{6} + \frac{1}{6} = \frac{4}{6} \text{ and } \frac{9}{12} - \frac{8}{12} = \frac{1}{12}$$

Step 3   If necessary, write the fraction in its simplest form.
$$\frac{4}{6} = \frac{2}{3}, \text{ and } \frac{1}{12} \text{ cannot be simplifed.}$$

Multiplying Fractions

To **multiply fractions**, multiply the numerators and the denominators together, and then simplify the fraction to its simplest form.

Example

$\frac{5}{9} \times \frac{7}{10} = ?$

Step 1   Multiply the numerators and denominators.
$$\frac{5}{9} \times \frac{7}{10} = \frac{5 \times 7}{9 \times 10} = \frac{35}{90}$$

Step 2   Simplify the fraction.
$$\frac{35}{90} = \frac{35 \div 5}{90 \div 5} = \frac{7}{18}$$

Dividing Fractions

To **divide fractions,** first rewrite the divisor (the number you divide by) upside down. This number is called the reciprocal of the divisor. Then multiply and simplify if necessary.

Example

$\frac{5}{8} \div \frac{3}{2} = ?$

Step 1   Rewrite the divisor as its reciprocal.

$$\frac{3}{2} \rightarrow \frac{2}{3}$$

Step 2   Multiply the fractions.

$$\frac{5}{8} \times \frac{2}{3} = \frac{5 \times 2}{8 \times 3} = \frac{10}{24}$$

Step 3   Simplify the fraction.

$$\frac{10}{24} = \frac{10 \div 2}{24 \div 2} = \frac{5}{12}$$

Using Significant Figures

The **significant figures** in a decimal are the digits that are warranted by the accuracy of a measuring device.

When you perform a calculation with measurements, the number of significant figures to include in the result depends in part on the number of significant figures in the measurements. When you multiply or divide measurements, your answer should have only as many significant figures as the measurement with the fewest significant figures.

Examples

Using a balance and a graduated cylinder filled with water, you determined that a marble has a mass of 8.0 grams and a volume of 3.5 cubic centimeters. To calculate the density of the marble, divide the mass by the volume.

Write the formula for density: $\text{Density} = \frac{mass}{volume}$

Substitute measurements: $= \frac{8.0 \text{ g}}{3.5 \text{ cm}^3}$

Use a calculator to divide: $\approx 2.285714286 \text{ g/cm}^3$

Answer Because the mass and the volume have two significant figures each, give the density to two significant figures. The marble has a density of 2.3 grams per cubic centimeter.

Using Scientific Notation

Scientific notation is a shorthand way to write very large or very small numbers. For example, 73,500,000,000,000,000,000,000 kg is the mass of the moon. In scientific notation, it is 7.35×10^{22} kg. A value written as a number between 1 and 10, times a power of 10, is in scientific notation.

Examples

You can convert from standard form to scientific notation.

Standard Form	Scientific Notation
720,000	7.2×10^5
5 decimal places left	Exponent is 5.
0.000291	2.91×10^{-4}
4 decimal places right	Exponent is −4.

You can convert from scientific notation to standard form.

Scientific Notation	Standard Form
4.63×10^7	46,300,000
Exponent is 7.	7 decimal places right
1.08×10^{-6}	0.00000108
Exponent is −6.	6 decimal places left

Math Refresher

Making and Interpreting Graphs

Circle Graph

A circle graph, or pie chart, shows how each group of data relates to all of the data. Each part of the circle represents a category of the data. The entire circle represents all of the data. For example, a biologist studying a hardwood forest in Wisconsin found that there were five different types of trees. The data table at right summarizes the biologist's findings.

Wisconsin Hardwood Trees	
Type of tree	**Number found**
Oak	600
Maple	750
Beech	300
Birch	1,200
Hickory	150
Total	3,000

How to Make a Circle Graph

1 To make a circle graph of these data, first find the percentage of each type of tree. Divide the number of trees of each type by the total number of trees, and multiply by 100%.

$$\frac{600 \text{ oak}}{3,000 \text{ trees}} \times 100\% = 20\%$$

$$\frac{750 \text{ maple}}{3,000 \text{ trees}} \times 100\% = 25\%$$

$$\frac{300 \text{ beech}}{3,000 \text{ trees}} \times 100\% = 10\%$$

$$\frac{1,200 \text{ birch}}{3,000 \text{ trees}} \times 100\% = 40\%$$

$$\frac{150 \text{ hickory}}{3,000 \text{ trees}} \times 100\% = 5\%$$

2 Now, determine the size of the wedges that make up the graph. Multiply each percentage by 360°. Remember that a circle contains 360°.

$20\% \times 360° = 72°$ $25\% \times 360° = 90°$

$10\% \times 360° = 36°$ $40\% \times 360° = 144°$

$5\% \times 360° = 18°$

3 Check that the sum of the percentages is 100 and the sum of the degrees is 360.

$20\% + 25\% + 10\% + 40\% + 5\% = 100\%$

$72° + 90° + 36° + 144° + 18° = 360°$

4 Use a compass to draw a circle and mark the center of the circle.

5 Then, use a protractor to draw angles of 72°, 90°, 36°, 144°, and 18° in the circle.

6 Finally, label each part of the graph, and choose an appropriate title.

A Community of Wisconsin Hardwood Trees

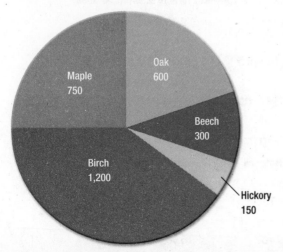

Line Graphs

Line graphs are most often used to demonstrate continuous change. For example, Mr. Smith's students analyzed the population records for their hometown, Appleton, between 1910 and 2010. Examine the data at right.

Because the year and the population change, they are the variables. The population is determined by, or dependent on, the year. Therefore, the population is called the **dependent variable,** and the year is called the **independent variable**. Each year and its population make a **data pair**. To prepare a line graph, you must first organize data pairs into a table like the one at right.

Population of Appleton, 1910–2010	
Year	Population
1910	1,800
1930	2,500
1950	3,200
1970	3,900
1990	4,600
2010	5,300

How to Make a Line Graph

1 Place the independent variable along the horizontal (*x*) axis. Place the dependent variable along the vertical (*y*) axis.

2 Label the *x*-axis "Year" and the *y*-axis "Population." Look at your greatest and least values for the population. For the *y*-axis, determine a scale that will provide enough space to show these values. You must use the same scale for the entire length of the axis. Next, find an appropriate scale for the *x*-axis.

3 Choose reasonable starting points for each axis.

4 Plot the data pairs as accurately as possible.

5 Choose a title that accurately represents the data.

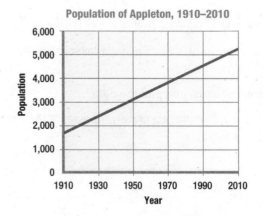

Population of Appleton, 1910–2010

How to Determine Slope

Slope is the ratio of the change in the *y*-value to the change in the *x*-value, or "rise over run."

1 Choose two points on the line graph. For example, the population of Appleton in 2010 was 5,300 people. Therefore, you can define point A as (2010, 5,300). In 1910, the population was 1,800 people. You can define point B as (1910, 1,800).

2 Find the change in the *y*-value.
(*y* at point A) − (*y* at point B) =
5,300 people − 1,800 people =
3,500 people

3 Find the change in the *x*-value.
(*x* at point A) − (*x* at point B) =
2010 − 1910 = 100 years

4 Calculate the slope of the graph by dividing the change in *y* by the change in *x*.

$$slope = \frac{change\ in\ y}{change\ in\ x}$$

$$slope = \frac{3{,}500\ people}{100\ years}$$

$$slope = 35\ people\ per\ year$$

In this example, the population in Appleton increased by a fixed amount each year. The graph of these data is a straight line. Therefore, the relationship is **linear**. When the graph of a set of data is not a straight line, the relationship is **nonlinear**.

Math Refresher

Bar Graphs

Bar graphs can be used to demonstrate change that is not continuous. These graphs can be used to indicate trends when the data cover a long period of time. A meteorologist gathered the precipitation data shown here for Summerville for April 1–15 and used a bar graph to represent the data.

Precipitation in Summerville, April 1–15			
Date	**Precipitation (cm)**	**Date**	**Precipitation (cm)**
April 1	0.5	April 9	0.25
April 2	1.25	April 10	0.0
April 3	0.0	April 11	1.0
April 4	0.0	April 12	0.0
April 5	0.0	April 13	0.25
April 6	0.0	April 14	0.0
April 7	0.0	April 15	6.50
April 8	1.75		

How to Make a Bar Graph

1 Use an appropriate scale and a reasonable starting point for each axis.

2 Label the axes, and plot the data.

3 Choose a title that accurately represents the data.

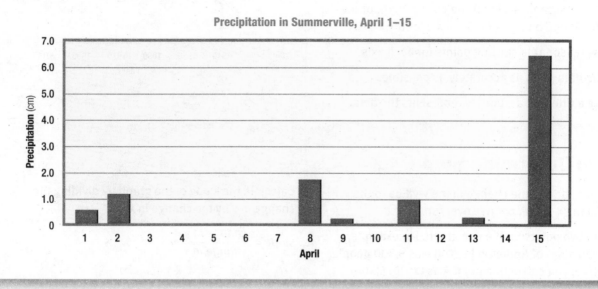

Precipitation in Summerville, April 1–15

Glossary

			Pronunciation Key				
Sound	**Symbol**	**Example**	**Respelling**	**Sound**	**Symbol**	**Example**	**Respelling**
ă	a	pat	PAT	ŏ	ah	bottle	BAHT'l
ā	ay	pay	PAY	ō	oh	toe	TOH
âr	air	care	KAIR	ô	aw	caught	KAWT
ä	ah	father	FAH•ther	ôr	ohr	roar	ROHR
är	ar	argue	AR•gyoo	oi	oy	noisy	NOYZ•ee
ch	ch	chase	CHAYS	o͝o	u	book	BUK
ĕ	e	pet	PET	o͞o	oo	boot	BOOT
ĕ (at end of a syllable)	eh	settee lessee	seh•TEE leh•SEE	ou	ow	pound	POWND
ĕr	ehr	merry	MEHR•ee	s	s	center	SEN•ter
ē	ee	beach	BEECH	sh	sh	cache	CASH
g	g	gas	GAS	ŭ	uh	flood	FLUHD
ĭ	i	pit	PIT	ûr	er	bird	BERD
ĭ (at end of a syllable)	ih	guitar	gih•TAR	z	z	xylophone	ZY•luh•fohn
ī	y eye (only for a complete syllable)	pie island	PY EYE•luhnd	z	z	bags	BAGZ
				zh	zh	decision	dih•SIZH•uhn
				ə	uh	around broken focus	uh•ROWND BROH•kuhn FOH•kuhs
îr	ir	hear	HIR	ər	er	winner	WIN•er
j	j	germ	JERM	th	th	thin they	THIN THAY
k	k	kick	KIK				
ng	ng	thing	THING	w	w	one	WUHN
ngk	ngk	bank	BANGK	wh	hw	whether	HWETH•er

adhesion (ad·HEE·zhuhn) the attractive force between two bodies of different substances that are in contact with each other (10)
  adhesión la fuerza de atracción entre dos cuerpos de diferentes sustancias que están en contacto

air mass (AIR MAS) a large body of air throughout which temperature and moisture content are similar (184)
  masa de aire un gran volumen de aire, cuya temperatura y cuyo contenido de humedad son similares en toda su extensión

air pressure (AIR PRESH·er) the measure of the force with which air molecules push on a surface (107, 160)
  presión del aire la medida de la fuerza con la que las moléculas del aire empujan contra una superficie

aquifer (AH·kwuh·fer) a body of rock or sediment that stores groundwater and allows the flow of groundwater (36)
  acuífero un cuerpo rocoso o sedimento que almacena agua subterránea y permite que fluya

atmosphere (AT·muh·sfir) a mixture of gases that surrounds a planet, moon, or other celestial body (106)
  atmósfera una mezcla de gases que rodea un planeta, una luna, u otras cuerpos celestes

channel (CHAN·uhl) the path that a stream follows (34)
  canal el camino que sigue un arroyo

cirrus cloud (SIR·uhs KLOWD) a feathery cloud that is composed of ice crystals and that has the highest altitude of any cloud in the sky (169)
  nube cirro una nube liviana formada por cristales de hielo, la cual tiene la mayor altitud de todas las nubes en el cielo

climate (KLY·mit) the weather conditions in an area over a long period of time (226)
  clima las condiciones del tiempo en un área durante un largo período de tiempo

cloud (KLOWD) a collection of small water droplets or ice crystals suspended in the air, which forms when the air is cooled and condensation occurs (166)
  nube un conjunto de pequeñas gotitas de agua o cristales de hielo suspendidos en el aire, que se forma cuando el aire se enfría y ocurre condensación

cohesion (koh·HEE·zhuhn) the force that holds molecules of a single material together (10)
  cohesión la fuerza que mantiene unidas a las moléculas de un solo material

condensation (kahn·den·SAY·shuhn) the change of state from a gas to a liquid (19)
  condensación el cambio de estado de gas a líquido

conduction (kuhn·DUHK·shuhn) the transfer of energy as heat through a material (124)
  conducción la transferencia de energía en forma de calor a través de un material

continental margin (kahn·tuh·NEN·tl MAR·jin) the shallow sea floor that is located between the shoreline and the deep-ocean bottom (59)
  margen continental el suelo marino poco profundo que se ubica entre la costa y el fondo profundo del océano

convection (kuhn·VEK·shuhn) the movement of matter due to differences in density; the transfer of energy due to the movement of matter (122)
  convección el movimiento de la materia debido a diferencias en la densidad; la transferencia de energía debido al movimiento de la materia

convection current (kuhn·VEK·shuhn KER·uhnt) any movement of matter that results from differences in density; may be vertical, circular, or cyclical (87)
  corriente de convección cualquier movimiento de la materia que se produce como resultado de diferencias en la densidad; puede ser vertical, circular o cíclico

Coriolis effect (kohr·ee·OH·lis ih·FEKT) the curving of the path of a moving object from an otherwise straight path due to Earth's rotation (83, 135)
  efecto de Coriolis la desviación de la trayectoria recta que experimentan los objetos en movimiento debido a la rotación de la Tierra

crest (KREST) the highest point of a wave (68)
  cresta el punto más alto de una onda

cumulus cloud (KYOOM·yuh·luhs KLOWD) a low-level, billowy cloud that commonly has a top that resembles cotton balls and a dark bottom (169)
  nube cúmulo una nube esponjada ubicada en un nivel bajo, cuya parte superior normalmente parece una bola de algodón y es obscura en la parte inferior

deep current (DEEP KER·uhnt) a streamlike movement of ocean water far below the surface (86)
  corriente profunda un movimiento del agua del océano que es similar a una corriente y ocurre debajo de la superficie

deep-ocean basin (DEEP·oh·shuhn BAY·sin) the ocean floor under the deep-ocean water (59)
  cuenca oceánica profunda el fondo del océano, que se encuentra bajo aguas profundas

dew point (DOO POYNT) at constant pressure and water vapor content, the temperature at which the rate of condensation equals the rate of evaporation (157, 167)
  punto de rocío a presión y contenido de vapor de agua constantes, la temperatura a la que la tasa de condensación es igual a la tasa de evaporación

divide (dih·VYD) the boundary between drainage areas that have streams that flow in opposite directions (35)
  división el límite entre áreas de drenaje que tienen corrientes que fluyen en direcciones opuestas

elevation (el·uh·VAY·shuhn) the height of an object above sea level (230)
  elevación la altura de un objeto sobre el nivel del mar

evaporation (ee vap uh RAY shuhn) the change of state from a liquid to a gas that usually occurs at the surface of a liquid over a wide range of temperatures (18)
  evaporación el cambio de estado de líquido a gaseoso que ocurre generalmente en la superficie de un líquido en un amplio rango de temperaturas

fog (FAWG) a cloud that forms near the ground and results in a reduction in visibility (172)
  niebla una nube que se forma cerca del suelo y causa una reducción de la visibilidad

front (FRUHNT) the boundary between air masses of different densities and usually different temperatures (184)
  frente el límite entre masas de aire de diferentes densidades y, normalmente, diferentes temperaturas

G

global warming (GLOH·buhl WOHR·ming) a gradual increase in average global temperature (246)
  calentamiento global un aumento gradual de la temperatura global promedio

global wind (GLOH·buhl WIND) the movement of air over Earth's surface in patterns that are worldwide (136)
  viento global el movimiento del aire sobre la superficie terrestre según patrones globales

greenhouse effect (GREEN·hows ih·FEKT) the warming of the surface and lower atmosphere of Earth that occurs when water vapor, carbon dioxide, and other gases absorb and reradiate thermal energy (110, 244)
  efecto invernadero el calentamiento de la superficie y de la parte más baja de la atmósfera, el cual se produce cuando el vapor de agua, el dióxido de carbono y otros gases absorben y vuelven a irradiar la energía térmica

groundwater (GROWND·waw·ter) the water that is beneath Earth's surface (32)
  agua subterránea el agua que está debajo de la superficie de la Tierra

heat (HEET) the energy transferred between objects that are at different temperatures (118)
  calor la transferencia de energía entre objetos que están a temperaturas diferentes

humidity (hyoo·MID·ih·tee) the amount of water vapor in the air (157)
  humedad la cantidad de vapor de agua que hay en el aire

hurricane (HER·ih·kayn) a severe storm that develops over tropical oceans and whose strong winds of more than 119 km/h spiral in toward the intensely low-pressure storm center (198)
  huracán una tormenta severa que se desarrolla sobre océanos tropicales, con vientos fuertes que soplan a más de 119 km/h y que se mueven en espiral hacia el centro de presión extremadamente baja de la tormenta

ice age (EYES AYJ) a long period of climatic cooling during which the continents are glaciated repeatedly (243)
  edad de hielo un largo período de enfriamiento del clima, durante el cual los continentes se ven repetidamente sometidos a la glaciación

jet stream (JET STREEM) a narrow band of strong winds that blow in the upper troposphere (138, 189)
  corriente en chorro un cinturón delgado de vientos fuertes que soplan en la parte superior de la troposfera

latitude (LAT·ih·tood) the distance north or south from the equator; expressed in degrees (228)
  latitud la distancia hacia el norte o hacia el sur del ecuador; se expresa en grados

lightning (LYT·ning) an electric discharge that takes place between two oppositely charged surfaces, such as between a cloud and the ground, between two clouds, or between two parts of the same cloud (197)
  relámpago una descarga eléctrica que ocurre entre dos superficies que tienen carga opuesta, como por ejemplo, entre una nube y el suelo, entre dos nubes o entres dos partes de la misma nube

local wind (LOH·kuhl WIND) the movement of air over short distances; occurs in specific areas as a result of certain geographical features (140)
  viento local el movimiento del aire a través de distancias cortas; se produce en áreas específicas como resultado de ciertas características geográficas

mechanical wave (mih·KAN·ih·kuhl WAYV) a wave that requires a medium through which to travel (70)
onda mecánica una onda que requiere un medio para desplazarse

mesosphere (MEZ·uh·sfir) the layer of the atmosphere between the stratosphere and the thermosphere and in which temperature decreases as altitude increases (108)
mesosfera la capa de la atmósfera que se encuentra entre la estratosfera y la termosfera, en la cual la temperatura disminuye al aumentar la altitud

meteorology (mee·tee·uh·RAHL·uh·jee) the scientific study of Earth's atmosphere, especially in relation to weather and climate (210)
meteorología el estudio científico de la atmósfera de la Tierra, sobre todo en lo que se relaciona al tiempo y al clima

mid-ocean ridge (MID·oh·shuhn RIJ) a long, undersea mountain chain that forms along the floor of the major oceans (60)
dorsal oceánica una larga cadena submarina de montañas que se forma en el suelo de los principales océanos

ocean current (OH·shuhn KER·uhnt) a movement of ocean water that follows a regular pattern (82)
corriente oceánica un movimiento del agua del océano que sigue un patrón regular

ocean trench (OH·shuhn TRENCH) a long, narrow, and steep depression on the ocean floor that forms when one tectonic plate subducts beneath another plate; trenches run parallel to volcanic island chains or to the coastlines of continents; also called a trench or a deep-ocean trench (61)
fosa oceánica una depresión larga, angosta y empinada que se encuentra en el fondo del océano y se forma cuando una placa tectónica se subduce bajo otra; las fosas submarinas corren en forma paralela a cadenas de islas volcánicas o a las costas continentales; también denominada fosa o fosa oceánica profunda

ocean wave (OH·shuhn WAYV) a disturbance on the ocean that transmits energy and takes the shape of a swell or ridge (68)
ola de mar una alteración del océano que transmite energía y adopta la forma de onda o cresta

ozone layer (OH·zohn LAY·er) the layer of the atmosphere at an altitude of 15 to 40 km in which ozone absorbs ultraviolet solar radiation (110)
capa de ozono la capa de la atmósfera ubicada a una altitud de 15 a 40 km, en la cual el ozono absorbe la radiación solar

polarity (poh·LAIR·ih·tee) a property of a system in which two points have opposite characteristics, such as charges or magnetic poles (8)
polaridad la propiedad de un sistema en la que dos puntos tienen características opuestas, tales como las cargas o polos magnéticos

precipitation (prih·sip·ih·TAY·shuhn) any form of water that falls to Earth's surface from the clouds (19, 158)
precipitación cualquier forma de agua que cae de las nubes a la superficie de la Tierra

radiation (ray·dee·AY·shuhn) the transfer of energy as electromagnetic waves (120)
radiación la transferencia de energía en forma de ondas electromagnéticas

relative humidity (REL·uh·tiv hyoo·MID·ih·tee) the ratio of the amount of water vapor in the air to the amount of water vapor needed to reach saturation at a given temperature (157)
humedad relativa la proporción de la cantidad de vapor de agua que hay en el aire respecto a la cantidad de vapor de agua que se necesita para alcanzar la saturación a una temperatura dada

salinity (suh·LIN·ih·tee) a measure of the amount of dissolved salts in a given amount of liquid (54)
salinidad una medida de la cantidad de sales disueltas en una cantidad determinada de líquido

solvent (SAHL·vuhnt) in a solution, the substance in which the solute dissolves (11)
solvente en una solución, la sustancia en la que se disuelve el soluto

specific heat (spih·SIF·ik HEET) the quantity of heat required to raise a unit mass of homogeneous material 1 K or 1 °C in a specified way, given constant pressure and volume (11)
calor específico la cantidad de calor que se requiere para aumentar una unidad de masa de un material homogéneo 1 K ó 1 °C de una manera especificada, dados un volumen y una presión constantes

station model (STAY·shuhn MAHD·l) a pattern of meteorological symbols that represents the weather at a particular observing station and that is recorded on a weather map (214)
estación modelo el modelo de símbolos meteorológicos que representan el tiempo en una estación de observación determinada y que se registra en un mapa meteorológico

storm surge (STOHRM SERJ) a local rise in sea level near the shore that is caused by strong winds from a storm, such as those from a hurricane (199)

marea de tempestad un levantamiento local del nivel del mar cerca de la costa, el cual es resultado de los fuertes vientos de una tormenta, como por ejemplo, los vientos de un huracán

stratosphere (STRAT·uh·sfir) the layer of the atmosphere that is above the troposphere and in which temperature increases as altitude increases (108)

estratosfera la capa de la atmósfera que se encuentra encima de la troposfera y en la que la temperatura aumenta al aumentar la altitud

stratus cloud (STRAY·tuhs KLOWD) a gray cloud that has a flat, uniform base and that commonly forms at very low altitudes (169)

nube estrato una nube gris que tiene una base plana y uniforme y que comúnmente se forma a altitudes muy bajas

sublimation (suhb·luh·MAY·shuhn) the change of state from a solid directly to a gas (18)

sublimación cambio de estado por el cual un sólido se convierte directamente en un gas

surface current (SER·fuhs KER·uhnt) a horizontal movement of ocean water that is caused by wind and that occurs at or near the ocean's surface (82, 233)

corriente superficial un movimiento horizontal del agua del océano que es producido por el viento y que ocurre en la superficie del océano o cerca de ella

surface water (SER·fuhs WAW·ter) all the bodies of fresh water, salt water, ice, and snow that are found above the ground (32)

agua superficial todas las masas de agua dulce, agua salada, hielo y nieve que se encuentran arriba del suelo

temperature (TEM·per·uh·chur) a measure of how hot (or cold) something is; specifically, a measure of the average kinetic energy of the particles in an object (116)

temperatura una medida de qué tan caliente (o frío) está algo; específicamente, una medida de la energía cinética promedio de las partículas de un objeto

thermal energy (THER·muhl EN·er·jee) the kinetic energy of a substance's atoms (116)

energía térmica la energía cinética de los átomos de una sustancia

thermal expansion (THER·muhl ek·SPAN·shuhn) an increase in the size of a substance in response to an increase in the temperature of the substance (117)

expansión térmica un aumento en el tamaño de una sustancia en respuesta a un aumento en la temperatura de la sustancia

thermocline (THER·muh·klyn) a layer in a body of water in which water temperature drops with increased depth faster than it does in other layers (55)

termoclina una capa en una masa de agua en la que, al aumentar la profundidad, la temperatura del agua disminuye más rápido de lo que lo hace en otras capas

thermosphere (THER·muh·sfir) the uppermost layer of the atmosphere, in which temperature increases as altitude increases (108)

termosfera la capa más alta de la atmósfera, en la cual la temperatura aumenta a medida que la altitud aumenta

thunder (THUHN·der) the sound caused by the rapid expansion of air along an electrical strike (197)

trueno el sonido producido por la expansión rápida del aire a lo largo de una descarga eléctrica

thunderstorm (THUHN·der·stohrm) a usually brief, heavy storm that consists of rain, strong winds, lightning, and thunder (196)

tormenta eléctrica una tormenta fuerte y normalmente breve que consiste en lluvia, vientos fuertes, relámpagos y truenos

topography (tuh·PAHG·ruh·fee) the size and shape of the land surface features of a region, including its relief (230)

topografía el tamaño y la forma de las características de una superficie de terreno, incluyendo su relieve

tornado (tohr·NAY·doh) a destructive, rotating column of air that has very high wind speeds and that may be visible as a funnel-shaped cloud (200)

tornado una columna destructiva de aire en rotación cuyos vientos se mueven a velocidades muy altas y que puede verse como una nube con forma de embudo

transpiration (tran·spuh·RAY·shuhn) the process by which plants release water vapor into the air through stomata; also the release of water vapor into the air by other organisms (18)

transpiración el proceso por medio del cual las plantas liberan vapor de agua al aire por medio de los estomas; también, la liberación de vapor de agua al aire por otros organismos

tributary (TRIB·yuh·tehr·ee) a stream that flows into a lake or into a larger stream (34)

afluente un arroyo que fluye a un lago o a otro arroyo más grande

troposphere (TROH·puh·sfir) the lowest layer of the atmosphere, in which temperature decreases at a constant rate as altitude increases (108)

troposfera la capa inferior de la atmósfera, en la que la temperatura disminuye a una tasa constante a medida que la altitud aumenta

trough (TRAWF) the lowest point of a wave (68)

seno el punto más bajo de una onda

tsunami (tsoo·NAH·mee) a giant ocean wave that forms after a volcanic eruption, submarine earthquake, or landslide (75)

tsunami una ola gigante del océano que se forma después de una erupción volcánica, terremoto submarino o desprendimiento de tierras

U

upwelling (UHP·well·ing) the movement of deep, cold, and nutrient-rich water to the surface (88)
　surgencia el movimiento de las aguas profundas, frías y ricas en nutrientes hacia la superficie

V

visibility (viz·uh·BIL·ih·tee) the distance at which a given standard object can be seen and identified with the unaided eye (161)
　visibilidad la distancia a la que un objeto dado es perceptible e identificable para el ojo humano

W–Z

water cycle (WAW·ter SY·kuhl) the continuous movement of water between the atmosphere, the land, the oceans, and living things (16)
　ciclo del agua el movimiento continuo del agua entre la atmósfera, la tierra, los océanos y los seres vivos

water table (WAW·ter TAY·buhl) the upper surface of underground water; the upper boundary of the zone of saturation (32)
　capa freática el nivel más alto del agua subterránea; el límite superior de la zona de saturación

watershed (WAW·ter·shed) the area of land that is drained by a river system (35)
　cuenca hidrográfica el área del terreno que es drenada por un sistema de ríos

wave (WAYV) a disturbance that transfers energy from one place to another; a wave can be a single cycle, or it can be a repeating pattern (68)
　onda una alteración que transfiere energía de un lugar a otro; una onda puede ser un ciclo único o un patrón repetido

wave period (WAYV PIR·ee·uhd) the time required for corresponding points on consecutive waves to pass a given point (69)
　período de onda el tiempo que se requiere para que los puntos correspondientes de ondas consecutivas pasen por un punto dado

wavelength (WAYV·lengkth) the distance from any point on a wave to the corresponding point on the next wave (68)
　longitud de onda la distancia entre cualquier punto de una onda y el punto correspondiente de la siguiente onda

weather (WETH·er) the short-term state of the atmosphere, including temperature, humidity, precipitation, wind, and visibility (156, 226)
　tiempo el estado de la atmósfera a corto plazo que incluye la temperatura, la humedad, la precipitación, el viento y la visibilidad

weather forecasting (WETH·er FOHR·kast·ing) the process of predicting atmospheric conditions by collecting and analyzing atmospheric data (210)
　pronóstico del tiempo el proceso de predecir las condiciones atmosféricas reuniendo y analizando datos atmosféricos

wind (WIND) the movement of air caused by differences in air pressure (134, 160)
　viento el movimiento de aire producido por diferencias en la presión barométrica

Index

Page numbers for definitions are printed in **boldface** type.
Page numbers for illustrations, maps, and charts are printed in *italics*.

© Houghton Mifflin Harcourt Publishing Company

W